THE NAXALITES AND
THEIR IDEOLOGY

THE NAXALITES AND THEIR IDEOLOGY

Third Edition

RABINDRA RAY

OXFORD
UNIVERSITY PRESS

OXFORD
UNIVERSITY PRESS

Oxford University Press is a department of the University of Oxford.
It furthers the University's objective of excellence in research, scholarship,
and education by publishing worldwide. Oxford is a registered trademark of
Oxford University Press in the UK and in certain other countries

Published in India by
Oxford University Press
22 workspace, 2nd Floor, 1/22 Asaf Ali Road, New Delhi 110002

© Oxford University Press 1988

The moral rights of the author have been asserted

First Edition published in 1988
Second Edition published in 2002
Oxford India Paperbacks 2002
Third Edition published in 2011

ISBN-13: 978-0-19-807738-1
ISBN-10: 0-19-807738-6

Typeset in Adobe Garamond Pro 10.5/12.5
by Bespoke, Pondicherry
Printed in India by Repro India Limited

Contents

Acknowledgements

I would like to thank my supervisor Gavin Williams for his constant help and encouragement, and the staff of the Centre for Studies in Social Sciences, Calcutta, particularly Nirmala Bannerjee and Hitesh Sanyal, for their help when I visited Calcutta in 1983. Librarians, Jonathan Katz at Oxford, others at the Centre for Studies in Social Sciences, and at the Institute of Development Studies in Sussex, guided me to invaluable materials.

Without a scholarship from the JCR of Lincoln College it would have been impossible for me to pursue this study at Oxford. The Overseas Research Students Fees Support Scheme of the Universities and Colleges in Great Britain assisted with my fees. On various occasions Lincoln College, the Board of Graduate Studies, the Radhakrishnan Memorial Bequest, and friends who would rather remain anonymous helped financially.

André de Vries and Wendy Olsen helped prepare the manuscript for presentation.

My debt to Gyanendra Pandey and David Goldey is not so easy to pin down.

Prologue

To people of good will, the revolutionary seems a well-intentioned person enough, almost one of their own. But, whatever else he or she may be, the revolutionary or the terrorist, as he or she is known nowadays, would certainly balk at being considered a person of good will and no different from people who try to lead correct and blameless lives. The revolutionary is a creature of postures, forever viewing himself or herself as engaged, and about matters of world-embracing import. The revolutionary is not infrequently trapped in his or her own posturings, the way out of which seem to him or her closed on grounds of principle. Inhabiting this destitute prison of his or her making, the revolutionary orients him- or herself in the light of a grand heroism, to which the run of humanity is so much material to cope with or shape. People who bring about or effect revolutions are not necessarily revolutionaries, just as revolutionaries themselves may forever be busy with the tasks of a revolution that never arrives. Such indeed is the plight of Western and Indian communist revolutionaries, wedded to a utopia of a classless society, while nevertheless either themselves occupying positions of considerable privilege or committed to the task of the elite vanguard, however humbly, who gift the deluded and enslaved masses the ideological weapons of their liberation.

Unlike terrorism, revolution is a word in very good odour—and not only among communists. There seems to be a veritable tide of rhetoric presuming the unsurpassable excellence of revolution and revolutionary perspectives and claiming revolutionary status or consequences for any and everything new. Of course, among communists and those familiar with their debates, the distinction between terrorism and revolution has been of some importance since the Bolsheviks. Indeed, where the early Naxalites viewed themselves as a breed apart, who not only preached but practiced revolution, those they broke from, the communists who participated in electoral politics, considered Naxalism an adventurist politics of individual terror. The contenders have not yet revised their views of each other, though there are now Naxalites who participate in elections as well.

At the end of the phase described in this book, the effective organizations of the Naxalites were destroyed, both through the strong counter-measures of the government and the internal dissension and lack of unity among the surviving Naxalites themselves. For a relatively protracted period, the Naxalites were not in the news and no events of Naxalite violence were reported. Naxalite ideologues were however active through this period in the towns and cities, proselytizing and propagandizing, establishing countrywide and international links. I am not familiar with the issues they debated amongst themselves, but two elements of their orientation in continuing to remain Naxalites or in becoming fresh recruits to the cause are reasonably manifest—first, the belief in violent revolution as a long protracted process on the Chinese model as the only solution for India's poor, and second, the unwillingness or inability to come to terms with the bloody history of the early period with respect to a clarity about themselves and their own motives. This externalization of what is an internal matter, this projection onto the world of what are concerns of the revolutionary's intimate soul is a matter that has only been fomulaically advanced in this book as the distinction between literate and existential ideology, and not adequately elaborated and fleshed out. In the course of time, the Naxalites did regroup, though in several different contending factions, and most of the rural areas in which they were successful in finding some kind of support, changed.

The intellectual profile of the Naxalite movement as a whole also changed. There were two significant respects in which this change is allied to the intellectual situation within the country and the world at large. Within the country, leftists, socialists and communists had been a significant presence right through the later phases of nationalism and onwards, but the early period of Naxalism detailed in this book and the period of the emergency and the resistance to it that followed slightly later, led to a quantum jump in the respectability of such views. The post emergency period saw the hallowing of such views by parliament by the inclusion of socialism in the very constitution of the Republic to describe its nature and aspirations. This was neither a cosmetic change, nor solely an outcome of the Naxalite events, but allied to a slow drift of the changing intellectual climate of which the Naxalites themselves indeed, were a constituent element. Leftist intellectual hegemony did not go unchallenged, but no party in India, even today, is a party of the right with the defence of private property and the private rights of individuals on its agenda. In academic matters, political correctness is dictated by prevailing leftist prejudices. Such currents have not left the world at large untouched, where paradoxically, the collapse of the Soviet dictatorship and the market orientations of surviving socialist regimes, including India, have not laid the socialist ghosts, but spread their prejudices wider and deeper in the following generation. This change in the very atmosphere in which the Naxalites operate is coupled with a change in the sections of the student population who get drawn to Naxalism to the point of becoming active revolutionaries. Though the general influence of Naxalism and leftist ideas is far more powerful today than the time of the events set forth in this book, the universities and especially the apex institutions of higher education are relatively peaceful and not hotbeds of revolutionary ideology, though a consistent and steady stream of the educated young sympathizes with Naxalite perspectives, even sometimes to the point of plunging into active revolutionary activity. The intellectual standards of the Naxalites were never high, but during the early period treated in this book they attracted to their fold some of the most academically accomplished. Activism of various other reform-oriented sorts has surfaced in the interim, and the universities of the country are just as actively engaged in non-academic political activity as ever they were.

As for the Naxalites themselves, they continue to be essentially and cultically wedded to violence, though it seems the pitch of bloodlust characteristic of the period of the terror in Calcutta is no longer prevalent. The Naxalites continue to pride themselves in the practice of violence, setting themselves, in their own opinion, as a breed apart. Nevertheless, some of them, while essentially so committed to the practice of violent methods, do not refrain in principle or indeed practice from peaceful parliamentary and electoral politics, and of course, as ever, are willing to utilize the efforts of all of those, however peaceful even in principle, who sympathize with them. And the ranks of these latter spreads tentacularly through society and politics into parliament itself and into the opinion-making circles in the world at large.

The Naxalite, however much committed to the welfare of the dispossessed, is a Naxalite on grounds of conviction having to do with intellectual proclivities and dilemmas. The roots of the Naxalite

phenomenon do not lie in the poverty of India's labouring rural population, but in the psychological traumas of its urban educated young.
These traumas are inextricably enmeshed in the oral and intellectual
problems of the leading thought of our times. Without coming to grips
with the moral and intellectual source, all activity, pro and con, is likely
to prove only a sop to the inability to confront our world and ourselves
with as much clarity as is possible.

It might seem contentious to argue that the Naxalite problem is primarily related to the intellectual climate of our times and principally a
question of the orientations of urban educated youth, when even sections of informed police opinion incline to the view that it is a problem
of the rural dispossessed, for, true enough, quite a few of those engaged
in Naxalite violence in principally Bihar and Andhra now are village
folk, and in the actual attempt to check or contain violence, it is they
who must be contended with. But even in the period described in this
book this was the case in most of the rural areas of Naxalite activity.
What is being argued is that the continuing organizational tenacity, its
effective continuance as a threat to peace and security rests not in the
labouring rural population, but in the urban educated and the respectability such views enjoy among those who consider themselves
enlightened. The possibility of the recurrence of such violence on a continuing basis remains so long as the centrality of the urban educated is
not understood. Indeed the very re-emergence of Naxalite activity after
a period of quiescence following the events detailed in this book is living
evidence of the cogency of my argument.

Without coming to terms with the ideology of the Naxalites and all
that that means with regard to our own ways of thinking and participating in politics, an effective resolution of the problem posed by the
Naxalites is likely to prove illusory. The collapse of Soviet Marxism or
Chinese collectivism, true enough, is not a *result* of the Western bloc's
persuasions and dissuasions, but it is certainly related to the intellectual
climate within these countries and the orientations of educated opinion,
right into the Central Committees of the ruling parties and even its very
apex. Bengal, after these bloody events, has never seen the resurgence of
Naxalite violence. It has had a change of heart. None of the survivors of
the Naxalite arm in Bengal still live by the same principles. How is this
to come about elsewhere? Fortuitous events contributed to such an outcome in Bengal. If Naxalite violence is to be checked and contained in
the regions where it has resurfaced, it demands the meeting of violence

with violence, for which already public opinion has to be contended with, and also, more importantly, it needs the persuasion and dissuasion in urban enclaves that will prevent more young people from being led astray.

It is a wonder how a veritably full-blown philosophy of bloodthirsty murder and general mayhem can appeal to educated, sensitive people, otherwise accustomed to the most civilized of everyday behaviour, as the highest altruism by which India and indeed the world is to be redeemed. And this in the country of the Buddha and Mahatma Gandhi. True enough, the legacy of the Buddha is a distant prospect, but the more proximate example of the life and work of the Mahatma—and its astonishing practical political success!—might otherwise have given pause to such a precipitate advocacy of brutal and naked violence only if those so committed had not felt the example of the Mahatma to be only a cruel hoax perpetrated on a gullible, long-suffering, population, its vaunted success a hollow hypocrisy belied by the persistent desperate destitution and oppression left untouched by the achievement of Indian independence.

The Naxalite reversal of values is only part of a far larger intellectual tendency of appeal to the highest moral principles to justify, vindicate and positively advocate what is usually considered the grossest and coarsest immorality. It seems to have become indeed, the most influential current of thought which, by a twist of subtle dialectical transformation, then accuses the highest forms of morality hitherto revered as brutally and fundamentally immoral. The Naxalite adventure originating in this general querulousness about values and of the very sense of values, in turn feeds into its stream again. It strengthens and consolidates the turn of thought to what are considered criminal recourses in the name of the very highest law and justice. It is not possible to take issue with this global pervasive drift within the space of such a brief preface or even to limn adequately its more important features. Nor would it be altogether appropriate to do so for a book devoted principally to the Naxalites. In the space that remains I wish to review some of the features of socialism, become an altogether respectable doctrine and inscribed into the very constitution of the republic of India indeed related to some of the events considered in this book. The collapse of Soviet socialism has disenchanted some with its perspectives, but not to the point of a theoretical reconsideration of its principles.

Socialist and socialistically inclined ideas still enjoy great prestige in India and are indeed influential in intellectual circles all over the world. In the relatively brief period that it has been current, socialist thought has assumed a vast variety of forms, not only accidentally or occasionally at loggerheads with each other—even murderously—though all socialist creeds seem agreed in principle that rights of private property are merely a customary social convenience, not in any way essential or fundamental, and to be flouted and disrespected at will either in the public interest or in principle, as the principal obstacle to a just and equitable social order. The doctrines of socialism are relatively recent and of European provenance though I have seen booklets after the event, touting a 'Vedic Samajwad'. True enough, disputes as to the nature of the right to private properly are hardly recent, and codified Hindu law of fairly distant origin is divided in its opinions both about the nature of the right and the details of its governing legislations. Whereas the earlier Mitaksara, more prevalent over the western and northern parts of the country, regards the right to private property and its rules as rooted in, and derived from sastra (scriptural injunctions in dharma—and thus inflexible and relatively unchangeable), the later Dayabhaga more prevalent in the eastern parts and principally Bengal, regards the right to private property and its rules as much more subject to change, and merely of laukik import, i.e. validated as custom and subject to variations of time and place. The two schools differ in their legislations and by implication their view of the rightful share of governance. But, it is worth mentioning here that the British when they came to India, to trade and then to rule, were puzzled by Hindu and Indian rules and customs of ownership, not infrequently arriving at the opinion that private property as it was known in England and Europe was not to be found in India. The subject of the nature of property in India is highly interesting and complex and I will not go further into it here, referring the reader interested in a brief overview of my opinion to my review of Hira Singh's work on Rajputana in colonial times. Nor will I purpose further here the complexities of the issues of the intelligibility of socialism in settings other than the European and its understanding of the nature of private property. I shall take for granted the European and Europeanist elaborations, which have been employed in any case by most avowed practicing socialists, both in their rhetoric and in their policies, i.e. where they have been in a position to formulate policy. The recourse has the merit of an overt intelligibility of principle, uncomplicated by the finer points of adequacy to actual practices, more in keeping with the aspects I wish to discuss here.

It bears mention with respect to the egalitarian rhetoric that underwrites the so-called socialist moralities, that for very good and cogent reasons the contention of a non-hierarchical society is a sociological absurdity. Concerning the issues of property, personal and private access to the wealth of the world seems to me not only inevitable and untranscendable but positively desirable and a natural and civilized good. The contrary contention, i.e. the socialist alternative, poses the problem of who is to decide authorized shares if personal and private acquisition is an abomination, and who is to decide the legitimate share of those who delegate to themselves the parceling out of shares. In any case, acquisition for personal gain, spiritual or material, is the inflexible principle of human conduct and no parceling out of just shares is going to prevent the vast majority of mankind from trying to improve its personal and private material position. Nor to my mind, is the principle of inheritance in any way morally corrupt. There is hardly an escape from it. It remains for the privileged to discharge the responsibilities of privilege as best they can and for those who feel they have been unjustly treated to sue for justice to such as are privileged to dispense justice.

Acquisition is necessarily and appositely personal. If the socialist contention that property is theft' is to be taken seriously, it is worth remembering that it is disrespect for the rules of property that is customarily theft. All socialism thus criminal in itself, makes criminals of the greater majority of the population, busy acquiring gain for private and personal ends. The consequences are the criminalization of the economy and politics, i.e. the reduction of the greater part of the population to criminality, with the law and its effective enforcement leading to and actively favouring the advancement of the deliberately criminal, and the invasion of the legitimate political domain by active criminals. A spritually, morally pure socialism can only begin—and end—with oneself and the surrender to others of what is mine, without coveting what is thine.

Indeed, the complexity of moral life is centered on the handling of the tension between mine and thine. Superior and inferior personal moralities exhibit themselves in the way in which they negotiate the difficulties of selfishness and altruism. Whereas most seem agreed on the moral superiority of altruism, only those who have some thing worthy of giving can actually make a meaningful gift. Renunciation in and of itself is of little use if it does not lead to the acquisition of some higher, greater good. That is not, however, to deny the centrality of the mystery of sacrifice to the human condition, where everthing is at risk, parents sacrifice routinely for their children, and the ambitious sacrifice all to the cultivation of their potential.

'Social justice' is the first value aspiration inscribed into the Indian Constitution, it underwrites later outright advocacy of socialism. To my mind, it can only be a figment of a deluded imagination of megalomaniac proportions. Social justice is not a humanly justiciable matter and all attempts at so-called social engineering are more pronounced in the achievement of unforeseen consequences, than in the solution of perceived problems for which they were purportedly invented. As to the workings of these attempts at social justice and its criminal outcomes, the first example is the first act of the newly constituted republic which led to the first Constitutional Amendment, in the very first year of its operation, and not on some minor peripheral issue but the guarantee of fundamental rights. Zemindari Abolition was set into motion to honour the promises the Congress party had made to its supporters in the struggle for independence. Such zemindars or their subordinates as evaded the law or used subterfuge have prospered and flourished. Such as respected the law were wiped out as landlords. The Maharaja of Darbhanga chose to move the courts not on the issue of the legality or justice of the Abolition itself, but on the issue of rightful compensation, claiming more than was offered to him by the Government. The Patna High Court upheld his plea and the defeated Government appealed to the Supreme Court, which also upheld the Maharaja's plea. Not to be outdone, the Government then took the matter to Parliament, where an overwhelming Majority of the Congress and in any case an even more socialistically inclined opposition, amended the fundamental right to private property so that the government could renege on the demanded payment. One wonders what the Mahatma who is on record as also being a socialist, albiet of a pure kind, would have made of this. Land-grabbing followed the abolition of zemindari and the successive legislations on a ceiling on holdings and the consolidation of holdings. It continues even today. It favours only the more aggressively criminal, so that, as I mention in the book, the ownership of cultivable land in the country is a complete mysterious maze which one investigates only at the risk of life and limb. All this, under the threat of criminal appropriation by the government itself, either in the individual capacity of a government appointee or functionary flouting the law, or entirely legally as governmental expropriation with little or no compensation. Needless to say, the problem of adequate increased production to feed the burgeoning towns and cities was not solved by all this land reform, but by the subsidizing of agricultural production with urban surplus through the Green Revolution.

The criminalization of the countryside was followed during the events detailed in this book by the criminalization equally of urban commerce and industry by the outright adoption of socialism. In financial straits due to the tax-liability concealment and tax evasion of the larger part of the commercial population to escape the punitive tax structure in the interests of 'social justice', the government seized and nationalized fourteen private Indian banks without paying a penny in compensation. The Congress Party still had an overwhelming majority in Parliament, but Indira Gandhi could not carry the party with her and the matter could not be ratified in the legislature. V.V. Giri, then President, came to Indira Gandhi's rescue and promulgated an ordinance legalizing the acquisition. The years of avowed socialism and the continuing licensing Raj have seen criminals flourishing in every economic activity. The government seems to be busy these days trying to bring back to the legal fold all this criminal wealth. Politics itself is riddled with convicted criminals. Whether any review of the constitution will ever raise the issue of socialism is doubtful.

To the Naxalites and to a large section of similar leftist opinion, all this constitutional socialism is completely bogus. The Naxalites want blood and the murder of the propertied, except for the propertied who kowtow to them. While not so bloodthirsty, a large section of leftist and liberal opinion sympathizes with the Naxalite cause. Shades of the advocacy of violence differ considerably. At its most civilized, the Nobel Laureate, Amartya Sen advocates welfare spending by governments without thought as to how the money is going to come, when all governments in the world are deeply in debt and getting deeper into debt. Individuals, now given the opportunity, are beginning to live in a similar fashion on credit. Perhaps our children or their children's children will need to settle the account.

The Naxalite beginnings are by now history and not a little nostalgia tinges the memory of these dread events. But the tragedy of it should not remain out of view. And whereas tragedy makes for beautiful and instructive literature, as history it can only be regretted.

Chapter One

Introduction: Perspectives and Problems

When we try to examine the mirror in itself we discover in the end nothing but things upon it. If we want to grasp the things we finally get hold of nothing but the mirror.—This, in the most general terms, is the history of knowledge.

—Nietzsche

In attempting a sociological interpretation of the ideology and practice of the 'Naxalite' terrorists in West Bengal we must have recourse to the meaning of this practice for the Naxalites themselves. However, their overt ideological statements do not reveal the meaning and significance of their actions. Hence I shall seek to distinguish their 'existential ideology' from their 'literate ideology'.[1]

It is perhaps desirable to understand. But if we can agree on what we wish to understand, we have not yet agreed on how we are to understand it. It does not help to appeal to an objective reality, for in posing the problem of how anything is to be understood we already confront the problematic character of the reality we seek to understand.

Reality never establishes itself except as an appeal to self-evidence, the unproblematic and unambiguous nature of that which presents itself and can be talked about. Objects, things, artefacts have a clarity which makes it easy for us to use them as evidence, to point where words fail. But human reality is not itself such an external artefact, even though it is in such artefacts that it often manifests itself. Being an internality, it lacks both the definiteness and sensuousness of tangible things, even when expressed in the communicable form of language. This does not

[1] Weber defines the sociologist's task as an 'interpretive understanding' of social action. While committed to this Weberian perspective this study rejects his distinction between 'subjective' and 'objective' meanings. Meanings are shared and it is the extent and depth of sharing that varies.

render human reality either imperceptible or incommunicable: it is of course the consciousness of this shared human reality that makes communication possible and renders it meaningful. But for the most part this reality remains as assumption, shaping the course of communication without being made explicit.

Social reality presents itself as that alien reality that confronts the individual in the pursuit of his goals, or even constitutes the condition of his existence.[2] However, it ceases to be as obvious or as clearly defined as soon as one attempts to grasp it or render it intelligible. Simultaneously external to the individual and yet a matrix of intersubjectivity that implicates him, the nature of this social reality can only be formulated and communicated to the historicity of the society it attempts to grasp, and to the human and personal awareness that gives it its form. Such a formulation is engaged with things, with objects of human creation in space and time, with institutions, with manifestos, and with more directly tangible artefacts. It is engaged with the awareness of others, with persons—as particular individuals or as more general stereotypes. But social reality is in itself neither things nor persons. It is constituted as that fundamental abstraction that invests both it, and by contrast the sense of self, with concreteness.

Sociology, as fundamentally concerned with social and human reality, cannot escape either their relativism or their absoluteness. In delineating these realities, sociology incorporates its awareness of the questionableness of such realities in the concept of ideology. The word ideology, which supposes such an awareness, poses as its first mystery that word itself, and, as its first manifestation, sociology, the discipline to which it has become central.

The Naxalites

The Naxalite occupies an ambiguous niche in history. Exemplary idealist to some, he indicates to others an expression of immature disaffection that has nothing constructive to offer. In either case, he embodies the reinstatement of man as a moral agent if only because Naxalites so radically challenged the premises of established morality. This might indeed

---

[2] See Durkheim's conception of society as constraint. Emile Durkheim, *The Rules of Sociological Method*, trans. Sarah A. Soloway and John H. Mueller, eighth edition, New York, The Free Press, London, Collier-Macmillan, 1964.

seem an untenable proposition, considering the brief flicker of the Naxalite challenge and their almost fore-ordained failure. True, there are still Naxalites around, provoking perhaps the same mixed responses that they did when they first appeared, but today they represent little beyond an insignificant irritant to those whose authority they question. Perhaps they have never in actual fact amounted to very much more than that. And yet there was a time when the word Naxalite was not just a characterization of another political tendency by the media, a casual throw-away phrase conveying broadly a belief in political violence in the interests of the dispossessed, but a word loaded with nameless fears and aspirations, stirring hopes or despair, and always strong passions. There are some of course who claim that this is still the case, though any examination of the scale and depth of contemporary Naxalite activities or expression of opinion will not bear this out.[3] But still, even if the Naxalites do not provoke the controversy they once did and belong so clearly to the past, it is only because there are very few fresh recruits to the cause and not because the issues raised by the Naxalite revolt have been satisfactorily explored, or indeed even explicitly stated. Their failure seems to have set the seal on the questions they raised as a dead letter, and no one is perhaps more reticent to discuss these than the ex-Naxalite himself.[4]

And yet the Naxalite revolt provokes a whole battery of vexed questions—some of them posed as such by the Naxalites themselves, others implicitly entailed in their activity, and yet others exposed in the consideration of Naxalite events in hindsight. Perhaps the questions people choose to ask are themselves more significant pointers to the nature of their involvement with the events, their standpoint and prejudices, than the answers that they finally arrive at.

To the historian the most important question is probably—how did the Naxalites arise? Or, to put it with a more mundane conventionality, what were the causes of the Naxalite outbreak? There are some, Marxists among them, who see sufficient cause for the origin of the Naxalites in the ideals they professed, and the root of the whole outbreak in the

---

[3] See Mahasweta Debi's contention that the Naxalite events have precipitated two camps in the world of contemporary Bengali literature, in 'Sattarer Dashak O Tarpore', *Sattarer Dashak*, Calcutta, n.d.

[4] This I found to be the case when I visited Calcutta in 1983 on a field trip in connection with this study.

abysmal poverty of the Indian dispossessed.[5] And yet as others notice, Marxists among them, however significantly the discontent of poverty may be related to the Naxalite disaffection with the status quo, it is not quite this disaffection that explains their activity, for the Naxalites fought in the cause of a class other than their own. During the course of events themselves, prominent leaders of the other communist parties dismissed the Naxalites as middle-class romantics and adventurists.[6] This obviously reopens the question of causation at a more immediate and profound level, for we are then led to the question of what it is that leads a person to rebel, and, even more generally, what the elements of a social revolution are.

The partisan on the other hand, whether he happens to be a Naxalite or not, will not see anything problematic about the Naxalites' commitment. What concerns him is rather why the Naxalites failed. This only increases the focus on the literature that the Naxalites produced, and even more particularly on disputes, both within the CPI(M-L) and those between the CPI(M-L) and other communists. In this undertaking it is assumed that at the root of the Naxalite failure lies an erroneous understanding of the world and an erroneous strategy that flows from this understanding; also that this understanding is found expressed in the documents and disputes of the Naxalites.[7] Obviously, this assumes that in politics 'truth always triumphs', i.e. people with a more correct or adequate understanding of circumstances win out in politics. However one may react to the naive optimism of such premises, the more fundamental issue that does not even come to light in such a discourse is the nature of the understanding of circumstances that the texts and disputes codify. In other words, when it is assumed that a given strategy follows from a stated evaluation, not only is the procedure questionable but it may in fact reverse the order of actual priority. To illustrate the confusion of this procedure one example will suffice: To most CPI(M) activists at the time the error of the CPI(M-L) formulations lay in the premise

---

[5] Such indeed seems to be the premise of Sumanta Banerjee, *In the Wake of Naxalbari*, Calcutta, Subarnarekha, 1980; India's Simmering Revolution London, Zed Press, 2nd edn., 1984.

[6] See, for instance, Biplab Dasgupta's dismissal of the Naxalites, quoted later in this work.

[7] Biplab Das Gupta's argument against the Naxalites is based on these premises, in *The Naxalite Movement*, New Delhi, Allied Publishers, 1974.

that the time was ripe for Revolution, a judgement that they see validated by the subsequent failure of the CPI(M-L). Leaving aside for the moment the responsibility of the CPI(M) itself in accomplishing this failure, in such a judgement the meaning of Revolution itself remains unexplored on account of a prejudice—that the use of the same word by the CPI(M) and the CPI(M-L) necessarily refers to the same 'thing', equally desired by both.

More generally than these specialized concerns with the origin and fate of the Naxalites, the question that arises in the mind of an observer not closely familiar with the events, or indeed concerned with them, is the question of the legitimacy of Naxalite violence and the question with which it is inextricably connected—that of the validity of their 'world-view'. Superficially the least specialized or demanding of the questions raised so far, this poses the most difficult problems, necessitating a recourse to metaphysical considerations and an attempt to establish the meaning of Naxalite discourse to the participants themselves. And, here, for the first time the paradoxes of the history of the CPI(M-L) present themselves, the most striking of which of course is that of a party committed to agrarian mass revolution being intimately involved in the exercise of urban terror. It is indeed this observation, more than any other, which provokes my principal argument, namely that the meaning that the literature of the CPI(M-L) is apt to convey to an observer (on the purely linguistic level) is very different from the meaning it 'contained' (at an existential level) for the participants. Separated in meaning, this literate ideology and existential ideology are nevertheless related to each other and transformed into each other, if by nothing else than the activity of the Naxalites. The study of this interrelation forms the crucial concern of this book.

At the centre of the CPI(M-L) concern with theory lie certain sociological premises and prejudices which implicitly challenge not only the existing state of the discipline but the very premises on which it is based.[8] In this, as a Marxist current specific to the time, the revolt of the CPI(M-L) is bound up with other 'leftist' student revolts of the late 1960s and early 1970s. As specifically student revolts these movements as a whole represent a challenge to the totality of academic disciplines and also perhaps to the philosophy of education. But it is in the attack on sociology and sociological wisdom, whether of the orthodox

[8] For an explicit statement see Nanterre Students, 'Why Sociologists?' in *Student Power*, ed. A. Cockburn and R. Blackburn, Harmondsworth, Penguin, 1969.

American variety (in the case of the Nanterre students), or the orthodox Marxist variety (in the movement as a whole generally, and particularly in the CPI(M-L) in its assault upon revisionism), that the intellectual aspiration of the New Left, to give it its proper name, achieves explicit expression. In a sociological work it would be impossible not to treat this challenge with the respect it deserves.

Arching over the whole discourse of the New Left, the Naxalites, and subsequent discussion of their theory and activity, is the unformulated and relatively unmentioned question of poverty, including that of the spirit. As far as the question of material poverty is concerned—its causation and the means of its eradication—the Marxist tradition sees the cause of the poverty of the Indian masses in the 'semi-feudal, semi-colonial' character of the country, in the exploitation of these masses by a feudal ruling class. The use of these terms in Naxalite discourse is somewhat problematic and I shall comment at some length on it later, but superficially this ties them to the mainstream of Indian liberal thought, while they provide an answer that ties them to the mainstream of communist thought in India. The Naxalites have no philosophic statement on the nature of the methods for achieving their aims. Their claim to being Marxist-Leninists would seem to argue that they share with the Marxist-Leninist sensibility the accomplishment of these ends through violence and revolution, a recourse that is simultaneously desirable and inevitable. However, their divergence from this materialist teleology into an essentially spiritual awareness of the relation between means and ends presents itself in the way in which the Naxalites formulate and resolve questions pertaining to the details of their tactics.

The question of spiritual poverty, again, is not tackled explicitly by the Naxalites. Though the New Left philosopher Marcuse is concerned with it, the Naxalites cannot be shown to share this view, though certainly a view of spiritual poverty is entailed in 'dropping out' of the 'rat-race' to make Revolution.

From quite another point of view the Naxalite outburst needs to be compared with other contemporary and historical forms of terrorism, either from motives of its prevention and containment, or from a purely scholarly interest. Such comparisons highlight the Bengali focus of these events and demand consideration of the problem of whether the Naxalite revolt is rooted in the peculiarities of Bengali social life and culture.[9]

---

[9] Richard Hula comments on 'the propensity of Bengal to erupt in spasms of political violence and disorder' in Richard C. Hula, 'Political Violence and

None of these questions has been tackled adequately, though questions such as the consonance of Naxalite practice with Maoist theory,[10] with Marxist theory in its Indian form,[11] and the validity of the term 'semi-feudalism',[12] have been broached, and the last discussed at some length. The literature on the Naxalites has, however, tended to remain partisan. Significant events have been described, but because of the superficial nature of the partisanship a distortion of the significance of the events has been inescapable.[13] A profounder partisanship that locks horns with the ambivalence of the Naxalite experience, though it must in passing treat of these questions, finds itself confronted with an even more fundamental question, namely the meaning and significance of the Naxalite terror. Where the fundamental issue at stake is not the desirability or undesirability of the Naxalite understanding and activity but rather the attempt to comprehend what it expresses and how this is related to its milieu, attention will necessarily be focused in a different direction.

My own concern with the Naxalites dates back to my first graduate year in Delhi in 1969. I began to work with a student organization, the Student-Youth Federation, that was pro-Naxalite. Together with some other students from this group I left Delhi in 1970 to preach Revolution in the north Bihar countryside and remained there for a couple of years under the direction of the North-Bengal North-Bihar Border Region Committee of the CPI(M-L). I returned to my parents' home with the disintegration of the Naxalite organizations and, after a while, to Delhi. There I associated with a small Trotskyist nucleus attempting to build up organizations of factory workers in the adjoining industrial districts of Ghaziabad and Faridabad. Still within a Marxist revolutionary perspective, I argued then that the Naxalite failure lay in its disregard of the revolutionary potential of the industrial proletariat, and in its Stalinist

---

Terrorism in Bengal', *The Politics of Terrorism*, ed. Michael Stohl, New York and Basel, Marcel Dekker Inc., 1983, p. 419.

[10] Especially in Mohan Ram, *Maoism in India*, Delhi, Vikas, 1971.

[11] See, for instance, Mohit Sen, 'The CPI and the Naxalites', *Communist Party and Naxalites*, ed. Pratap Mitra and Mohit Sen, Communist Party Publication, November 1971.

[12] A discussion scattered through various journals over a long period on the issue is reviewed in Alice Thorner, 'Semi-Feudalism or Capitalism', *Economic and Political Weekly*, 4 Dec. 1982, pp. 1961–8, 11 Dec. 1982, pp. 1993–9, 18 Dec. 1982, pp. 2061–6.

[13] Particularly as occurs in Sumanta Banerjee, *In the Wake of Naxalbari*.

authoritarian organization. It was in the course of my association with this group that I deepened my understanding of Marxist theory and began to criticize it. It was then that I first began to attempt an evaluation of the Naxalite revolt from a sociological point of view. My ideas crystallized over a long period and took more or less their present shape at Oxford.

The principal problem I address here is the ideology of the Naxalites and its meaning. Questions about the failure of the Naxalites or the validity of their 'world-view' cannot be suitably understood, let alone tackled, until this question about the meaning of the Naxalites' ideology has been settled. The CPI(M-L) literature has often been seen as requiring no interpretation, as a transparent medium wherein meaning is manifest. The present study suggests that such literature conceals a framework of self-definition and aspiration that appropriates this manifest meaning in action, that invests it with the meaning requisite for terror. It is in this concealed existential ideology that the spiritual crisis constitutive of the terrorist commitment takes shape. It is in this sense that such existential ideology is the origin or the cause of the emergence of Naxalism. Elements of it find expression in the formulated doctrine. Certain key concepts constitutive of the ethos of Naxalite terrorism span the gulf between the formulated doctrine and the perception of self, which is resolved in activity.

Ideology

The problem of ideology does not appear so long as we are concerned solely with biology, the whole realm of culture then being relegated to some instinctual reflex that conceals instincts in some obscure way. But even the apes are not instinctual creatures.[14] With psychology the problem first begins to appear as the problem of civilization or morality or religion that is related in some fundamental way to instincts or human desire, if only negatively. It is here that one finds formulated as principle the necessity of ideology, if not as concealment, certainaly as repression.[15] The realm of values is postulated as necessary and at a

[14] See for instance the discussion in Eugène N. Marais, *The Soul of the White Ant*, trans. Winifred de Kok, London, Penguin Books, 1973, pp. 51–2.
[15] Sigmund Freud, *Civilization and its Discontents*, trans. Joan Riviere, London, The Hogarh Press, 1951.

fundamental remove from man's knowledge of his individual self. With the intrusion of the social the problem begins to take shape, either as a collective awareness, conscious or unconscious, that is different from a person's identity as individual though fundamentally related to it, perhaps even constitutive of it;[16] or as the realm of the interaction of persons with others through which the self is defined. As long as one is concerned with psychology the problem is fundamentally a mythical one, for the mediation of culture, through which the social presents itself to the individual, the immediate reality of sexuality, language, values, and knowledge (not to speak of work) from which the social is constructed, as indeed is the sense of selfhood, is not examined. Only in the disciplines essentially concerned with society—sociology and anthropology—is an encounter with the problem of ideology possible and necessary. Ideology is indeed the problem of the social form of consciousness, historically the problem of the determination of individual consciousness by social circumstances and that of the social consequences of consciousness, either individual or collective.

The problem of ideology obviously posits the realms of biology, sociology, psychology and anthropology simultaneously. It is impossible to dissociate it from any of these and still retain the sense that is conveyed to it in ordinary speech, or indeed even in a more theoretical exposition. It gathers up the counterposed realms of the social and the individual into a totality from which the two cannot be dissociated. This totalizing, far from being a 'dialectical' manoeuvre, is merely a reclamation of the original unity of the person. It is only through socialization that individuation becomes meaningful, and only as individuation that socialization is expressed.

In the rival materialist determinisms of academic American sociology (structural functionalism) and orthodox Marxism the concept of 'ideology' surfaces as the principle of cohesiveness of social groups, in the former as a 'value system', in the latter as 'class consciousness'. Simultaneously epiphenomenon and regulative principle, it serves to order existing relationships at the same time as it merely expresses these. At a remove from fundamental structural determination it provides nevertheless the crucial, if unexplored (and unexplorable) locus of structural

---

[16] See Jung's discussion of the collective unconscious in Carl G. Jung, *The Integration of the Personality*, trans. Stanley Dell, London, Kegan Paul, Trench, Trubner and Co., 1940.

change. Within these parameters the very exploration of the meaning, content and integration of ideology is transformed into a partisan enterprise that threatens the validity not only of the logical premises that serve to underpin these parameters but the social premises as well. And indeed who, schooled in these determinisms, would not be led to believe that an examination of values could not be dissociated from a revaluation, if not indeed a devaluation.

It is a profound devaluation of these doctrines (emphasizing their emphasis on partisanship), among others, that one finds expressed in the world-wide student revolts of the late 1960s. Ideological in the primary sense of upholding the priority of ideology and its necessity, they experienced a disillusionment with the fairly recent pronouncement of an 'end of ideology', dismissing it as 'mere' ideology, at the same time that they enacted their opposition to the most cherished ideals of their society and their reality. Committed paradoxically to a truth denied in the use of the term ideology, they upheld an ideology of revolt to unmask the reality of the prevalent ideology and overthrow it. The terms in which this revolt and this unmasking were expressed varied. What did not vary was the extremity of the impulse to action that overflowed merely ideological bounds into social and political action, sometimes in a wholly personal, never far removed from a symbolic, way.

Politically, if there was one issue that unified these various cultural tendencies, it was an opposition to the American involvement in Vietnam. By the Marxist-Leninist sects that formed significant ideological foci, this opposition was formulated as an opposition to US imperialism, serving to link up their own revolt with the revolutionary Marxist-Leninist discourse. Elsewhere over the globe other concerns occupied the centre-stage, especially so in the Third World. China, convulsed by the Great Proletarian Cultural Revolution, was occupied with predominantly internal concerns, though the rhetoric of leadership in the World Revolution was not lacking. In India there were the Naxalites, primarily concerned with the prospect of a revolution in India. Much more important than the political issue of Vietnam, which superficially was the only unifying issue, was the more fundamental redefinition of the 'political' attempted by the radical sects that chose to define their revolt in political terms. This was nowhere explicitly stated but formed the undercurrent to all the statements and actions of these groups. In this more far-reaching sense the political student revolts of the 1960s were ideological.

'Student unrest' is of course a phenomenon that has characterized the Indian scene for a long time—at least since the opposition to British rule.[17] Certainly, the Naxalite development is rooted in this phenomenon. But to overlook its crucial departure from the customary pattern of 'student unrest', in the form of the intrusion of principles (or 'ideology' in one of its popular usages) would be to lose sight of its distinctiveness and significance. Indeed there have been ideologically oriented student movements in Bengal before—the nationalist, and even earlier that of Young Bengal. Such student movements serve to highlight nodes in the evolution of the Bengali, and more generally Indian, spirit. The location of these crises in the student population is a matter of considerable sociological importance and needs explanation. It is in fact of almost as great a significance as the form that this crisis takes and its resolution, for it poses questions overlooked in the ideological form of the crisis, namely the social content of this crisis, or the *structural* distinctiveness of the ideology and the form that the crisis I takes for those who do not participate in it. This in no way 'demystifies' the ideology. It merely indicates that element of the ideology of which it itself is unaware—the construal of the ideology by those not involved in or sympathetic to its activity, and, more generally, its location in the culture in which it participates and which, in its ideological way, it opposes.

The word 'ideology' itself gained fresh currency in the course of and thanks to the student revolts. An investigation of their ideology is thus fraught with the difficulty posed by their self-consciousness in the adoption of ideology. It is impossible not to consider seriously the question of 'bad faith' involved in their acts, though it is all too easy to dismiss them as parent-supported revolutionaries.[18] Whatever their fate, and they were not without their successes, it is necessary both to settle accounts with their ideology and to see where it leads us in the understanding of ideology.

[17] See, for instance, Philip G. Altbach, 'The Transformation of the Indian Student Movement', *Asian Survey*, vol. VI, no. 8, Aug. 1966, and Philip G. Altbach, ed., *Turmoil and Transition: Higher Education and Student Politics in India*, Bombay, Lalvani, 1968.
[18] A. C. Macintyre, *Marcuse* (Modern Masters), London, Fontana, 1970.

The problem of ideology is not constituted, let alone solved, by postulating the connection between matter and ideas. The problem surely is how action is related to ideas. As a principle of course it can be stated that action does not flow from ideas (at least that form of it which I call literate ideology), though it is related to them. Still less are ideas a mere *post-hoc* justification of action, though they can be this (and nowhere more so than in 'Sasanka's' justification of the Naxalite 'cultural revolution'),[19] More importantly ideas, or literate ideology, and action are mediated by existential ideology.

The Marxist attempt to find a 'rational' content, if not indeed form itself, to this existential ideology as 'interest' and more particularly 'class interest' runs into difficulties when faced with 'irrational' action. The existential grounds (again in the sense of a material and therefore rational basis) of such 'irrational' action is not merely postulated but explored (or so the claim runs) by disciplines such as psychoanalysis. But that action should thus constitute itself into a rational explicable part, and an irrational aspect (needing explanation if not indeed presumed to be inexplicable) should not really surprise us, for the existential ideology in which action is rooted is neither rational nor irrational in the way these terms are used to describe literate ideology, nor an explanation of action in the terms of a literate ideology that seeks to unravel it. Existential ideology, to which access is provided by phenomenology, is the domain of manipulated or manipulable experience in terms of which the self and the world are apprehended, whether or not these are simultaneously or later conceptually defined.

The immediate form in which the problem of the relation of 'ideas' to action presents itself, to men in general no less than to the philosopher or student of thought, is the problem of choice. In the form in which a choice presents itself, the ground of this choice—the question of the will, the need for action or inaction, the very character of needs themselves, or any of a host of similar philosophic or mundane formulations—is already determined, and thus too are in a sense the possibilities of the resolution of this choice. The rising to awareness of this choice—whether considered illusory as in a theory of inaction or metaphysically revealing as in the prophetic forecast of a saint or a sage—is itself the product of the interaction of 'ideas' with action in the

---

[19] As in *Prob Akash Kal*, CPI(M-L), publication cited in Sumanta Banerjee, *In the Wake of Naxalbari*, p. 238.

constitutive acts of self- and world-definition. The only standpoint from which to grasp this simultaneous positing of a self and a world in which it is located is a phenomenological one—i.e. one located in a subjective Transcendental Ego, which for all its subjectivity, if not indeed because of it, is transcendentally (and thus necessarily inter-subjectively) intelligible.[20]

The necessity to choose obviates as a needless metaphysic any attempt to explain away this necessity by either the bio-chemical reduction of thought, or the recourse to a historical inevitability. The only materialist thesis worth considering in this regard is the thesis of materialism in ethics, i.e. the contention that men pursue material goals cloaked, where necessary, in idealistic garb.

Materialism is not merely a rejection, though it certainly is this, but an affirmation as well. And yet nothing is rejected or affirmed explicitly. It is a return to what is felt and declared by those who profess to be non-materialists (of any kind), and even by some who call themselves materialists (of some particular, perhaps 'dialectical', kind), to be the natural state.

The first explicit awareness that materialism entails is 'I', not as a defined creature in a complicated scheme of things or thoughts but as an entity sufficient unto itself, needing neither justification nor outcome, pursuing or not pursuing its ends as it chooses to formulate them, doing its own thing. Implicated in this awareness is a claim to stand beyond all moral judgements in the conventional sense—anything goes. With this claim the primacy of reason or doctrine, particularly in matters of ethics but also as access to truth generally, is dismissed, in whatever way this truth may be interpreted. It entails the rejection of universal prescriptions, and is thus at odds with philosophy in the conventional sense.

Materialism is certainly concerned with the good life, but its formulation as an ism entails a necessary paradox. As an ism it defines itself negatively as an opposition to the professed goodness of others, under which it sees the same meanness they choose to ascribe to materialists, and defiantly holds this meanness forth as the unravelling of the complexities of non-materialist and anti-materialist thinking. This low view of oneself—and of the world generally—is the defining feature of materialism as a doctrine. It demystifies, deflates and thereby claims it

[20] Edmund Husserl, *Cartesian Meditations, An Introduction to Phenomenology,* trans. Dorion Cairns, The Hague, Martinus Nijhoff, 1973.

enlightens. But its intimate concern with the good life transcends this epistemological reduction. As an opposition, still within its life-circumscribed circumstances, it affirms the this-worldly character of its aspirations in contrast to any theoretical validation or excursion into cosmology. Nevertheless, obviously, the nature of the world itself remains in doubt—though only philosophically—for in life both the materialists and those who oppose them know perfectly well where they stand.

The world of the materialist is not a construct within which the 'I' is located, it is the horizon-delimited obviousness in which the 'I' strives, to which thought is incidental except occasionally, and if the radicals are to be believed, tragically, as instrument. Its reality is not a matter of proof or argument, nor in need of grounding if only in the 'I' but one the materialist knows for a fact. Facticity is neither the opposition to will nor the possibility of its fulfilment, but that which the 'I' recognizes or chooses, accessible in desire which exists independent of the will. The investiture of this desire with necessity is the last escape from materialism, as it happens into history. The worldhood of the world of the materialist is conferred by the recognition of the finality of death.

Nihilism, which is wedded to this last awareness, dissolves the self-evidence of reality, philosophically truth. It affirms the personal character of the world and the nothingness of both (though certainly it seems to make some kind of difference where this nothingness is primarily located, if only to the philosophers). To the idealist, nihilism is the logical outcome of materialism. Nihilism itself, however, sees itself as standing beyond the idealism-materialism divide, not merely as the escape from the epistemological dilemma (pragmatism?) but as providing access to the amoral universe that the formulation of materialism as an ism, or the consistent rationality which idealism seems to dictate, entails. It claims to be the realization of philosophy and its dissolution, in contrast to historical materialism, which claims to achieve this through a praxis oriented to idealistic goals. Nihilism knows for a fact that I am everything and nothing.

These considerations, of some value for an understanding of the Naxalites and of the radicalism of the 1960s generally, do not however either exhaust the implications of materialism in a consideration of those events, or indeed provide the phenomeno-logical frame in which the choice presented itself to the revolutionaries. The anti-capitalist, neo-socialist rhetoric (or literate ideology) in which their opposition to the state of affairs expressed itself is fairly well known by now, if only obscurely understood. But neither this nor the existential ideology within which the self was constituted for these revolutionaries was materialist in the sense that I have been discussing. Both ethically (as in the affirmation of ideals) and epistemologically (in the principle of the power of the idea to penetrate an illusory appearance to its true reality, i.e. the reality of the idea) it was through and through idealist (as indeed in the case of so many contemporary Marxists). No doubt this idealism was rooted in certain material facts, in certain social conditions, to which I shall devote some attention. But neither this idealism nor these conditions can be considered constitutive of the choice that confronted the revolutionaries. True, in a superficial sense the idealism is a choice which negates the conditions with which the revolutionaries are faced. But this superficial view overlooks the fact of the constitution of the choice as such, the spiritual crisis that defines both the idealism and the conditions with which it is faced in a way that makes the 'professional revolutionary' the only possible self-definition (or ideal to be realized).

The existential ideology of the Naxalites was fundamentally a nihilist one, consisting in immediate experience of the devaluation of the highest values. Both the aspiration to these highest values and the simultaneous awareness of their nothingness gave to the attitude its simultaneously authentic and theatrical character. But this nihilism was an *active* nihilism—one which undertook to destroy the sham of values it had seen through. It defined itself positively only as an opposition, and nowhere more explicitly—and originally—than in its attack upon 'revisionism'. This revisionism however was not attacked by defining the revolutionism to which it stood counterposed but by enacting this revolutionism. Where the theory of the Naxalites concerned itself with technique, their activity assumed a symbolic and theoretical cast. The underlying and unstated ontology, the existential ideology, was nothing else than the very collapse of ontology, the loss of veritable being—nihilism. In its political implications this ontology, or collapse of ontology, was nothing other than a concentrated orientation which can only be called *anti*-political. The opposition of the Naxalites to the existing manifestations of politics was overt enough and thus indisputable. But even more fundamentally the 'political' in the name of which the Naxalites attacked these (formulated in the literate ideology as an attempt to end exploitation) was in an existential sense only a conceptualization of a fundamentally anti-political stand. This was in fact the extremity and urgency of their nihilism.

The Literature and History

The literature that has appeared on the Naxalites to date has been severely limited in its character, choosing either to ignore the questions raised by the Naxalites, or considering them an un-problematical phenomenon. Certainly all the existing accounts have lost sight of the central paradox—a party of agrarian revolution involved in urban terrorism on a large scale. Mohan Ram deplores the 'degeneration' of a Maoist movement into 'individual' terrorism.[21] Biplab Dasgupta is quick to point out that the (urban) targets of the CPI(M-L) terror were mainly policemen and members of the CPI(M), and hardly qualify as 'class enemies' as communists construe them.[22] And to Sumanta Banerjee this was a 'spontaneous youth upsurge', relatively peripheral to the main thrust of the movement that spawned it, though it was important and provoked a 'backlash'.[23] One looks in vain for any attempt to comprehend the connection of this 'spontaneity' with the CPI(M-L) rhetoric that extolled it as a 'cultural' revolution, and in vain for any attempt to grasp the logic of the transformation. It is the blindness to this most glaring of contradictions between the so-called CPI(M-L) theory and its practice that vitiates all attempts at presenting its history.

The first fact of this history is that it rests on a myth, namely Charu Mazumdar's contention (offered much later than the event, as also Kanu Sanyal's 'Report') that in Naxalbari in mid-1967 poor and landless peasants had fought for political power and not for land.[24] One looks in vain for the organs of this political power, when ministers of the United Front government, then in power in Calcutta, came to parley with the leaders of the Naxalbari disturbances. These ministers talked with the Communist radicals leading the movement in a purely personal capacity rather than as representatives of some constituted political power. And the subsequent government policy of isolating this handful of radicals—and its success!—leaves little doubt that, apart from the unstructured respect that these radicals received from the population, there were no on-going institutions of political authority. To the apologist, of course, this does not serve to show the mythical character of Charu Mazumdar's contention, for

---

[21] Mohan Ram, *Maoism in India.*
[22] See the discussion in Biplab Das Gupta, *The Naxalite Movement,* p. 83.
[23] Sumanta Banerjee, *In the Wake of Naxalbari.*
[24] Kanu Sanyal's 'The Report on the Peasant Movement in the Terai Region', *Liberation*, vol. 2, no. 1, Nov. 1968, *Deshabrati*, 24 Oct. 1968.

The peasant obviously knew what he was doing when he rose in revolt. The fact that this was designed primarily to destroy the authority of the superordinate élite and carried no elaborate blueprint for its replacement, does not put it outside the realm of politics. On the contrary, insurgency affirmed its political character precisely by its negative and inversive procedure. By trying to force a mutual substitution of the dominant and the dominated in the power structure it left nothing to doubt about its own identity as a project of power.[25]

However accurate or inaccurate this may be concerning the psychology of the peasant, the fact to notice here is that in such a defence politics has been psychologized, transformed into symbol—the very process of symbolization by which the peasant is transformed into the redeemer in Charu Mazumdar's Maoist rhetoric, stood on its head! First one sees in the peasant the symbol of one's hopes, and then by a leap of rhetoric attributes to him the symbolism of this hope!

Matters are most confused in Sumanta Banerjee's account, which apologizes for the 'rhapsodic, even exaggerated' style of CPI(M-L) reports by arguing 'that those who were writing the reports from the areas of struggles, were seeing everything through the eyes of the landless peasants.'[26] It would perhaps have been truer to say that they were writing the reports as they believed the landless peasants should see them. Unaware (deliberately?) of the gulfs between the sensibilities of revolutionaries and landless peasants, between the jargon of revolutionary discourse and the language of rural life, between the vocabulary of the CPI(M-L) and the ethos that shaped it, Banerjee unfurls the account of the Naxalites as a Maoist beginning that failed to reach the 'higher stages' of the organization of a People's Army largely because of 'the behaviour pattern of the CPI(M-L) leadership, particularly of Charu Mazumdar, which was shaped by the socio-economic environs …'.[27] As to whether these 'socio-economic environs' were merely the 'band of devotees'... who elevated him to the sacrosanct position of the 'revolutionary authority' or also 'his limited experience as a participant in the Tebhaga movement in North Bengal in 1940s', Banerjee does not make clear.[28] He seems to share the revolutionary perspectives of that leader without being 'cramped' by his limited experience. How little he

[25] Ranajit Guha, *Elementary Aspects of Peasant Insurgency in Colonial India*, Delhi, Oxford University Press, 1983, p. 9.
[26] *In the Wake of Naxalbari*, p. vi.
[27] Ibid., p. 350.
[28] Ibid., pp. 357, 356.

understands it is demonstrated by his inability to distinguish the urban intelligentsia as the section most moved to action by these perspectives.

Agrarian conditions in Bengal have been an area of ignorance in the nineteenth century, and continue to remain so today, despite the fact that most of Bengal is rural. One might even say that the twentieth century has rather exacerbated this ignorance through the very legislation which was intended to alleviate the lot of the rural poor. The rural propertied, because of the illegitimacy of their position, can now actively conceal aspects which might otherwise have come to light. 'Enlightened' legislation—and its enforcement—was responsible in no small degree for the isolation of the Indira Gandhi government during the Emergency. Though not in the same way or to the same extent, legislation against 'feudalism'—the practice of taking half the produce as rent by proprietors of agricultural property—is likely to isolate any group or party advocating it, as also any group fulminating against it, because the practice is not limited to a small handful of rich exploiters but forms part of the fabric of rural society. In the same way as many industrial workers act as money-lenders, so too the practice of leasing out land is not restricted to rich or powerful families. But at any rate that is not what most of the communist groups are fighting against at the moment. Their strategy is, rather, geared to realizing the legislation already passed regarding land holdings. And even with their zeal and recourse to violence, they have not been able to illuminate the structure of agrarian society. The communists in Bengal have been concerned with agrarian agitation for quite some time now, and yet they too are unable to provide a clear picture of the relations obtaining. This can only be explained in the following way: the urban élites are ignorant of rural conditions and function with a sketchy schema that they take to be the case, without thoroughly investigating their postulated ends—social justice or the increase of production, or optimistically both. Their rural cohorts, not called upon to enlighten anyone, keep matters to themselves, either because they constitute that small fraction to which the abstract schema applies or because they themselves are 'implicated' in it and, through cunning or inertia, are unwilling to enlighten their superiors.

Less confused, because more alive to the urban content of the failed revolution of the CPI(M-L), Biplab Dasgupta is, perhaps for two reasons, not puzzled by this urbanism in the face of rural rhetoric. Intimately involved with the CPI(M), its revolutionism and eclectic theory, he sees nothing strikingly incongruous in this contradiction of doctrine and is more concerned with demonstrating how the logic of the CPI(M-L)'s politics was principally directed against the CPI(M). However true it may be that the CPI(M) became the CPI(M-L)'s principal enemy, the direction in which Dasgupta pushes it denies autonomy to CPI(M-L) initiatives, and that on a crucial matter. He distinguishes between 'cultural revolution' (the smashing of statues, etc.) and 'urban guerrilla activities', citing a precise date for the former—the attack on the Gandhi Centre at Jadavpur University on 21 April 1969 (after the fall of the second UF), and no fixed date for the latter, though the former is to him relatively spontaneous and the latter a calculated move.[29] The distinction, however sound it may seem, will not help in understanding the logic of events, for both originate in a far more public event just *before* the fall of the United Front, when Naxalites attacked seven cinema houses screening the film 'Prem Pujari'. Despite this Dasgupta is alive to the distinction between both Maoism and Naxalism, and Marxism and Naxalism. Nevertheless, though he notices that the Naxalites flourished only in areas with a history of communist activity, he does not explore the nature of their relation to communism in India, being content to find 'the Naxalite attitude to violence' their most striking divergence from it.[30] He believes that they failed because their 'assessment of the Indian situation and characterization of the ruling class were wrong'.[31]

In this context, Manoranjan Mohanty's work needs to be mentioned as providing a more adequate approach to the mediation of theory in its final conclusion that 'this movement was pre-organizational in character because it was confined basically to mass activity without a network of organization'.[32] This highlights a feature of Naxalite organization that Dasgupta notices as 'conspiratorial' and 'decentralized'. The features of this 'pre-organizational organization are not discussed as this entails, again, an investigation of the ideology of the CPI(M-L), though the motions of an attempt at a taxonomy are made.

These avowedly partisan works seem to be implicitly in agreement 'that Naxalism is basically a socio-economic problem and only superficially

[29] Biplab Das Gupta, *The Naxalite Movement*, pp. 68–93.
[30] Ibid., p. 210.
[31] Ibid., p. 229.
[32] Manoranjan Mohanty, *Revolutionary Violence, A Study of the Maoist Movement in India*, New Delhi, 1977, p. 221.

a law and order problem'.[33] The sense of the distinction seems easy enough to understand. To the construal of the government that these events constitute a breakdown of law and order, and therefore must be tackled as such a problem, the distinction argues that the events involve more than merely a breakdown of law and order. They are an expression of economic injustices and constitute a political challenge to the state. In retrospect it is plain that *all* political parties, and the ruling party among them, saw and reacted to the Naxalites as a political problem, in the sense in which those who insist on this aspect of the events call it a political problem. The *political* ground on which the various parties who opposed the Naxalites united was the breakdown of law and order that the politics of the Naxalites entailed. The Naxalites themselves are aware of this political dimension of law and order. But to them, and to another section of opinion close to them, the question is not that of a disintegration of law and order at all but rather that of the competing legitimacy of two opposed systems of law and order. (As in the previous case, legitimacy is seen to be rooted in the notion of economic justice, and politics its 'concentrated expression.') This seems to be the only adequate explanation of the importance attached to the Naxalbari revolt as a fight for political power rather than land or economic benefits as maintained by Charu Mazumdar. And here, in retrospect, it seems obvious that of the parties in power at the time it was only the CPI(M) who perceived the Naxalites as a challenge to their political legitimacy—for reasons internal to the constitution of the CPI(M) itself. Witness the frantic overtures of the CPI(M) to the dissenting rebels of Naxalbari. And again, in retrospect, it is equally clear that the Naxalites' *later* claim to have in the period established a viable political organization in the region, i.e. a firm basis of their alternative law and order, is largely hot air. Thus the Naxalites can be seen to have triggered off *and* spearheaded a disintegration of law and order in the Naxalbari region, and all the subsequent regions in West Bengal including Calcutta.

This of course does not in any way tarnish their claim, so dear to them, to being revolutionaries, even in the Leninist sense, for central to the Leninist philosophy of revolution is the need to destroy the state, the formulator and executor of law and order.[34] But it brings to the fore the

---

[33] Haridwar Rai and K. M. Prasad, 'Naxalism: A Challenge to the Proposition of Peaceful Transition to Socialism', *Indian Journal of Political Science*, xxxiii, 4 Oct.–Dec. 1972, p. 480.

[34] V. I. Lenin, *The State and Revolution*, London, Martin Lawrence, 1933.

aspect of revolutions that Marxists, and Leninists among them, in their formulae of the replacement of the rule of one class by another, characteristically ignore. The aspect is one that is central to the notion and reality of social revolutions—the complete disintegration of the legal fabric and the breakdown of order. Everyone goes his own way and political organizations can do little but attempt to ride out the storm, or give it direction. In this sense, the attempt of the government to characterize the Naxalite events as a 'law and order' problem, far from belittling their significance attached to them a profound importance, for 'law and order' lie at the very basis of the government's own claim to legitimacy.

But away from this ideological theorizing, the insistence on the 'socio-economic' character of the 'Naxalite problem' invokes Marxist demystifications of the ideological. It states, paradoxically, the Naxalite thesis itself as its own causation. From economic causes superstructural events ensue—entirely overlooking that but for the Naxalites there would be no Naxalbari.

The spontaneous movement as it figures in Leninist theory only refers to the fact that such a movement is not led by the Leninists. The implication, though, seems to be that such a movement is inchoate, directionless and doomed to failure without their leadership. Lenin's own appreciation of spontaneity underwent some modification after the Bolsheviks were in power, though not essentially. The desertion of Russian soldiers from the front presented a 'movement' that was spontaneous (as indeed did the election of the Soviets themselves) with which the Bolshevik party had to cope. It was not, because of that, inchoate or directionless, though it did not rule out the necessity of the party to lead—in today's uncharitable terminology—to retain its credibility. Other considerations intervened in the 'justice' meted out to the Kronstadt sailors and workers. Spontaneity in general creates the situations in which the Leninist party is expected to lead.

As this situation, the spontaneous movement is a product of developments, organizations, forces and desires to which the Leninist party is largely peripheral. Above all it is an activity that takes place without direct recourse to the Leninist party or its functionaries. Some of it can be traced directly to active agencies other than this party, but for the large part it represents the outcome of social and psychological processes that have been a long time in the making. The disputes about the character of the Indian revolution among Indian communists, as also to a large extent those about the mode of production among Indian Marxists, are attempts to label, if not understand, these social and psychological processes. What vitiates these attempts is not so much the predominantly economic character of these analyses as the unstated assumption of such analysis that, given an economic characterization, the situation has been explained and a strategy implied. Concessions have of late been made to 'super-structural' aspects, but only in terms of the need for philosophizing and cultural criticism among Marxists.

What is totally lacking from this Leninist perspective is any conception of the integration of culture and economy in which culture is not dependent on the economy. Far less is there an anthropological awareness of the economy as life-process in which culture forms an essential component. And anathema of course (perhaps the principal ideological enemy) is the view that the economy constitutes merely an element, of greater or lesser importance, of an overarching and composite culture. It is only within this last perspective that the 'spontaneous movement' of Leninist orthodoxy, or even the Leninist party itself, can be adequately understood.

Naxalism is far from exhausted if it is described as merely the ideology of terrorism (or even more narrowly the ideology of urban terrorism), just as the Naxalite practice is far from exhausted in the exercise of terror. There is on the one hand the Maoist perspective of peasant revolution in which it has its origin, and the subsequent concerns with issues of socialism in which it is expressed. But the heritage of the Naxalite events, dismissed by its critics as just this 'degeneration' into 'individual terrorism', has yet to take account of the terrorist form that the movement assumed.

It is difficult to pin a precise date on the turning point in this evolution of terrorism, partly because the formative influences of an event are at work far earlier than the event itself occurs, and partly because in the specific form in which this terrorism evolved in the case of the Naxalites it was never a part of the formulated doctrine. Tendencies towards elements of the outlook characteristic of the Naxalite terrorists existed in at least Charu Mazumdar's thought long before this outlook became an explicit and dominant one, just as on the other hand Charu Mazumdar's leadership, even in the end, remained purely a spiritual and inspirational one rather than a conscious shaper of the organization (if that is the right word) that grew out of this leadership. In saying this, however, one has identified the leadership of the terrorist phase as distinctly that of Charu Mazumdar, and thus the evolution of the terrorism and its organization of the Naxalites with the event that establishes his leadership—the founding of the CPI(M-L) on 22 April 1969. True, at that time, the organization of the party, though already largely urban (as always), was not yet a terrorist one. In its emergence the formulation of the line of annihilation is an essential prerequisite, and more importantly its advertisement in the *Liberation* article in February 1970. But with the formation of the party and its subsequent announcement, the leader, as formulator of doctrine, and the large mass of the revolutionary youth as shapers of the organization and its executors (in more senses than one), were brought together into a single fold, and in circumstances in which another outcome seems altogether improbable. It was obviously not Mazumdar alone who was responsible for the evolution of the urban terror—for it was rather the mass of urban youth who interpreted his teachings in the particular way essential to the evolution of this terror. But in the support that Mazumdar extended to them, and in the devotion they claimed towards him lay the mutual recognition as 'revolutionaries' that understood this revolutionary as a terrorist. There is already an indication of this in the *staged* character of the formation of the party itself. The party is not born in the press of circumstance, coping with events with which it must keep pace, as e.g. was the CPI(M), but is theatrically composed on a 'historic' date—Lenin's birthday, 22 April—and equally theatrically announced on May Day. Already the element of unreality characteristic of the terrorist experience and ethos has entered inextricably into the picture.

Who is a terrorist? For governments in power the question is an easy one to answer—anyone or any group attempting to overthrow the established regime by recourse to violence, or more specifically terror. For governments in power, whether or not the terrorists themselves see their acts as inducing terror is usually immaterial, relevant only being the fact that their acts provoke terror among the population, or at least among those sections of it that feel threatened by the terrorists' existence, whether or not the terrorists intend to threaten them in the first place. The passing of legislation to curb terrorism is usually the way in which terrorists are identified as terrorists. Central to this legislation is an extension of the scope of activities considered criminal and a relaxation of the rules of rigorous evidence deemed permissible to convict. This happens in a situation where the attempt to cope with terrorism has not itself passed out of the rigorous framework of the law (as is to a lesser or greater extent always the case) and has not assumed out and out the dimensions of a civil war.

The rhetoric of civil war is, however, fundamental to the terrorists' justification of their own actions, on whatever limited scale these actions may be mounted, the vindication of the terrorists' claims being a matter that is decided by the outcome of their actions themselves. There is no paucity of examples of groups who had been called terrorist subsequently coming to power either as a group, or more usually individuals involved with the group later coming to power through involvement with some other group. The effect of this is to produce a situation that is even more usual than these cases of immediate involvement, in which those who had been called terrorists by an earlier regime occupy an honoured, even sanctified, position in a later one, if only as martyrs.

'Terrorists' thus occupy somewhat the same position that 'revolutionaries' occupied in the last century, and there seems to be no way of examining the denotation, let alone the connotations, of the epithet without involving oneself in an examination of the claims of legitimacy and the charges of illegitimacy espoused by the terrorists themselves.

Significance

The three concepts central to this study, namely ideology, nihilism and terrorism, are all words that pose definitional problems. To a large extent these stem from the evaluation of these concepts themselves, the open spectrum of significations it is possible to read into them. But if this is so, it is largely because each of these is in origin an evaluative word, loaded with judgement on the state of things it undertakes to describe. In this sense, apart from being modern in their occurrence, i.e. occurring in modern times, they are modern in their very being (or essence or spirit):

The fourth distinction (being and the ought) was only remotely foreshadowed by the designation of the *on* (the essent, that which is) as *agathon* (the good). It belongs wholly to the modern era. And since the end of the eighteenth century it has determined one of the dominant positions of the modern spirit toward the essent in general.[35]

The fact of their centrality does not need belabouring and can be validated through other arguments as well. Whereas it is possible to subsume the literate ideology of the Naxalites under some such rubric as modernization, a consideration of their existential ideology leaves no doubt that here we are essentially concerned with modernism—and the modern itself.

[35] Martin Heidegger, *An Introduction to Metaphysics*. trans. Ralph Manheim, Yale University Press, 1959, pp. 94–5.

Chapter Two

Ideology

It will be obvious, therefore, that to ask a man why he does a certain thing is by no means an invariably efficient method of discovering the genuine causes underlying his action. Introspection, however honestly it may be carried out, frequently fails when it attempts more than the mere recording of the superficial contents of consciousness. So soon as it aims at the elucidation of the real springs of action, there is always the possibility that either no result whatever is obtainable, or one vitiated by the mechanisms of rationalization. This fact is of primary importance, even to the psychologist who concerns himself only with the normal mind.
—Bernard Hart, *The Psychology of Insanity*

Ideology, when not itself an ideological word, is usually polemical. The everyday use of the term is aptly defined in the counterposition of the ideological to the pragmatic. The *Encyclopaedia Britannica* rejects this polarity as neither exhaustive nor unambiguous. Nevertheless, within the ambiguities of everyday political discourse the ideological and pragmatic points of view are seen to constitute an exhaustive polarity that is at its very root polemical. Whether the ideological is extolled (as a commitment to principles) or denigrated (as a recourse to beliefs and rhetoric that obscure the problem at hand), it none the less exists as an altogether different approach to politics from the pragmatic. And according as ideology is seen as something positive or something negative, conversely is pragmatism seen as something negative (selfish opportunism and unprincipled time-serving) or something positive (a no-nonsense approach to the real issues at stake). Obviously, in the counterposition, opposed perceptions of reality are pitted against each other.

If the *Encyclopaedia Britannica* is keenly aware of the politically significant content of ideology, the American *Encyclopaedia of Social Sciences*,

though aware of this content, is equally concerned with the vexed relation of ideology to science, and finds it necessary to offer an apologia for
the dubious attempt of American scholars in the fifties to proclaim an
end of ideology. Harry Johnsson's article in the *Encyclopaedia*, 'Ideology
and the Social System', while arguing that ideological beliefs are fallacious (though they may indeed be functional), ambitiously argues for a
definitive establishment of the truth or falsity of an ideology:

social science is not the *direct* criterion by which we judge whether or not particular ideas are ideological. The direct criterion is what Parsons (1959) calls a
'value-science-integrate'. The ideas to be judged purport to describe a particular
social system or some of its aspects. The corresponding value-science-integrate is
an objective description of the same social system, a description made with reference to the conceptual schemes of social science but showing to what extent in
fact the cultural value system of that particular social system is carried out or
realized in the various levels of its structure. If the ideas to be judged depart from
this value-science-integrate, the departures are said to be ideological ... to deny
the possibility of such a test is in effect to deny the possibility of social science.

Edward Shils in his article on 'Ideology' in the same *Encyclopaedia*,
though sharing the view of ideology as distortion, is not quite as categorical in distinguishing ideology from science, preferring to see the
false claims of ideologists as based on their dogmatism and their denial
of the free spirit of dispassionate inquiry.

Both these contemporary usages of the term 'ideology' see it as a
system of ideas which, desirable, or not, stands at a remove from the
perception of a manifest reality that it undertakes to describe or master.
Totally missing in this usage is the original sense in which the word first
came into being as a science of ideas.[1] The *Oxford English Dictionary*
highlights the contradictory meanings clustering about the word ideology when it gives as its two meanings:[2]

1. The science of ideas; that department of philosophy or psychology which
deals with the origin and nature of ideas.
a. *spec.* Applied to the system of the French philosopher Condillac, according to
which all ideas are derived from sensations.

---

[1] It is in this meaning that the French Ideologists of Napoleonic times originally
coined the word. Their science of ideas was to serve, however, political goals, an
enterprise that led Napoleon to use the term of them in a pejorative sense, a
sense that Marx appropriated.
[2] *OED*, complete edition.

b. The study of the way in which ideas are expressed in language, and, on the other hand,
2. Ideal or abstract speculation; in a depreciatory sense, impractical or visionary theorizing or speculation.

The former, original, meaning has largely fallen out of use, to be replaced by the 'sociology of knowledge', whereas the latter remains. The problem clustering around the contemporary use of the word ideology centres rather on the question of the possibility of such a 'sociology of knowledge' (which appropriates the Marxian concept of ideology), or indeed of the possibility of a science of ideas at all. Exemplified in the tortuous explorations of the Marxist Althusser,[3] the problem raised by the very nature of the conception of ideology is whether it is possible to have a non-ideological, i.e. scientific (or truthful), perception of reality, or more particularly social reality. This form of the problem is *largely* the outcome of the Marxian and Marxist development of the concept of ideology.

Marx's use of the concept of ideology in 'The German Ideology' ascribes to it a fallacious or distorted character. In that book the ideas of the Left Hegelian philosophers are criticized and dismissed as ideology, with a sketching out in opposition to these ideas the programme of a science that is to replace such ideological theorizing. The premises of this science, justly famous, appeal to 'real individuals, their activity and the material conditions under which they live, both those which they find already existing and those produced by their activity' as the unravelment of the true or actual meaning of their ideas.[4] The ideological character, i.e. fallaciousness, of the ideas of the Left Hegelians is seen to consist of their unawareness of the social conditions in which their ideas are rooted. In opposition to the ideological, i.e. ideational or ideal, universality claimed by the Left Hegelians, Marx sets up a scientific and material universality, namely the necessity and the production of material life. No obvious logical connection is established, however, between the ideas of the Left Hegelians and their social circumstances beyond the postulation of such a connection.

[3] Louis Althusser, *Reading Capital*, with Etienne Balibar, trans. Ben Brewster, London, NLB, 1970.
[4] Karl Marx and F. Engels, *The German Ideology*, ed. C.J. Arthur, London, Lawrence and Wishart, 1970, p. 42.

The assumption of a logical and necessary relation between ideology and social circumstance runs throughout the whole of Marx's work. Both its necessary character and its fallaciousness are seen to be rooted in its concordance with social circumstance, which it takes as unproblematical and seeks to justify. This is explicitly the case in Marx's evaluation of religion. Simultaneously 'the opium of the people'[5] and the injunction to 'Accumulate',[6] the Judaeo-Christian religion, particularly in its Protestant forms, is seen to be particularly suited to the evolution of capitalism.[7] The most striking and revealing (as far as Marx's own method is concerned) comment on religion occurs, however, in the 'Theses on Feuerbach,' where the disjunction between the religious and wordly realms (man's 'religious alienation' if you like) is seen to be merely a reflection of a disjunction in the social fabric that gives it form.[8] Philosophy, too, is bound up in this ideologizing, though its content is seen to be liberating. In some way a quintessential expression of reality, it suffers from the defect of stopping short at mere comprehension of the world when the 'point' is to change it.[9]

In all of this, however, no positive conception of the reality that ideology distorts appears. It is only with the formulation that 'the anatomy of civil society is to be sought in political economy that a principle is established which will permit the accurate investigation of reality and demystification of the concealments and mystifications of 'ideology'.[10] With this the whole of non-economic thought is relegated to a superstructure that can at best merely reflect the economic base. But this for Marx poses two kinds of problems. The first, to which Marx devotes less

[5] K. Marx, *Introduction to the Contribution to the Critique of Hegel's Philosophy of Right*, trans. Annette John and Joseph O'Malley, Cambridge University Press, p. 131.

[6] K. Marx, Capital, vol. I, trans. Samuel Moore and Edward Aveling, Moscow, Foreign Languages Publishing House, 1961, p. 595.

[7] Ibid., p. 79.

[8] K. Marx, *Theses on Feuerbach, no. 4, Collected Works*, vol. 5, K. Marx and F. Engels, London, Lawrence and Wishart, 1976, p. 4.

[9] K. Marx, 'Difference between the Democritean and Epicurean Philosophy of Nature in General', *Collected Works*, vol. 1, pp. 22–105. See also Leading Article in no. 179 of the *Kölnische Zeitung*, ibid., p. 195.

[10] K. Marx, 'Introduction to A Contribution to the Critique of Political Economy', in David Horowitz, *Marx and Modern Economics*, London, MacGibbon and Kee, 1968.

thought but more activity, is the problem that it is only in these ideological forms that men become aware of economic circumstances and
conflicts and fight them out.[11] Marx's involvement as a socialist agitator
is informed on the one hand by the attempt to raise this agitation above
moral dispute and on the other to identify it with the real movement of
the working class. The second concerns the ideological character of political economy itself. It is to this that Marx devotes his mature thought.
But whereas in the case of the criticism of 'The German Ideology' Marx
appeals against the ideologists to a manifest material reality, namely that
investigated by political economy, in his critique of political economy he
appeals to abstract principles implicit in the activity of individuals, of
which they are unaware.[12] The word ideology is not used for this, but it
adds a complexity to the notion of ideology significant for later Marxist
use. The resolution of both kinds of problems is in a recourse to the
'economic', but as we shall see this 'economic' aspect, as the materialism
Marx espouses generally, has a metaphysical dimension.

The fundamentally economic character of social relations in capitalist society appears to Marx in the prevalence of commodities as the
repository of wealth, and the transformation of labour power itself into
a commodity.[13] Certainly, Marx's assumption of the fundamentally economic character of social relations is not restricted to capitalist society,
but whereas for Marx pre-capitalist societies are easily revealed as fundamentally economic organizations by the very appearance of capitalist
society, the economic character of capitalist society itself produces its
own mystifications.[14] Such mystifications are threefold. There is, first,
the ideological mystification of liberty and the doctrine of property,
belied both by the emergence of the capitalist form of property from the
feudal[15] and the very dynamic of capitalist appropriation as an outcome
of commodity production.[16] There is, second, the political-economic
mystification of the character of wages as the value of labour which
masks the capitalist appropriation of surplus value.[17] And there is, finally,

[11] Ibid.
[12] K. Marx, *Capital*, esp. pp. 75–83.
[13] Ibid., p. 35 and p. 167.
[14] K. Marx, 'Introduction to A Contribution to the Critique of Political Economy'.
[15] K. Marx, *Capital*, p. 77 and pp. 713–16.
[16] Ibid., pp. 613–14, p. 762, p. 774, and esp. p. 587.
[17] Ibid.

commodity fetishism which gives reality to the abstractions of political economy by concealing the social character of the labour process in the garb of private exchange.[18]

Of these mystifications it is only commodity fetishism that poses perhaps intractable problems for the Marxist perception of the 'economic', for here the actual consciousness of the people engaged in the labour process ceases to be a point of reference, in favour of a system of thought that abstracts from and represents this consciousness. It is a concept central to the philosophy of Marxism that overtly contradicts the programme of 'The German Ideology':

In the first method of approach [i.e. the idealist Hegelian] the starting point is consciousness taken as the living individual; in the second method [Marx's own materialist one], which conforms to real life, it is the real living individuals themselves, and consciousness is considered solely as *their* consciousness.[19]

The commodity is, in general, 'a very mysterious thing'[20] to Marx when 'the value-form, whose fully developed shape is the money-form, is very elementary and simple'.[21] It is this relocation of the mystery of economic life that characterizes the metaphysical element in Marx's category of the 'economic', and makes it possible to reconcile idealist, revolutionary aspirations with a materialist philosophy. It does not, however, exhaust the peculiarity of the economic domain that is fundamental for Marx. Of equal importance is the economic character of force, for not only is force 'the midwife of every old society pregnant with a new one. It is itself an economic power.'[22] The economic domain is thus only fully understood as a 'this-worldly' domain in opposition to the postulated other-worldliness of religion, or indeed of ideological thought in general. It is as the unravelling of the mystifications of ideological thought that Marx's economics establishes itself as both materialist and scientific.

Much Marxist apologetic has felt the need to modify this insistence on the economic with which Marx lays his claim to science. Impressed perhaps by the absurdity of the contention that 'being determines consciousness', when human being is as Marx himself recognizes obviously

---

[18] Ibid., pp. 72–4.
[19] K. Marx and F. Engels, *The German Ideology*, p. 47.
[20] K. Marx, *Capital*, vol. 1, p. 71.
[21] Ibid., pp. 57–8.
[22] Ibid.

'conscious being', or the logical and empirical contradictions of holding by a doctrine of economic determinism, many Marxist thinkers have demanded a reinterpretation of the Marxist conception of ideology. At its most succinct and polemical extreme, such a view contends 'that the old notion of ideology as a gaseous effect of the economic structure is inadequate and must be replaced by a conception of ideology as an integral and substantive element of all social practice.'[23] There are on the other hand Marxists such as Perry Anderson who hold that the ideologization of Marxism, in the sense of its turning to philosophy, characteristic of European Marxism, is a product of the ebb of the working class movement in Europe.[24] More consistent with Leninist materialism, such a view holds fast to the Marxian interpretation of the distinction between ideology and science, ignoring the ideologization of the whole of social science characteristic of Lenin's thought and that of the Third Communist International.

Two aspects of Lenin's thought are relevant to the present discussion, both theoretical and both inextricably connected with his organizational perspectives. The first and perhaps more important in the present context is his transformation of the use of the word ideology from a pejorative sense to a neutral one, and the theory of consciousness with which it is connected. Socialist consciousness for Lenin was not something that developed spontaneously in the workers' movement but had to be brought to it from the outside.[25] As the bearer of this consciousness the Russian Social Democratic Labour Party (RSDLP), composed largely of intellectuals connected with the workers' movement, was engaged in a primarily ideological task. Socialist ideology was thus counterposed to bourgeois ideology, without the question of the distinction between ideology and science occupying the prominence that it did in Marx's thought. Whereas for Marx, all that was entailed in the scientificity of the socialist thinker was the necessity merely to become the mouthpiece of the workers' movement, to give expression to what he saw unfolding under his very eyes, Lenin was more concerned with

[23] Colin Sumner, *Reading Ideologies, An Investigation into the Marxist Theory of Ideology and Law*, London, Academic Press, 1979, p. 290.
[24] Perry Anderson, *Considerations on Western Marxism*, London, NLB, 1976.
[25] This is the commonplace of Lenin's teaching on the proletarian party. See for instance his 'What is to be Done?', *Collected Works*, vol. 5, London, Lawrence and Wishart, Moscow, Foreign Languages Publishing House, 1961, esp. p. 375.

organizing and leading such a movement. The closest Lenin got to the vexed question of the truth of polemical ideologies was the philosophical tract 'Materialism and Empirio-Criticism'. This is not to deny Lenin's concern for the truth, or more acceptably perhaps, his commitment to science, but to indicate that in his thought the theoretical problem of the distinction between ideology and science has ceased to matter.[26]

Lenin does not see himself as significantly at odds with Marx in this matter, or at least does not show his awareness of it. Nevertheless, the second aspect of his thought worthy of consideration here is a conscious departure from Marx's prejudices. It is intimately connected with Lenin's materialist, theory of ideology and is of some political significance. Imperialism, formulated by the theorists of the Second International as a higher stage of the capitalism that Marx undertook to describe, analyse and attack, and which essentially consisted of the export of capital by industrially developed (capitalist) countries to others less developed, is also construed by Lenin to have rendered the European working class non-revolutionary.[27] Fed on imperialist super-profits, the great hope and cornerstone of Marx's theoretical edifice, this class had lost its concern for social revolution.[28] As point of fact it is worth mentioning here that the capitalism Marx undertakes to exhibit, that in Britain, is already inextricably connected at the time Marx is writing with the plunder of profit from the colonies. But, though aware of this fact in his writings on India, Marx refuses to allow this in any way to alter his presentation of capitalism as anything other than a self-subsistent development.[29]

The implications of the Leninist view of consciousness are caught up with two kinds of problems. The first of these is the fundamental paradox of Leninist revolutionary theory—the concept of class-consciousness. If indeed socialist consciousness is imported into the working class from outside itself, this argues for an altogether different relation between

[26] His avowal of Marxism is indeed related to some such commitment to science. See his polemic against the Narodniks, *The Heritage We Renounce*, *Collected Works*, vol. 2, London, Lawrence and Wishart, Moscow, Foreign Languages Publishing House, 1960, pp. 493–534.

[27] As for example R. Hilferding, *Finance Capital*, ed. Tom Bottomore, London, Routledge and Kegan Paul, 1981.

[28] V. I. Lenin, *Imperialism and the Split in Socialism*, in *Collected Works*. pp. 105–20.

[29] K. Marx, and F. Engels, *On Colonialism*, London, Lawrence and Wishart, n.d.

social groups and the ideas or ideologies to which they subscribe than the one assumed by Marx. True, even in the Marxist view, the disjunction between the ideas held by the working class and those that it should have had if the Marxist theory of ideology were true had already come to the surface, both in the question of the truth of the ideas of political economy, and implicitly in Marx's own theoretical revolutionary activity. But these questions are not addressed directly in either the work of Marx or that of Lenin.

The paradoxical notion of class-consciousness that derives logically from Lenin's views on the subject is explored explicitly by Lukács. Lukács, however, given the nature of Lenin's understanding of ideology, can only explain class-consciousness as a consciousness imputed to a particular class.[30] He leaves unexplored what the ground of such an imputation is to be, leaving us to presume perhaps that it would consist of a 'logical' inference from the Marxist understanding of classes. This too is rather uncertain, considering that for Luákcs what is crucial in the appellation 'Marxist' is not this or that pronouncement of Marx but Marx's method. Marx's own views on his method are notoriously obscure, offering only the observation that he claims his method is dialectical and the precise reverse of the mystifying Hegelian formulation of dialectic. If Engels' presentation of the materialist dialectic is to be taken as one that Marx shared (about which there is some dispute),[31] this dialectic resolves itself into three general laws of development, which Engels would contend are—as all philosophy—general laws abstracted from the process of development.[32] Thought, reason, or human comprehension is significantly absent in this schema, which thus bypasses the whole problem.

Where Lukács' partisan work explores the implications of Leninist thought or Marxist theory, Mannheim is at greater pains to extend this thought into a theory of consciousness in general. In his work all thought, and political thought in particular, is seen to be ideological, i.e. distorted. Varieties of ideological thought—Utopias or ideology proper—are possible, but the approach to the truth of affairs is made possible only on the

[30] Georg Lukács, *History and Class Consciousness* (esp. 'Class Consciousness', pp. 46–82), trans. Rodney Livingstone, London, Merlin Press, 1971.
[31] Jeff Coulter, 'Marxism and the Engels Paradox', *The Socialist Register,* 1971, eds. Ralph Miliband and John Saville, London, The Merlin Press, pp. 129–56.
[32] F. Engels, *Dialectics of Nature,* trans. C. Dutt, Moscow, 1954.

basis of a free-floating declassed intelligentsia.[33] In sum this view presents a logical outcome of the Leninist theory and practice, but where Lenin is partisan Mannheim aspires to the truth that is possible for the intelligentsia. Contemporary fulminations against ideology paradoxically see the intellectuals of a society as the source of this evil influence, rather than a ground for its demystification.[34] At all events, whatever one's response to ideology or the possibility of its transcendence, in addition to the classes that in the Marxist schema underlie and explain ideology the stratum of intellectuals—or more generally the intelligentsia—emerges as a significant locus of ideology or its demystification.

Difficulties in the Instrumental Understanding of Ideology

When used pejoratively ideology indicates a disjunction between the state of affairs and the way in which this state of affairs is perceived. The source of error in the Marxian schema is postulated to lie in the social circumstances in which it is located, and reference to which both explains the distortion and indicates its 'true' meaning. Whereas Marxists generally lay emphasis on the social character of ideology, leaving the motivation and lives of ideologists or scientists in relatively obscure irrelevance, Mannheim and contemporary donouncers of ideology draw attention to the intellectuals or intelligentsia as a stratum, distinct from classes in the Marxian sense, involved in the production of ideology or its demystification. Despite certain expressive overtones to the meaning of ideology in the work of Marx, this whole Marxist-Leninist conception of ideology can be called instrumental. It does indeed share this instrumentality with the conception of ideology as positive and necessary ideals in politics. What I mean by its instrumental character is the assumption that ideology as it occurs and is produced is located in a social dynamic and is aimed at activity in the social milieu, whether this activity is conservative, ameliorative or revolutionary. In the Marxian schema of course this instrumentality is identified with the ontology of the social classes. But even where, as in Mannheim's work, this social distortion can be surmounted by the free enquiry of intellectuals, the

[33] Karl Mannheim, *Ideology and Utopia*, trans. Louis Wirth and Edward Shils, London, Routledge and Kegan Paul, 1936.
[34] See, for instance, Lewis S. Feuer, *Ideology and the Ideologists*, Oxford, Basil Black well, 1975.

fundamentally ideological and social character of thought in general, as also its instrumentality, is not denied.

In India and in Indian writing on the subject (perhaps most markedly in the discipline of history) ideology, far from being a pejorative term, has a positive validating character. Ideology is a high-minded idealism opposed to the selfish and petty scrabbling for power that others see as the content of politics.[35] But even here ideology is seen to be instrumental in character, aimed at uniting group identities and positing (metaphysical?) goals for them. This might indeed well be the case. But the point to be made is that the postulation of ideology, or the realm of ideas, on the one hand, and social groups or classes on the other, overlooks the way in which ideology is appropriated and understood. The assumption of a logical identity between certain groups and the ideologies to which they subscribe rests on a prejudice that promises little in the elucidation of the dynamics of ideology.

There have of course been explorations of the dynamics of ideology other than the instrumentalist one, notably the work of Pareto, and if one is willing to forage further in philosophy, the work of Nietzsche. Neither of these, however, explicitly uses the word ideology, though much of their writing is concerned with the relationship of ideas, and distorted ideas particularly, with human and social life. Where Marxists and those who adopt their conception of ideology trace this ideology to a rationalist social metaphysic of class interest, Pareto and Nietzsche are concerned with a psychological interpretation of ideologies and their meaning. Premised on a non-rationalist (if not indeed irrationalist) conception of the human psyche in general and motivation in particular, these views emphasize the expressive character of ideology. That this expression is implicated in action itself remains a dogma even here, the attempt of these thinkers being to relate received or transmitted ideology to a universal and familiar psychology. Because of this, despite its richness and fruitfulness, locked in polemical confrontation with the rationalist Marxist interpretation of ideology, this approach is also committed to the instrumentalist view of ideology. Only here it is a psychological substrate rather than a rational class interest that is conveyed in the ideology.

[35] T. Raychaudhuri, 'Indian Nationalism as Animal Politics', in *The Historical Journal*, 22, 3 (1979), pp. 747–63.

The main difficulty with an instrumentalist understanding of ideology is that the interpretation of any ideology is itself an independent enterprise. Whether through specific acts of interpreters who constitute an organization or the evolution of a discourse which appropriates an ideology to the purposes of a group, an ideology remains at a remove from the psychology and indeed the activity that it is meant to codify. It is indeed this distance that gives an ideology its ideological character. The distortion characteristic of ideological consciousness lies not so much in its patent falsity, but its distance from the focus of its concern, the masking of the frame of reference within which it acquires significant meaning.

It is in this context that the counterposed concepts—the Marxist 'class consciousness' and the American sociological 'end of ideology'— geared to a theory of ideology, themselves emerge as ideological in the pejorative sense that it is their aim to transcend. Class-consciousness in the Marxist usage certainly does not refer to the awareness of a person in society of belonging to a particular class that influences, say, his or her choice of partner in marriage. It is a more embracing philosophical concept, concerned with the evolution of a political identity in conformity with Marxist guidelines or under Marxist leadership. Its meaning cannot be dislocated from the Leninist theory in which it lies embedded. And the Leninist theory itself remains opaque without reference to the revolutionary ethos that informs it. In this more comprehensive context, class-consciousness, far from being a concept that describes an empirical existent, emerges as an Ought in two senses. First, it postulates that there is a particular way in which its saviour, the proletariat, ought to think; and second it presents an Ought for the revolutionary—a moral or even categorical imperative. This dual Ought is more fundamentally concerned with how these people should feel and think, and only as a corollary of this with how they should behave. Keeping in view the revolutionary intellectual stratum in which the concept originates, class-consciousness is rooted in the awareness of a self as 'bourgeois' and a speculative construction of a 'proletarian' as the opposite of this bourgeois. This implicit and expanding meaning that the word 'class-consciousness' codifies, is however not accessible in the theory in which it appears. That theory, manifestly refuted by electoral behaviour, continues to be meaningful and relevant on the grounds of this, its concealed connotation. A departure from the facts but codifying nevertheless a relevant orientation towards them, the concept of class-consciousness (in the Marxist sense) can thus be seen to be ideological.

Matters are not much different with regard to the formulation (programme? proclamation?) of an 'end of ideology'. Employing the pejorative sense of the word ideology, the formulation expresses as fact the wish for the elimination of ideology. Its short-lived popularity indicates, as nothing else, the ideological, i.e. distorted or fallacious, character of its conception of ideology and its origins. Located in the pragmatic point of view so sharply opposed to the ideological in popular discourse, it highlights the weakness of this counterposition and the shallowness of the pragmatic understanding of ideology, which seeks to set itself apart from ideology. Indeed it is the instrumental frame of reference of both pragmatism and ideology (in the Leninist sense) that leads to their being so sharply counterposed in appearance and so difficult to disentangle in essence. Ideology springs from the same sources as pragmatism—the wish to make meaning of the world—and, so long as both are committed to the instrumental understanding of ideas, remain radically counterposed while fundamentally the same.

The difficulties involved in an instrumental understanding of ideology do not end there. The evolution, or historical development of ideologies throws not only the counterposition between ideology and pragmatism into doubt but threatens the coherence and continuity of ideology itself. The accommodations necessary to allow an ideology to cope with circumstances that in their generality it undertakes to describe soon necessitates distinctions between 'fundamental' and 'operative' ideology.[36] We have already considered a subtle but decisive shift in the Marxist conception of ideology itself, a shift perhaps as significant as that between the Hegelian system and the Marxian, and yet the shift maintains its direct descent from the Marxian, accommodating its innovations to some tenets enshrined as central in the Marxian doctrine. Though the very usage and contemporary Marxist concern with ideology subverts the original intent of Marx to distinguish between ideology

---

[36] 'Party ideologies, and also the more abstract political philosophies (when they refer to matters of immediate political significance), must relate to circumstances which demand compromise over, and even contradiction of, some of their basic tenets. Since in the course of such deviations fundamental principles are not necessarily renounced or altered, all political argumentation normally bifurcates into two interacting and intersecting dimensions: the dimension of fundamental and of operative ideology, as I call them'. Martin Seliger, *The Marxist Conception of Ideology*, Cambridge University Press, 1977.

and science, it is this ideological tendency itself that feels called upon to uphold the Marxian heritage. Equally striking is the Maoist modification of Marxist tenets. To a Marxist, of course, these may represent only the 'creative development' of the Marxist doctrine. To the student of ideology, however, they necessitate some thought on the nature of ideology.

In the events with which we shall be concerned we will need to consider not only such an evolution in ideology but a split. The dynamics of the split can of course be related to social groups—but that only as a partial outcome and implicit direction. As itself, the split poses insuperable problems for the instrumental conception of ideology. At stake are not only different conceptions of Marxism (parliamentary or revolutionary) and not only different conceptions of revolution (theoretical-academic or scientific-revolutionary), but different conceptions of ideology (theoretical or practical) and of politics. The opposition between the CPI and the CPI(M), which could perhaps be seen *in retrospect* to centre on the question of support for the Congress regime, and that between the CPI(M) and the CPI(M-L), so inscrutable on the surface, are in actual fact perceived and enacted with a certainty that permits violence. With the purely instrumental understanding of ideology this confrontation cannot be understood. We need a more immediate conception of ideology than the bare formula that it reflects class interests, a more fundamental appreciation of its meaning than that proclaimed by documentary artifacts.

Within the Marxist discourse itself such an awareness had already manifested itself philosophically, long before the events with which we shall be concerned. Both in the existentialism of Sartre and the Critical Sociology of the Frankfurt School, there emerged an encounter with social facticity at a more immediate and fundamental level than that of the constitution of classes. Abandoning even the Lukacsian claim to the expression of implicit class interest, these thinkers rescued from the determinism of Marxist problematic and its reification of social existence the quality of lived existence as the primary datum of human life. Their partisanship with Marxism was caught up in the need to stand in judgement on, and to criticize, this quality. But as formulations of the human reality itself, both Sartreian Existentialism and Critical Theory brought forward a conception at odds with the instrumental conception of ideology. Where Critical Theory saw its continuity with the Marxist project in its critical vocation, Sartre saw existentialism as an *ideology* located within an overarching Marxist *philosophy*. This is the logic of his simultaneous avowal of existentialism and Marxism. For our purposes here, because of its clarity, the Sartreian separation of two realms of discourse fused in the question of partisanship is particularly valuable. As in the partisanship and independence of the Surrealists of an earlier time, the partisanship and independence of Sartre's existentialism draws attention to the dissociation between the theoretical universe of instrumental ideology and the personal universe of existence in which the problem of partisanship is posed. It is these developments therefore that both criticize the instrumental understanding of ideology and provide a possibility of exploring the dynamics of ideology.

To put the matter in simple terms, whereas Marx attempted to replace the Hegelian Idea as the-demiurgos of History by real living men, he did so in a form in which ideas were bound by ties of interest to social groups. The evolution of Leninism, which began from this premise, related the whole realm of the ideological (i.e. that concerned with ideas) to a class interest and paved the way for an avowal of the class character of thought itself (an idea one also finds in Mao's writings). In this process ideas were seen to be related by some inner affinity with groups that could be expected to be receptive to them. The development of Critical Theory, and Existentialism particularly, in keeping with other significant developments in European philosophy, distanced ideas as ideas from the lived world in which they might be presumed to become effective. Though Critical Theory presumed and explored some kind of immanent relation between ideas and experience,[37] relating these on a civilizational rather than class scale, Sartre devoted himself to the exploration of the existential world postulating a necessary connection between the theoretical ideological universe and the subjective existential.[38]

Literate and Existential Ideology

So long as our attention is focused merely on the observable facts—on the one hand documents that elaborate an ideology and on the other the behaviour of people committed to such an ideology—there seems little possibility of comprehending either the significance of an ideology or its

---

[37] As explicitly in Horkheimer and Adorno, *Dialectic of Enlightenment,* trans. John Cumming, London, Allen Lane, 1973.
[38] It is in this light that he sees existentialism as an *ideology* within an overarching Marxist *philosophy* and writes his literary biographies, Particularly 'Saint Ceenet'.

development and elaboration. Certainly, this polar analysis, so neatly sepa-
rating the realm of ideas from the realm of behaviour, makes no allowance
either for the creativity of the ideologist or the business of interpretation so
crucial to the propagation of an ideology. This interpretation may well be
the appointed task of an organization of ideologists. But even where this is
the case, so long as some initiative is exercised by those who subscribe to
the ideology and it is not merely a case of commands and obedience, there
is always a residue of purely personal interpretation as well. This personal
domain of interpretation may well expand to become the only legitimate
or recognized principle of solidarity, as in the case of some Protestant sects.
But whatever the range of freedom of interpretation, a doctrine or ideology remains at a distance from the lives of those who choose to be guided
by it, requiring a transformation of its principles and assertions into truths
relevant to them personally. Instrumental or immanentist views of ideology characteristically ignore this dynamic.

For a clearer comprehension of the dynamics of ideology we therefore need to postulate, in addition to the manifest texts on the one hand
and behaviour on the other, an internal existential domain through
which the two are related by the participants themselves. We could characterize this existential domain as that fundamental ground of experience
in which meaning becomes meaningful. More mundanely, one could
construe it as the frame-work of experience in which value judgements
concerning the person of the person making these judgements are made.
It is that domain of construal in which the categories of one's concern
define themselves as relevant. This inner world, postulated here as construct, does not define itself as an independent realm with definite
relations to doctrines on the one hand and action on the other; it is in
itself the domain of experience itself within which points of doctrine
and assertions of will are meaningfully located.

If the attempt to abstract this existential domain from doctrines and
actions is a speculative exercise, the chief experience with which it is
concerned needs no such analytical enterprise. It is the sense of self or
personhood defining itself, both with reference to the world of its concern and the nature of the choices with which it is concerned. Setting
aside for the moment the reality or illusory character of this selfhood or
selfness, it is on the ground of such an awareness that allegiance or, certainly, commitment to an ideology accrues.

It is through the medium of this existential ideology—to give the
domain of the construction of self a name—that the literate ideology

(that which we have been calling ideology so far) comes to be meaningful to persons. It is only as refracted through such an existential ideology that the propositions of a literate ideology are transformed into significant choices. It is only in the light of this existential ideology that the meaning of a literate ideology to those who subscribe to it becomes manifest. The logic of the transformation of idea into act is the groundedness of both in existential ideology. Certainly there are literate (documentary, documented) expositions of existential ideologies—tracts or manifestos or literary works that undertake to elaborate the awareness of selfhood. Most striking in the context of Marx's thought is the case of Max Stirner whom he criticizes as an ideologist.[39] More generally, they are connected in the Occidental tradition with what has come to be known as existentialist philosophy and, perhaps most significantly, connected to revolutionary events, in the case of the Russian nihilists.[40] But for the most part existential ideologies remain submerged premises of the culture in which they are located, and underpin the evolution of more articulated and explicit literate ideologies.

The distinction between literate and existential ideologies can perhaps be suggested by indicating that where literate ideologies are concerned with the nature of the world or the cosmos, existential ideologies pertain to the most intimate and immediate experience of identity in the context of which the cosmology presented in a literate ideology becomes meaningful. In a sense the distinction between literate and existential ideology overlaps with the distinction made in anthropology between text and context.[41] It is indeed a more precise rendering of this anthropological distinction in that it locates the relevant context of a text specifically in the awareness of self that is the ground of its interpretation. There is in addition a sense in which the distinction between literate and existential ideology is already contained in the very conception of ideology, in that ideology is an untruth to express a reality

---

[39] K. Marx and F. Engels, *The German Ideology, Collected Works*, vol. 5, pp. 117–452.

[40] The Russian nihilists were certainly revolutionaries, though not the instigators of a revolution. It would not be far-fetched to suppose that their sensibility contributed to that of those revolutionaries in Russia who ultimately did participate in a full-scale social revolution.

[41] Milton Singer, *When A Great Tradition Modernizes*, London, Pall Mall Press, 1972, p. 4.

which never appears. I do not mean here the class (or social) basis to which one variety of Marxist analysis (as that of Marx in 'The German Ideology') penetrates as the truth of ideology, providing it with a largely spurious Objective Basis. I do mean, however, the Marxist attempt at a 'demystification' of humanist and religious ideology which penetrates it not so much to a class basis as to a *real* meaning. I have here in mind Marx's comments on religion—that it is the heart of a heartless world and that the sum of the teaching of the Bible is to 'Accumulate'. Here the meaning of the text which forms the locus of interpretative discourse by the priests is not discarded as meaningless but reduced to essential existential meanings. A similar reduction is at work in Marx's criticism of political economy as bourgeois as the expression of an essential existential interest. This awareness of the existential domain is vitiated in Marx's case by ascribing to this fundamental existential domain an economic character, ruling out an investigation of the relation between literate and existential ideology in favour of a dogma about the existential domain (i.e. that it is economic).

Discarding this dogma, and indeed its general form where the existential domain is rooted in an objectness and determinacy which it only reflects, however, poses problems of another kind. Awareness of the original character of existential ideology raises indeed the question as to whether it can be shared at all. At bottom a construction that each is engaged in as the kind of person he or she takes himself or herself to be, there seems to be no logical or necessary way of relating the constructions of one person with those of another. It is quite possible to avoid this problem by denying the shared nature of existential ideology altogether—pointing on the one hand to the artifactual objectivity of the literate ideology and leaving the notions of selfhood through which this becomes personally relevant as a free construction of those who acknowledge the truth of the literate ideolgy. Obviously, the acknowledgement of the truth of a literate ideology is by itself grounds for some kind of social identity, but where the assertion of this social identity in action becomes crucial, the evolution of shared assumptions of selfhood which constitute an existential ideology become inescapable. To put it in other words, so long as existential ideology constitutes merely an article of personal faith it is possible to ignore its shared and social character; in its implication in a programme of social action in which one's experienced identity is pitted against what others perceive to be one's identity, the social and shared character of both this existential ideology and its social construal cannot be avoided. The coalescence of a social group oriented to action imposes not only an identity on this group but also an identity on its members as constituting the group. This identity has both an inwardness, the existential ideology of the group itself, and an outwardness, the group as it is perceived by those who do not belong to it, but neither of these must necessarily be aware of the other.

Where the truth or untruth of a literate ideology is open to investigation, in that it makes claims to explaining the world, the truth or untruth of an existential ideology turns rather on questions to do with its authenticity. Part of the fallaciousness of literate ideology as false consciousness is indeed nothing other than its reference to this concealed existential basis. But the fallacy or truth of an existential ideology cannot appeal to any objective determinants other than the validity or questionableness of a philosophy to which it refers. It is in this sense that Sartre's arguments of Existentialism functioning as an ideology within the framework of Marxist philosophy are to be understood.[42] In other words, where the literate ideology makes observations and statements about the nature of the world as reality—which can be examined, demonstrated or refuted— existential ideology is an awareness, or even conceptualization, of the nature of the self through which this world makes meaning. This awareness of self is only true or untrue to the extent that its prescriptive assumptions coincide with the actual actions in which this self is involved, and the individual's awareness of this conformity or disjunction.

Though existential ideology is not always explicitly elaborated, and certainly not in the case of the Naxalites, it is not entirely invisible. Connected with action, and deducible from it, it does also coalesce about key concepts in the literate ideology which provide access to the way it is being construed. The identification of those key concepts is both an analytical and an empirical exercise for an observer of the ideology who is not a participant in the universe delineated by it, for these key concepts are not significantly marked out by being the ones used most often. Their peculiarity lies in being related to the framework of analysis that underlies the conceptual structure and relates it to the experience of the adherent or activist. In particular conflicts, of course, these concepts enter into the construal of events by the adversaries in

[42] It explains the location of a work like Sartre's *Critique of Dialectical Reason*, New Left Books, 1976.

these conflicts, but not necessarily so. Their importance lies in their centrality to the self-definition of ideologists, whether or not this centrality is recognized by those whom they oppose or even support.

Before exploring the general assumptions and consequences of this distinction, it needs to be pointed out that it is as such an existential ideology that the Naxalite critique counterposes itself to both the ruling government and 'revisionism'. The pathos or urgency of the Naxalite events does not lie so much in the abstract theoretical principles they espoused but in their existentializing the theoretical enterprise. Unmentioned in the discourse but implicit in the action is the insistence on the proof of ideals espoused by deeds. It is as a question of life, of existence, that the Naxalite challenge takes shape, and as a particular perception of life that it assumes significance. Ignorance of this shift of concern, leading to an instrumental evaluation of Naxalism, will miss both the spiritual, moral, content of the Naxalite critique and the spiritual crisis that it represents.

Assumptions and Implications of the Distinction between Literate and Existential Ideology

In postulating the existential domain, not to speak of existential ideology, one assumes the freely creative character of the construction of selfhood and the world of its concern. Such an assumption does not alter in any way the question of reality or objectivity. It merely asserts the reality and priority of the constitution of this domain. Whatever epistemological implications it might have, the assumption is an ontological contention that grasps the human reality as subjective.

This subjectivity and the possibility of exploring it only become intelligible on a phenomenological ground. Whatever implications it might have for psychology, and however it may be related to it, it is not itself this psychology, as Husserl points out. It is as the intersubjectivity of subjectivity that existential ideology takes shape, and as the assertion of its reality that it relates itself both to literate ideology and action.

But if by postulating the existential domain the dynamics of ideology gains clarity, the formulation and propagation of literate ideology becomes even more obscure and enigmatic. If one contends that not only its relation to action but its very historical meaning is mediated by its appropriation in an existential ideology, one is confronted with the problem of why there is a literate ideology in the first place, and why it is this ideology that has continuity, and not the existential ideology that invests it with meaning.

This is not such a difficult problem as it seems at first sight if one restricts oneself to exploring particular examples of the emergence and development of ideologies. As a general problem, however, it has far-reaching implications that affect the very attempt at a theory of ideology. As a general proposition every literate ideology enunciates what, for lack of a better word, the status of this ideology is to be. The mode in which this status is enunciated relates it directly, if not unambiguously, to the existential ideology that gives it meaning. Psychologically speaking any set of attitudes is compatible with any literate ideology, but phenomenologically the possibilities of the correlation between particular literate ideologies and particular existential ideologies is fairly restricted and definitely finite. This is indeed part of the dynamic of the emergence and elaboration of literate ideologies.

This, obviously, does not yet touch upon the priority of either literate or existential ideology and the relation between them. It does not take into account the necessity of literate ideology. Though the Ought entailed in a bare description of what is may well pertain to the problematic of the literate ideology itself, it bears a direct relation to the existential ideology that invests it with meaning. But the historical persistence of literate ideologies and the ambiguity of their content is caught up in a retroactive way with the tension between what is and what ought to be. Literate ideology, which addresses itself to the question of what is, gains ascendancy in its relation with existential ideology because only it (literate ideology) assumes documentary form and development, and can thus fulfil the aspiration of existential ideology to Truth. And it is as an expression of this aspiration that the viable form in which ideology presents itself is literate ideology. It is only when (if indeed, ever) truth loses its significance (linguistically and ontologically) that existential ideology surfaces as the 'true' form of ideology.

Ideology, Society and the Terrorist

Social existence, the objectivity of ideology, can be viewed as the location in which existential ideology confronts the images that others place upon it, though it is not in this confrontation that existential ideology defines itself.

Ideology has as its basis, if not the meaningfulness of life itself, certainly the hope of this meaningfulness, so that whereas the fact of society encompasses ideology and the production of ideology, ideology as meaning subsumes society. The social is just as much an ideological matter as ideology is a social artifact. Where society (this or that institution or person) supports ideologues, ideologues legitimate society. In this perspective the terrorist emerges as the total ideologue. Not involved in the everyday business of society, his (or her) total existence is subordinated to the idea of society. That this society only exists for the terrorist as ideologized abstraction has its counterpart in the social perception for which he (or she) is merely the embodiment of an idea.

In this spiritual, abstracted, symbolic realm in which the terrorist moves—and is materially validated—society shrinks to the ideas meant to invest it with meaning, and meaning to the action designed to make it real.

The life of the terrorist is quite obviously not the life of society. The determinations in terms of which his (or her) life (i.e. existential ideology) are formulated are, far from being universal, not shared even by those who extend him (or her) material support. The literate ideology to which he or she subscribes, designed to bridge this (unbridgeable?) existential rift is simultaneously the distortion of his life into idea, and the distortion of his ideas into life. The reclamation of the existential ideology of the terrorist relocates him in the human reality which his idealism denies and indicates the historic ground of his idealism.

Chapter Three

Bengali Society

Though Naxalbari is in Bengal, Naxalism was not restricted to that province. Membership in the CPI(M-L) extended all over India, and the greatest successes of the party were, in the eyes of its members, in Srikakulam in Andhra. Bengalis, however, played a major role in the leadership of the party, and, more germane to this study, the party turned to urban terrorism only in Bengal, and particularly in Calcutta. This could quite easily be made the basis of an argument that sees affinities between Bengali society and the evolution of a terrorist ethos.[1] While contradicted by outbreaks of terrorism in western and north-western India in colonial times, such an argument might distinguish between anti-colonial terrorism and Naxalite terrorism. This difference concerns not only the ideals to which the terrorists subscribed and the contentious or acceptable character of their doctrines (nationalist terrorism was perhaps equally contentious), nor even merely the forms and scope of terrorism, but also, more comprehensively and fundamentally, a difference in the very ethos of terrorism itself.[2] Granting this difference between anti-colonial and Naxalite terrorism, it might perhaps be feasible to maintain a necessary connection between Bengali society and Naxalite terrorism. While unable to refute this, I rather see the emergence of Naxalite terrorism as governed by conditions and values in Bengal but not determined by them. And certainly the significance of this Bengali event is not restricted to Bengal.

To ascribe to Bengal the character of a society may seem somewhat questionable. It is more usual to identify nation-states as societies. Unlike nation-states Bengal is neither a self-sufficient economic entity nor a sovereign polity. It does, however, occupy a definite region, uses a particular language and, most significantly, there is a distinctive culture common to Bengalis. This culture is far from homogeneous or self-contained.

---

[1] As in Biplab Das Gupta, *The Naxalite Movement*, pp. 218–19.
[2] See Richard C. Hula, *Political Violence and Terrorism in Bengal*.

There are characteristics it shares with what can be considered more generally an Indian culture and, perhaps even more importantly, ways in which it is articulated with this Indian culture, not to mention particular relations with the dominant Anglo-American culture of our times. It is only in a limited sense that this culture is premised on practices and beliefs that are wholly local. Nevertheless, there are peculiarities that permit one to consider it more than merely an Indian sub-culture, and allow one, if only tentatively, to call it a society. Chief among these is the evolution of a Bengali cultural identity (rather than merely an ethnic one) based on the ideas, values and outlook of the so-called Bengali Renaissance. Not as easily demonstrable, but arguably the case, is a distinctiveness in the nature of Bengali social relationships, which this culture, so to say, expresses. I do not mean 'the ensemble of social relationships', but rather the character of each social relationship, the nature of 'socialty' itself.

Access to the distinctiveness of this socialty is possible in the current coin of social categorization—the popular terms in which a person's social standing is typified.

Bhadralok

'*Bhadralok*' is a Bengali compound word formed by the union of *bhadra* and *lok*. Both are today in as common use as the compound bhadralok itself, with essentially the same sense they possess in the compound. *Bhadra*, a *tatsama* word, is however tatsama only in form, for its customary usage in the sense of polite, particularly marked in its abstract noun *bhadrata* (politeness) is slightly but definitely removed from the original Sanskrit sense of fortunate or privileged. The association of both with the condition of being civilized is however indisputable. I am unable to say with the materials at my disposal as to when this decisive shift in meaning occurred, though I believe that the direct denotation of fortunate or privileged in the Sanskrit is important, though perhaps not as important as the more general connotation of civilized in the evolution of its meaning into 'polite' in Bengali. In other words the attributes of privilege and good fortune are indissolubly connected with the evolution of the word for politeness in the Bengali language. This is certainly so for the compound bhadralok indicates a civilized person (in the customary usage 'gentleman'), which, in addition to conveying the polite behaviour of an individual, unmistakably points to his privileged position, even if this refers merely to culture and not also, as is usual, material affluence. The word lok is also of Sanskrit origin. Though in Sanskrit it denotes as a suffix a place of the particular kind indicated by a prefix, or a collectivity, or even man, and though Bengalis still retain this sense of the word, the meaning of lok that denotes a person in Bengali is altogether lacking in Sanskrit. The Sanskrit senses of the word are shared by Bengali with other Indian languages, among them Hindi, which uses a variant, lok, to denote people. But the usage of lok for person, as in the compound bhadralok, is peculiar to Bengali, as is the usage of the word bhadra, and certainly bhadralok has no precise equivalent in other Indian languages. That there is such a close parallel in English, true more current in an earlier time, in the word 'gentleman', is at once revealing and confusing—revealing because of the aspiration to anglicization, or certainly an informed westernism, if only of a bygone age, characteristic of Bengali urban society; and confusing because too heavy a reliance on the English equivalent obscures the native nuances both of the use of the term and its social implications.

Bhadralok is used to refer to a member of polite society and is counterposed variously to *chotolok* or *garib lok*.[3] As such a way of referring to persons it defines a class of people to whom it is applicable, who by implication occupy a similar status in society. This is not to say that the class is not internally differentiated, but that as opposed to the chotolok or garib lok it possesses an internal principle of unity that elicits the description of a particular member of it as a bhadralok.[4] Though counterposed as, in principle, classes of the same kind, the chotolok or garib lok do not in fact constitute such classes, for they refer not to an internal principle of coherence but to a difference from the bhadralok in terms of which they define themselves. To begin with, the distinction between chotolok and garib lok, perhaps a mere terminological nicety to an outside observer, indicates a sharp dichotomy in the awareness of people of the way in which they construe their difference from the bhadralok. Beyond this, however, neither the garib lok nor the chotolok are internally differentiated on the lines of the principle that sets them off from the bhadralok. Whereas the bhadralok recognize amongst themselves types of bhadralok, the types in terms of which the chotolok and garib

---

[3] J. Sharma, *Caste Dynamics Among the Bengali Hindus*, Calcutta, Firma K. L. Mukhopadhyay, pp. 102–4.
[4] Sarma notices the division of the *bhadralok* into the *baniyadi*, the *sahebi* and the *madhyabitta*. Ibid.

lok are differentiated refer outside the bhadralok-chotolok dichotomy to considerations of caste, locality and the *jal-chal* and *jal-achal* divisions of Brahmin hierarchy.[5] These considerations indicate both the location of the bhadralok-chotolok/garib lok as centred on the bhadralok, and the asymmetry in the opposed poles in that the bhadralok, internally differentiated and articulated, form a cohesive entity and the chotolok or garib lok do not.

The bhadralok are not a class in the sense some observers give to the word of a specific and rigorous relationship to property in the narrow sense. It is thus possible to distinguish them from a class, and call them rather a 'status-group'.[6] But in the sense in which class is coversationally used, it is nothing other than such a status-group. Those criteria that are significant for distinguishing members belonging to different classes in this sense, as e.g. wealth and breeding, are also significant for distinguishing a bhadralok from a garib-or chotolok. In addition to these, in Bengal, caste considerations also intrude, though in a veiled and implicit way. None of the considerations enters explicitly into a formal judgement with regard to a person's location in the social hierarchy. The principle of differentiation is in its very essence (as in the conversational use of class) informal, and (as in the case of calling a person a gentleman) the appellation bhadralok entails a larger number of criteria with increasing intimacy. Overall, as observed, what seems to be important is a style of life, for which access to a certain modicum of wealth and education on the one hand, and subscription to a particular value-system on the other, are necessary.[7]

In Bengali society the bhadralok constitute the middle classes, distinct as has already been mentioned from the inferior chotolok or garib lok, and equally distinct from a superior class or classes, *for whom there is no term in the Bengali lexicon*. In colonial times this superior class was the colonizing Englishman, between whom and the Bengalis an ambiguous love-hate relationship existed and continues to exist. In independent

---

[5] S. Sengupta, *Caste Status Group Aggregate and Class*, Calcutta, Firma K. L. Mukhopadhyay, 1979, distinguishes the *jal-chal* (Nabsakha) castes from the *chotolok* as an intermediate stratum.

[6] Perhaps as a peer group of the Parsonian status roles. Also Max Weber, *Economy and Society*, vol. 1, eds. Guenther Roth and Claus Wittich, Berkeley etc., University of California Press, chapter IV.

[7] See S. Sengupta, p. 157, and J. Sarma, p. 126.

India dominance over bhadralok existence has passed commercially into the hands of the Marwaris, for whom the Bengalis have little respect, and politically—explicitly in the rhetoric of the CPI(M)—to the 'centre', i.e. the government at Delhi.[8] Bengali society, and Bengali Hindu society particularly, is in this sense a 'headless' society, has been so since Muslim times, and continues to be so today. For all that, the bhadralok still constitute the dominant class of Bengali society. What gives them this dominance is the dominance of their value-system in the society at large.

Bhadralok society, which prides itself on being the most 'advanced' on the Indian subcontinent, is in addition relatively free from the taint of an overwhelming mass of wage-labourers. To say that it is altogether free of them would be an exaggeration and would, moreover, overlook a characteristic peculiarity of Indian industry—its stratification into a more prestigious, relatively skilled stratum, and a less prestigious sector devoted to heavy manual labour. In the more prestigious, relatively skilled stratum the Bengalis preponderate, whereas in the heavy manual and menial occupations Biharis and Oriyas predominate. This awareness forms the accepted horizon of social discourse in industrial Calcutta, and the unspoken bedrock sentiment of the bhadralok sense of superiority. The vulgar derogatory terms for the Bihari immigrants performing heavy manual and menial tasks are *'khotta'* (a term having no precise meaning, only a derogatory intent) or *chatukhor* (meaning literally eaters of *chattu*—flour made from a variety of foodgrains, depending on the eater's purse, at its best a mixture of chick-peas and millets). The unprestigious sectors of industry consist of jute and textiles—the first outlets for Indian capital. The Bengalis predominate in the relatively more skilled engineering districts of Howrah and in the newer, more capital-intensive factories. As this skilled stratum the Bengali working class is not composed of rural migrants and partly shares the ethos of bhadralok society.

As industrial areas, Calcutta etc. could hardly exist without a working-class population. But much as independent India, through an exorbitant prudery, ceased to keep official records of castes, so too in the interests of national integration perhaps the stratification of industry and the provincial

---

[8] See S. C. Pandubhai, 'The Voluntary. Institutions of the Marwaris in Calcutta', in M. K. A. Siddiqui, ed., *Aspects of Society and Culture in Calcutta*, Calcutta, Anthropological Survey, 1982, and also Thomas A. Timberg, *The Marwaris*, New Delhi, Vikas, 1978.

composition of classes of workers has been ignored.[9] But only in official records. As far as the social organism itself is concerned, it goes its own way regardless of these taboos, recognizing, as any positivist, only the accomplished fact. The labour pool of the industrial districts of Bengal is thus not to be found so much in Bengal itself, certainly not in the Bengali countryside, but in Bihar, eastern UP, Orissa, and now Bangladesh. It is in these regions that the 'expropriation of the peasantry' has fuelled the demand of the industrial districts of Bengal for cheap unskilled labour.[10]

Bhadralok Society and Values

West Bengal is perhaps the most industrialized and urbanized state in India. It is also one of the most educated.[11] To a superficial observer these would seem sufficient reason to explain the most striking peculiarity of Bengali culture—that caste has apparently no role in politics, and certainly there are none of the caste hostilities of its neighbouring state, Bihar.[12] Such an estimation, i.e. that industrialization, urbanization and education taken together are sufficient to account for the disappearance of caste considerations in politics, would, however, be mistaken. For side by side with this 'feebleness' of caste considerations in politics we have the anomalous fact that the proportion of untouchables to the whole population of the state is the second highest in India, and that this untouchable population boasts no political leadership of its own, of any account.[13] The matter appears more mysterious when coupled with the fact that, for the most part, the Bengali Hindu population is largely

[9] Resistance to the tabulation of castes surfaced in colonial times. See Sarma, p. 27.
[10] P. Saha, *History of the Working-Class Movement in Bengal,* New Delhi, People's Publishing House, 1978, pp. 13 and 14. See also H. Lubell, 'Migration and Employment: The Case of Calcutta', in Alfred de Souza, ed., *The Indian City,* New Delhi, Manohar, 1978, pp. 115–16.
[11] Though it has declined from its pre-eminence. See Ranajit Roy, *The Agony of West Bengal,* 3rd edition, New Age Publications, 1973, p. 31.
[12] And this as early as the nineteenth century. See S. N. Mukherjee, 'Class, Caste and Politics in Calcutta 1815–1838', in Edmund Leach and S. N. Mukherjee, eds., *Elites in South Asia,* Cambridge University Press, 1970. See also C. von Fürer-Haimendorf, 'Caste and Politics in South Asia', in C. H. Philips, ed., *Politics and Society in India,* London, George Allen and Unwin, 1963, p. 65.
[13] According to the 1931 Census cited in P. V. Kane, *History of Dharmasastra,* vol. II, part I, Poona Bhandarkar Oriental Research Institute, 1941, p. 179.

Shakta, with other denominations as well, of course, and takes its religion, including caste (particularly in matters of marriage), as seriously as the rest of India.[14] Ideas about pollution[15] and untouchability are the same as elsewhere in India.[16] The matter is much more complex than it seems at first sight—a complexity that belies the easy identification of the bhadralok class with a social category to which considerations of birth and breeding are irrelevant.

The peculiarities of caste in Bengali Hindu society date back to pre-British and even pre-Muslim times. Perhaps due to a late Brahmanization, compounded by the relatively late date to which Buddhism was prevalent in the region, the castes of Bengal are not divided along the classical lines of four *varnas*, as elsewhere in India. The intermediate varnas, namely Kshatriya and Vaisya, are conspicuous by their absence, leaving the population divided into Brahmans and Sudras merely,[17] or rather, as is the case, into Brahmans and non-Brahmans, the latter being further subdivided into the jal-achal and jal-chal castes, i.e. castes from which drinking water is acceptable or unacceptable respectively for a Brahman.[18] This categorization dates back to at least the reign of Vallala Sena (dated variously AD 1158–79 or AD 1160–78), who, according to legend, brought order to the castes of Bengal, and divided them into *uttam-sankara, madhyam-sankara,* and *antyajas.*[19] The distinction into jal-achal and jal-chal (Navasakha), though of a later and uncertain dispensation, traces to this for its authority.[20]

---

[14] See Sarma, p. 89.

[15] One of the reasons why the profession of nursing is held in such low esteem. With 24,374 registered practitioners of medicine in West Bengal in 1968, there were only 4277 nurses. See General Statistical Organization, Deptt. of Statistics, Cabinet Secretariat, Government of India, *Statistical Abstract India 1970*, Delhi, published by Manager of Publications, 1972, Table 235 (p. 682), and Table 236 (p. 683).

[16] Though, apparently, untouchability does not exist in the metropolis of Calcutta. See S. Sengupta, 'The Hela Caste in Calcutta: A Study in the Nature of Untouchability', in M. K. A. Siddiqui, ed., *Aspects of Society and Culture in Calcutta.*

[17] See Sarma, pp. 9 and 10. Also Amitabha Mukherjee, 'The Transformation of Caste', in S. P. Sen, ed., *Modern Bengal A Socio-Economic Survey,* Calcutta, Institute of Historical Studies, 1973, p. 68; and N. K. Sinha, *The History of Bengal (1757–1905)*, University of Calcutta, 1967, p. 126.

[18] Amitabha Mukherjee, *The Transformation of Caste,* pp. 69–70.

[19] A. K. Sur, *Folk Elements in Bengali Life,* Calcutta, Indian Publications, 1975, p. 28. See also Sarma, p. 9.

[20] Ibid.

On this already modified orthodoxy, with its relatively extremely thin crust of *dvijas*, the entry of the Muslims, and developments in the native religion, built a structure that makes not only the Bengali caste system but the practice of Hinduism in Bengal peculiar to the region. Peculiar to the region in intensity are Caitanya (1485–1533) Vaishnavism and Tantrik Shaktism which developed principally after the Muslim conquest. Both, despite their differences (there are many), emphasize a devotionalism relatively less grounded in caste orthodoxy than is the case elsewhere in northern India. If Caitanya Vaishnavism had its heyday under Muslim rule, it is only under the sovereignty of the British, particularly in the eighteenth and nineteenth centuries, that Shaktism came into its own as a full-blown doctrine (the Mahanirvana Tantra dates to the early decades of the eighteenth century). Both Shaktism and Vaishnavism are of course doctrines which are dispersed all over India. What is peculiar to Bengal is the form and intensity which these doctrines acquired there. The nineteenth century, though, saw the evolution of religious sects peculiar to Bengal in the Brahmo Samaj and later the Saktism of Ramakrishna Paramahansa and the Vedanta of his disciple Vivekananda, which grew into the contemporary Ramakrishna Mission. As a social reformer Ramakrishna is credited with having offered worship at the temple at Dakshineshwar built by a rani of jal-achal caste come into money, though the image of social reformer is not entirely congruent with his essentially mystical message.

It is against the background of these developments peculiar to Bengal that the bhadralok class emerged under British rule. Under the combined influence of the British experiments with the land tenure system[21] culminating in the Permanent Settlement, which encouraged sub-infeudation and thus an urban population, and the spread of education, the bhadralok—as the Indian middle classes generally—came into being.[22] Two points are worth noting here as giving access to the distinctive nature of the bhadralok. The first is the relatively greater weight of

[21] See Ranajit Guha, *A Rule of Property for Bengal*, 2nd edition, New Delhi, Orient Longman, 1982. See also N. K. Sinha, *The History of Bengal (1757–1905)*.
[22] However, Sir Francis Floud, *Report of the Land Revenue Commission Bengal*, Alipore, Bengal Government Press, 1940, p. 33, rightly draws attention to ascribing too great a weight to the Permanent Settlement in this dynamic.

English and higher education in the Bengal Presidency,[23] and the other is the relatively higher proportion of the higher castes in Calcutta, and by implication in other urban centres (certainly Poona), compared to the countryside.[24] From this it would seem that the bhadralok are an urban phenomenon. Though this is largely true, it is not wholly so, for whereas the bhadralok constitute the urban middle classes, they are the socially dominant group in the villages in which it is customary to distinguish between bhadra-and chotolok.[25] Another fact that throws a great deal of light on the concept of the bhadralok is that, to begin with, the greater part of the industrial working class of Bengal was non-Bengali, and thus, in principle, outside the pale of Bengali society.[26] Though by and large it might seem true, as Kusum Nair observes, that 'apart from caste and property qualifications, the most distinctive feature of the *Bhadralok* is that they do not work with their hands. The *Chotoloks* are the "labouring" or the "serving" classes', such a typology does not do justice to the nature of labour or servitude nor to the necessity for being included in the ambit of the Bengali social horizon, before

[23] See N. K. Sinha, *The History of Bengal (1757–1905)*, p. 439; also Pradip Sinha, *Nineteenth Century Bengal*, Calcutta, Firma K. L. Mukhopadhyay, 1965, pp. 32–7. Also R. C. Majumdar, *Glimpses of Bengal in the Nineteenth Century*, Calcutta, Firma K. L. Mukhopadhyay, 1960.

[24] See N. K. Sinha, *The History of Bengal (1757–1905)*, p. 385. It has even been argued by Benoy Ghosh that social reforms were inaugurated in Bengal by the Radi Kulin Brahmins to safeguard their own interests. Cited in S. N. Mukherjee, 'Class, Caste and Politics in Calcutta 1815–1838', in Leach and Mukherjee eds., *Elites in South Asia*, Cambridge University Press, 1970, p. 70. See also Chittabrata Palit, 'Calcutta—The Primate City: A Study in Urbanisation', in S. P. Sen, ed., *Modern Bengal A Socio-Economic Survey*, which cites the 1901 census figures of the caste distribution of English education among the Hindus. Brahmins constitute more than 40 per cent.

[25] See S. Sengupta, *Caste Status Group Aggregate and Class*, which notices the adoption of food and water taboos by Adivasis and Musalmaans as well (p. 122). See also S. Chakrabarti, 'Concept of Bhadralok and Chotolok in Bengal Hindu Society: Some Observations', *Bulletin of the Anthropological Survey of India*, XIX/2, April 1970, which finds the Muslim community in the study free from considerations of bhadra-or chotolok, but finds they characterize the Hindus in the same way that they themselves, after some hesitation, do.

[26] N. K. Sinha, *The History of Bengal (1757–1905)*, pp. 410–11. See also P. Saha, *History of the Working-Class Movement in Bengal*, pp. 14–16.

one can lay claim to bhadralok status.[27] Both these considerations become relevant when considering the status of the industrial worker with respect to the bhadralok. Still more important perhaps from a general point of view, an analysis that attempts (as Kusum Nair's does) to penetrate a popular discourse to its hidden differentiating principles is suspect when it does not recognize that the popular distinction incorporates the distinction of the analyst without being determined by it, i.e. that the fact that bhadralok do not work with their hands is part of the understanding that all concerned have about the bhadralok.

The distinction however draws attention to what is, nevertheless, a distinguishing feature of the bhadralok sensibility, its system of values. And that is the inordinately high status ascribed to purely intellectual occupations, and this despite the relatively, weak incidence of Brahmanism in the orthodox sense. To anyone acquainted in any degree with the culture, the strikingly high status occupied by the 'intellectual' is a commonplace and constitutes an element of the effeminacy ascribed to Bengalis by non-Bengalis. This high status and an intellectual tradition that is often invoked as its origin and legitimation is, indeed a matter of pride to the bhadralok.[28] Pervasive as the sentiment is, it is reflected in the fact that despite the generally low status of academics in India, Presidency College in Calcutta used to be almost the only institution where the best students were encouraged to take up the academic profession.[29] Almost as interesting as this aspiration to intellectual attainments is the character of bhadralok intellectualism. Despite the contrary bias of the Bengali Renaissance (in its protestations rather than its own accomplishments), the type of intellectual revered among the bhadralok is the accomplished (and political, at least today) man of letters, par excellence a product of the liberal arts rather than of the sciences, but liberal arts in which the scientific philosophy of Victorian times has pride of place. The arts for all their impecuniosity have all the glamour.[30]

[27] Kusum Nair, *Blossoms in the Dust: The Human Element in Indian Development*, London, Gerald Duckworth, pp. 147–8, cited in S. Chakrabarti, 'Concept of Bhadralok and Chotolok in Bengali Hindu Society: Some Observations', p. 67.
[28] S. Bandopadhyay, 'Report on an Adda at Dr Surajit Sinha's House on 20th February, 1970', in *Cultural Profile of Calcutta*, Surajit Sinha, ed., Calcutta, The Indian Anthropological Society, 1972, p. 255.
[29] Edward Shils, 'The Academic Profession in India', in *Elites in South Asia*, p. 178.
[30] S. Bandopadhyay, 'Report on an Adda at Dr Surajit Sinha's House on 20th February, 1970', p. 255.

Bengali literature is among the richer bodies of literature in India, and though the language dates back to pre-British times it is only after the advent of the British and the proliferation of presses that literature in the modern sense developed. Poetry, music and drama (in the form of the *jatra*) were current prior to the arrival of the press and the spread of literacy, such as it is, but certainly both the novel and the drama (both as literary form and acted in the Western manner in a theatre)[31] owe their inception and development to the Western impact.[32] The leading lights of Bengali literature occupy an eminent place in Indian letters. This is perhaps not as true today as it has been in the past, particularly in the latter half of the nineteenth century and the first half of this one, the great flowering of Bengali literature which produced among others the most eminent of all Bengali artists, the Nobel Laureate Rabindranath Tagore.

To say anything about Tagore's art is a risky business, considering the respect and popularity his work enjoys, not because what I have to say is derogatory but that to draw interest to the sociological aspects of his work might be considered by some to be doing it an injustice. Nevertheless to escape doing so is impossible because of this very eminence and popularity. The young girls in bhadralok families are almost invariably encouraged to sing, and among songs Rabindrasangeet occupies pride of place. Rabindrasangeet or indeed Rabindranath's art is not however of importance only for the women of Bengal, encompassing as it does themes that concern men and women equally, and none more immediately than that of love. Rabindranath's 'love' is a creature of the mind, if sensual at origin, refined in its formulation and expression at all times. Romanticism in this sense pervades most of his work, which in its ethos elaborates the mystical humanism that is associated in the non-Bengali Indian mind with Bengali culture. His general humanist concern pervades his erotic romanticism, if only in the sense of his greater awareness of women's needs, in the same way that his sensuousness pervades his mysticism.[33] The delicacy of his romanticism, emphasized by a

---

[31] Classical Sanskrit drama was almost defunct when the British arrived. Kironmoy Raha, *Bengali Theatre*, New Delhi, National Book Trust, 1978.

[32] Ibid. Humayun Kabir, *The Bengali Novel*, Calcutta, Firma K. L. Mukhopadhyay, 1968, does not trace the evolution of the Bengali novel from the English, but nevertheless holds the western impact responsible as an indirect cause by having created the middle classes, who he believes are necessarily associated with this art form; pp. 4–5.

[33] Humayun Kabir, *The Bengali Novel*, p. 37. See also Manisha Roy, *Bengali Women*, Chicago and London, University of Chicago Press, 1975, p. 48.

passionate concern for Beauty, is nevertheless informed by a rationalism opposed to all superstition, and none more than those of everyday social life. It would however be wrong to call him a realist, even though he is not otherworldly. He is referred to reverentially, and sometimes mockingly, as 'Kobiguru'—the poet-sage. It might be too extreme to argue that bhadralok culture is created by the Bengali Renaissance of which he is the last and leading exponent.[34]

Though the poet is no longer considered a sage, as indeed few others besides Rabindranath have been, poetry is still a sought-after mode of expression—to the point even of becoming a joke.[35] But though the most ancient, and in this sense characteristic fine art of the Bengali tradition, poetry, apart from songs—be they those of Rabindranath, Nazrul, Atul Prasad, or even Bombay films—no longer enjoys the popularity it may once have had.[36] Poetry and literature, though still lively in Bengal, have been outstripped by the film. Theatre continues to be a prized pastime, but as almost everywhere else in the world, extremely limited in its audience, and thus the home of the avant-garde such as it is.[37] Bengali cinema is in the doldrums, despite the eminence of its leading exponent Satyajit Ray, and has been so since the late 1960s at least. Both Bengali and Western cinema have retreated from the eminence they enjoyed and yielded place in popularity to the Bombay film, though film festivals screening foreign films are popular and film clubs proliferate.

The treatment of love in Bombay films is in general more earthy, i.e. directly sexual, than its treatment in Rabindranath or any of the writers of the Renaissance. Bombay films emphasize, nevertheless, freedom of

[34] K. M. Chakravorti argues that 'Since the Bengal Renaissance was in fact the vanguard of the Indian Renaissance, a proper understanding of the former was a sine qua non of any study of the latter,' in the Foreword to *Studies in the Bengal Renaissance*, Jagannath Chakravorty, ed., revised and enlarged edition, Jadavpur, National Council of Education, Bengal, 1977.

[35] 'It is often said that in our country more people are writing poetry than buying or reading it. Even if these poets read poetry they read only their own.' Dipak Kumar Barua, 'New Poets with New Lines: An Overview', in *Studies in Modern Bengali Poetry*, Nirmal Ghose, ed., Calcutta, Novela, 1968, p. 207.

[36] J. C. Ghosh, *Bengali Literature*, London and Dublin, Curzon Press and Totowa, USA, Rowman and Littlefield, 1976, p. 11.

[37] ' "Avant-gardism" is a luxury which we cannot yet afford in our country'. Satyajit Ray, 'The Odds Against Us (1966)', in *Our Films Their Films*, Bombay etc., Orient Longman, 1976, p. 58.

choice in choosing a husband or wife based on sexual attraction, namely 'love marriage', though they are careful to distinguish between the legitimate and illegitimate sphere of this sexuality, and the transformation of love into duty in its legitimate development, particularly for the woman. It would not be untrue to say that it lacks the sensitivity of the Renaissance authors, and especially Tagore, particularly where women are concerned, even though both are concerned with imbuing legitimate eroticism with a modern form. That this 'modern form' is so much at variance with the current practice, where arranged marriages are still by and large the rule, says something not only about the escapist nature of this art but about the content of modernity for the cinema-going public in general.[38] The disjunction between enlightenment in public life and orthodoxy in private has indeed been the bane of bhadralok radicalism.[39] Though it is not on this ground that Bombay films can be faulted, in that their professed goal is to harness a potentially subversive sexual love to the fulfilment of a traditional marriage, the whole idea of sexual love even leading to marriage is one which for most Bengalis—and Indians (of the middle class)—is acceptable in principle so long as it does not touch one's own children. As such the Bombay film has universalized a dilemma that previously plagued mainly the radicals.

'Love marriages' do, however, occur, among the bhadralok. Indeed among those belonging to the Brahmo Samaj they have been the rule for some time now. What makes this possible in a society that is for the most part sexually segregated is the evolution of the Bengali social concepts of *attiyo* and *attiyo-sojon*. One's attiyo, literally 'one's own', are etymologically one's kin, but in the course of time this kinship terminology has extended to include one's neighbours, friends, acquaintances, all those with whom one establishes relations by choice. There are thus *parar attiyo* (neighbourhood intimates), even *buser attiyo* (intimates from the bus).[40] The complex attiyo-sojon comprising the whole (one's own

---

[38] Manisha Rov, *Bengali Women*.

[39] For some of its implications, see Myron Weiner, 'Notes on Political Development in West Bengal', in *Political Change in South Asia*, Calcutta, Firma K. L. Mukhopadhyay, 1963, pp. 255–6, cited in Marcus F. Franda, *Radical Politics in West Bengal*, MIT Press, 1971.

[40] Fruzzetti *et al.*, 'The Cultural Construction of the Person in Bengal and Tamil Nadu', in *Contributions to Indian Sociology*, (NS), Vol. 10, No. 1, 1976, p. 165.

intimates) of these is a reference that could extend as widely or as narrowly as the speaker chooses to interpret the intimacy of relations established by free choice. Both the original kinship terms, attiyo and attiyo-sojon, as well as their contemporary usage, are peculiar to Bengal. What the usage permits in addition to establishing free-choice intimates on the same ground as kin (in principle, of course), is to extend the innocuity and safety of the umbrella of kinship over inordinately delicate or disruptive relations so as to allow them to develop. Though it is in general true of the whole of Indian middle-class culture that intimates of any degree, except close friends of the same sex, are transformed into kin of one kind or another, the Bengali bhadralok culture is particularly rapid in transforming intimates into '*da*' and '*di*'—diminutions of '*dada*' and '*didi*', elder brother and elder sister respectively. Whether or not the permissible intimacies of such arrangements actually lead to love-marriages or not, they throw a network of sentiment (may one say sentimentality) over relations of free choice by dressing them in kinship terms. Into this one could also read the communitarian, as opposed to the societal, character of bhadralok society, in the sense in which that distinction is made by Tönnies without extending the distinction to characterize a transition from traditional to modern society, as he does.[41] Other cultures in India, far less industrial and certainly less westernized—as the Hindi speaking cultures of Bihar or UP—are not at all communitarian in this sense, though they are more ferociously partisan about caste.

The hard core of kinship, however, is constituted by one's *rokter attiyo* (one's own through blood). Fruzzetti and Östör say of *rokto* (blood):

Rokto is a Bengali construct which refers to blood as a substance, enduring and persistent, a permanent attribute which is recognized in the male line, transmitted by men through the reception and acceptance (*grohon kora*) of the male seed (*sukra*, *bij*) by women after marriage. Blood is shared by all persons in the male line, and the direction of the line itself is recognized through lines from male to male. Blood then is a symbol for a relationship among persons and groups of persons. It differentiates relationships and categories of related persons. It expresses one of the most important concepts in what, by now, we may call Bengali kinship: the idea for a certain kind of relatedness in conjunction with the idea of the person, the idea of relative, the idea of marriage, the ideas of issuance and lineality—all of which together define 'kinship' in Bengal.[42]

[41] Ferdinand Tönnis, *Community and Society,* trans. C. P. Loomis, Michigan State University Press, 1964.

[42] Fruzzetti and Östör, 'Seed and Earth: A Cultural Analysis of Kinship in a Bengali Town', in *Contributions to Indian Sociology* (NS), Vol. 10, No. 1, 1976, pp.111–12.

Further, 'The group of persons with whom one shares blood in a recognizable form by birth, male to male, is one's *bhaiyat*',[43] and, 'Blood (*rokto*) creates semen, several drops of the former to one of the latter.'[44]

Both the specifically Bengali character of this construct, considering the resonance 'blood' has in any language or culture, and its relevance, can be challenged. Certainly, Vedantist views of identity (also relevant to the Bengali context) emphasizing separation from the world would indicate an aloofness from the whole question of kinship epitomized in such *slokas* as

kastvam koham kut ayatah, ka me janani ko me tatah

(what am I, who am I, where have I come, who is my mother, who is my father).[45]

But the ubiquity of the symbolic associations of 'blood' are no grounds for dismissing this interpretation of its Bengali associations. And certainly the Tantrik mode of thought, so prevalent in Bengal, would indeed favour the implicit avowal of this or similar constructs. I shall have occasion to return to this interpretation later, while considering the ideology of the Naxalites, as rokto (blood) figures prominently in their rhetoric.

Here it would be relevant to note that if such an understanding were valid it would, perhaps, span the whole of Bengali society, both bhadralok and chotolok (or garib lok). But bhadralok and chotolok (or garib lok) differ in the concept of marriage, or at least are taken to by the individuals concerned. Certainly, there is an overt difference in the pecuniary transactions accompanying marriage, namely dowry among the bhadra-, and bride-price among the choto- (or garib-) lok.[46] As to whether this difference is indicative of a more fundamental difference in the attitude towards marriage, or a difference in the philosophy of marriage must remain a speculative matter, even though in the case of Muslims and Adivasis there is quite clearly a different rationalization of the act of marriage.[47] Functionally speaking there is no difference between these, though again

[43] Ibid., p. 112.
[44] Ibid., p. 121.
[45] A popular corruption of *kasya tvam kah kuta ayata*, in Mohamudgarah, *The Works of Sri Sankaracharya*, Vol. 18, Srirangam, Sri Vani Vilas Press, Memorial edition, p. 64.
[46] S. Sengupta, *Caste Status Group Aggregate and Class*, has a table on the difference in marriage patterns between *bhadraloks, chotoloks, Adivasis and Musalmaans*; pp. 117–18.
[47] Ibid.

the different practices of the bhadra- and choto- (or garib-) lok would seem to indicate different functions in the context of the larger social order in that the bhadralok practice of dowry seems to be bound up with hypergamy in marriage. Nicholas' study of the adoption of dowry by the Mahisyas of Radhanagar (a chotolok caste), intended to show how the marriage payment has been transferred as ritual without affecting the substance of marriage, has, however, the unintended consequence of leading one to doubt whether hypergamy of the sort usually ascribed to bhadralok marriage transactions is actually the case.[48] It highlights the ritual character of marriage payments, which in so far as they are ritual cannot easily be penetrated to either a social reality of functionality or an underlying philosophy of marriage. It points to the status of such attempts at a functional interpretation or the attempt to unravel a philosophy as by and large rationalizations. Nevertheless, in the sensibility of the bhadralok at least, if nothing else, a difference exists between the content of marriage among the bhadralok and that among the choto- (or garib-) lok. In fact in general superordinate and subordinate orders in a society, when they recognize themselves as such, usually find a focus for their opposed self-identities in marital customs and by general extension the character of eroticism ascribed to oneself and to the other. This is of course especially marked in the Hindu case, though not restricted to it. Bhadralok families and particularly the ladies amongst them are apt to consider the chotolok as marked by a licentiousness in sexual affairs and a vulgarity in speech.

Speech once again provides an adequate access to this whole realm of eroticism, with a view to distinguishing Bengali society from the rest of India. The most revealing element to my mind is constituted by customary and infuriating abuse. Among the *sahebi* bhadralok,[49] of course, abuse is customarily showered in English, and vernacular abuse other than *sala* (wife's brother) or *haramjada* (ill-begotten son) rarely find expression. But among other bhadralok males, both in their talk amongst themselves and with lower orders, and among the chotolok, the most common abusive word, as also the most insulting is *bokachoda* (idiot-fucker). Among friends in some groups it is quite freely used and

---

[48] Ralph W. Nicholas, 'Ritual Hierarchy and Social Relations in Rural Bengal', in *Contributions to Indian Sociology*, No. 1, Dec. 1967.

[49] 'The term *sahebi* refers to families or people who attempt to gain distinction through channels of activities related to the European world'. J. Sarma, *Caste Dynamics Among the Bengali Hindus*, p. 104, thus English-speaking and concentrated in and around Calcutta in West Bengal.

sometimes also amongst some as a term of endearment. Hostile intent, however, transforms it into the most insulting of abusive words. There is here no element of incest as in *bahinchod* (the equivalent Hindi term, meaning sister-fucker), for that seems to my mind precluded by the ease with which women are transformed into *di;* or motherfucker (the equivalent Americanism), for that seems to my mind precluded by the erotic mysticism of Shakta cults. The transgression that casts the greatest shadow in Bengali consciousness is copulation with a mental defective, whose gender remains undefined.

Classes and the Intelligentsia

From what has already been said it should be clear that the bhadralok occupy a middle position between the working classes below and the entrepreneurial classes above. This is not to say that the bhadralok do not incorporate entrepreneurial or business elements amongst their number. In actual fact at the origin of the bhadralok lies an entrepreneurial initiative unprecedented in the history of Bengali society. Yet as matters now stand, or, rather as matters stood before the crisis of the late sixties and early seventies, the bhadralok did not 'soil their hands with either trade or labour.'[50] The bhadralok were, par excellence, the educated classes, the epitome of that Anglicized education that B. B. Misra would make the sum of the Indian middle classes.[51] And yet the economic spine of the bhadralok consists of propertied classes of two kinds. The first, the traditionally propertied—the *boniyadi* or the *abhijat*—would cringe from including in their number the assorted owners of petty property, the tradesmen.[52] And yet both of these constitute in a way similar classes in that both are owners of traditional forms of property. The second, constituting the greater bulk of the bhadralok and, as a minority, its admired successes, the sahebi bhadralok are owners of cultural property, intellectual skills as it were, that guarantees them their livelihood.[53] There is no local lexicon that distinguishes between these two types of property

[50] Premen Addy and Ibne Azad, 'Politics and Society in Bengal', in *Explosion in a Subcontinent*, Robin Blackburn, ed., Penguin Books in association with New Left Review, 1975, p. 91.
[51] B. B. Misra, *The Indian Middle Classes*, Delhi, Oxford University Press, 1968.
[52] I am unaware of any nuance other than linguistic that separates the *boniyadi* from the *abhijat*.
[53] See footnote 49 above.

within the bhadralok, but as differing frameworks of aspiration they are clearly distinguished. The sahebi, with its prospect of mobility and westernization, and the boniyadi with its orthodoxy and stability, are contrasting points of reference for the *madhya-bitta*.[54]

The explicitly Marxist discourse, of course, shuns this terminology of bhadralok and chotolok and seeks rather to explain Bengali society in terms of 'classes' as construed in a Marxian fashion, even to the extent that the very use of a class terminology is taken to be the substance of a Marxist point of view. This poses definitional problems—and not only in India.[55] Leaving these aside for the moment, it should however be mentioned that this class problematic is taken to be a vocabulary that illuminates the actual structure of the society, regardless of the way in which its members themselves construe it. Bengali urban society thus seems to be composed of the bourgeoisie, the petty bourgeoisie and the proletariat, and rural society of landlords, rich peasants, middle peasants, poor peasants and landless labourers. In this characterization the nature of the bourgeoisie, whether comprador or national, formed a bone of contention between the CPI(M) and the CPI(M-L),[56] and the nature of the rich peasantry, or rather the attitude the proletarian party should adopt towards them, became a point of dispute within the CPI(M-L) itself.[57]

The definitional problem can be traced back to Marx's unfinished manuscript of vol. III of *Capital*, which ends without defining a principle of class. What makes it particularly urgent in the Bengali case is that it is not a vocabulary current in Bengali society itself. In their attempt to popularize the terminology, the Marxists have translated the term into Bengali—*sreni*. But in Bengali this term has a direct denotation of 'rank' that is lacking in the English word 'class'. The full range of the class categories is restricted to the Marxists, but a loose usage of the word is current in the 'middle classes', of whatever degree of anglicization, in

[54] 'The *madhya-bitta* people, as the words signify, are the undistinguished middle classes. They are the clerks, shopkeepers, teachers, or in general, all the salaried workers'. Sarma, p. 106.

[55] The problem of distinguishing the various strata of modern Occidental society as classes in the absence of property distinctions plays hob with the Marxian scheme.

[56] Overtly it was a question of characterizing the state, both being by and large agreed on the nature of classes. The question thus was whether any section of the bourgeoisie that ruled was national (and thus progressive) or not.

[57] See chapter v.

referring to themselves. In this loose sense madhyabitta is often used for the whole body of the bhadralok as well. Located thus in urban middle-class discourse, relatively free of the caste considerations that are so overwhelming in rural society, the terminology of class can in a certain way be seen to constitute an intellectual 'superstructure' (in the Marxian sense) of this society.[58] Rural society in Bengal, caste-ridden as it is, has another feature worth mentioning in this context. And that is the relatively 'sedentary' character of its population. The number of labourers from the countryside who migrate to the towns and cities is almost negligible, and even the labourers in the large tea gardens of the north (of which Naxalbari has a sizeable scatter) are mostly non-Bengali. From this it would perhaps be appropriate to deduce a relatively smaller proportion of landless labourers in the Bengali countryside than, say, in Bihar. It seems a paradox that with such a non-proletarian composition Bengali society should have produced such a vigorous communist movement, i.e. one that describes itself as having a proletarian character.

Whatever the relationship of myth to the intelligentsia, the intelligentsia itself forms a significant section not only of Bengali society but of Indian society at large.[59] And, as in Indian society at large, the Bengali intelligentsia is differentiated into the English-speaking intelligentsia and the vernacular intelligentsia.[60] Relations of concealed hostility obtain between these, with the English-speaking intelligentsia occupying a position of dominance, even though it is to the development and proliferation of the vernacular that nationalism owes its force. The cleavage between the English-speaking and vernacular intelligentsia in Bengal is, however, not as sharp as elsewhere in India, as for instance in the labour bowls of eastern UP and Bihar, largely because of the evolution of the bhadralok sensibility in the vernacular, thanks to the Bengali Renaissance. In the consideration of the Naxalite events, though, this distinction is particularly relevant as the leadership of the Naxalite movement belongs quite

[58] As for instance in marriage considerations discussed in Sarma, pp. 86–7, or the numerous cases of Sanskritization in the past—including that discussed by Nicholas (footnote 48).

[59] 'non-industrial, non-agricultural wage-earners are *more numerous than the wage-earning workers in the modern industries*'. C. Bettelheim, India Independent, trans. W. A. Caswell, London, MacGibbon and Kee, 1968, p. 90.

[60] The basis of this divide lies in the medium of instruction. The government currently in power in Bengal, headed by the CPI(M), has recently instituted education only through the vernacular in state-run schools.

clearly to the vernacular intelligentsia. It is indeed in the context of this distinction that the ordinary phrase *Bangla katha* ('in Bengali', equivalent to the English phrase 'in plain English') gains its force as meaning the hard, unadorned truth. Without the inferior position occupied by the Bengali language with respect to English, such an equation of hard, unadorned truths with the Bengali language *per se* in opposition to the cultural flights of English would not be possible.

Though the dominance of English has a social occurrence it is connected to fairly definite institutional arrangements that serve to perpetuate this dominance. Chief among these are the codification of law in English, though of necessity this is interlarded with terms from the vernacular, and the use of English as a medium of instruction for higher learning. The popularity of education in English, as an authentic access to Western learning and consequent dominance is, however, far more widespread than these official seals of approval. The proliferation of private education in English has been a feature of Bengali life since the early nineteenth century[61] and continues to be so today, even though the greater part of school education is in the vernacular.[62]

Structures

More significant than the intelligentsia in general, for our present purposes, are the students, for it is among these that the revolts of the sixties were primarily located. Constituting the formative phase of the intelligentsia in general, students are nevertheless distinguished from this intelligentsia by their conditions of life, whatever their aspiration. Student activism, or, as it has been called, student unrest, has been a feature of Indian life (unlike the situation in the West where it was non-existent earlier) since the early part of the twentieth century in the nationalist agitation,[63] with student radicalism

---

[61] R. C. Majumdar, *Glimpses of Bengal in the Nineteenth Century;* N. K. Sinha, *The History of Bengal (1757–1905)*, p. 439.

[62] 'The mother-tongue of the majority of pupils continued to be the medium of instruction in all secondary schools. In most schools this was Bengali and in a few cases Hindi, Urdu, Nepali, Oriya and Telugu. There were not many English medium schools in the state'. Government of West Bengal Education Directorate, *Septennial Review on the Progress of Education in West Bengal For the Period 1957–58 to 1963–64*, Alipore, Superintendent, Government Printing West Bengal Government Press, 1970, p. 24.

[63] Philip G. Altbach, 'The Transformation of the Indian Student Movement', in *Asian Survey*, vol. VI, no. 8, August 1966, p. 449.

going back to the days of the founding of the Hindu College in Calcutta. The consideration of this student activism as unrest, as an undesirable malaise, is however a feature of post-independence India.[64]

As a social group, certain sorts of modern-day students in many parts of the world are similar in some ways. They are young, unaccustomed to work in the ordinary sense, secluded from the cares of everyday living of the householder and, in my experience of India in the sixties, sexually inexperienced as a rule. This age group marks the onset of maturity in the cultural sense, i.e. that of legitimate sexual identity, and forms the crucial period of self-definition. The leisure of student life itself, as well as the leisure and comforts of the middle-class background of many students—inculcates at the same time the possibility of speculation, the formation of ideals (whether these are spriritual or worldly), and in many cases a boredom—an inability to utilize this leisure in a productive fashion on one's own. The absence of cares—as well as the associated lack of status—often encourages a hankering for responsibility and a partial distaste for student existence, no matter how enjoyable this life may be. This could perhaps be construed as the outcome of the process of socialization. The onset of maturity also argues very strongly for the development of sexual urges, suppressed far longer than the attainment of puberty and physical maturity, colouring all encounters with an increased meaningfulness. The classical Hindu description of the stage of *brahmachari* fits the status-role adequately.

The future that the majority of such students look forward to in the contemporary world is fundamentally related to their perception of this world in their present. As heirs of middle-class parents they are proletarian, i.e. they rarely have property that they can fall back upon to live out the course of their natural lives, far less work this property as a living to enrich themselves. Their education forms in most cases the most obvious and significant form of their inherited 'capital', a 'capital' of which they are as unaware and contemptuous for the most part as the world that faces them is aware of it and recognizes it as significant. Their future lies in the corporate establishments that demand this 'capital'—guarantee of applicants for their white-collar jobs. And yet it is not the future, bleak in the prognostications of the analysts of student unrest in India, that students are thinking of when they rebel. And certainly not in the

[64] Edward Shils, 'Students, Politics' and Universities in India', in Philip G. Altbach, *Turmoil and Transition: Higher Education and Students Politics in India*, Bombay etc., Lalvani, 1968, contends for the essential continuity of this unrest despite the changed attitudes of outsiders to it.

case of the rebellions of the sixties, and the Naxalite revolt in particular, which drew into its ambit students of élite institutions who had remained politically inactive since the nationalist agitations.[65]

Educated unemployment, however, has been a significant consideration of educationists in India since independence. A volatile issue, its shadow has lengthened with the post-independence boom in education, and has significantly coloured the philosophy of education, especially in Bengal.[66] There, indeed, the extension of facilities for higher education has even been seen as a means of preventing, or at least delaying, the precipitation of students into manual labour to which they are unaccustomed.[67]

The Economy

Educated unemployment is far from being the only or even the most important problem that faces West Bengal. An adequate rate of industrial growth (a concern that encompasses that with educated unemployment but is not exhausted by it) and the problems connected with it—adequate financial aid from and investment by the centre, adequate private investment, development of power generation, etc.—are far more pressing concerns today. Though these problems have originated in a tendency that can be traced back to independence and even earlier, it is only in the post-Naxalite period that they have come to the forefront to dominate attention.[68] In connection with the Naxalite

[65] 'In this atmosphere many of the better students (and there is some evidence that this is particularly true for those in the sciences and in engineering) have consistently refused to have anything to do with politics, and it is likely that most students are fundamentally opposed to the present structure of political authority'. Thus Marcus Franda, *Radical Politics in West Bengal*, MIT Press, 1971, referring to his own 'Perceived Images' of 1963–4 before the Naxalite movement had risen to awareness.

[66] See the table on page 5 in the *Septennial Review on the Progress of Education in West Bengal;* also G. S. Mansukhani, 'Crises in Indian Universities', in G. S. Mansukhani, ed., *Crises in Indian Universities*, New Delhi etc., Oxford and IBH Publishing Co., 1972.

[67] K. P. Chattopadhyay, *et al.*, 'Undergraduate Students in Calcutta: How They Live and Work', *The Calcutta Review*, vol. 132, no. 1, July 1954, in the Foreword to it by the Vice-Chancellor, Dr J. C. Ghosh, p. 2.

[68] Perhaps to the end of Bengal's leadership of the nation. Ranajit Roy, *The Agony of West Bengal*, p. 60, quotes Nehru on the cause—Calcutta 'had been

events, however, these problems had only just begun to become acute, expressed in a concern for the flight of capital away from West Bengal. The concern with educated unemployment was much more overt at that time, and even more important than the concern with the shortfall in the grains' production of the state, which necessitated the setting up of a public distribution system in urban areas.

As early as 1965, however, an article by Nirmal Kumar Bose on Calcutta in the *Scientific American* had been introduced in the volume by a blurb which contended: 'Calcutta has become a metropolis without benefit of the industrial revolution that gave rise to the cities in advanced nations'.[69] Contradicting the fallacy that the cities of the 'advanced nations' are products of the industrial revolution is easier than to rebut the charge of Calcutta's pre-industrial character, which seems to be emphasized by the ubiquitous poverty of India. This is here raised to a higher power, along with the concern for industrial growth in responsible and official circles to meet the demands of the burgeoning population. It is not just the population of Calcutta that has increased but that of the whole of West Bengal. Between 1951 and 1961 the population of the state rose from 263 lakhs to 349 lakhs, an increase of 32.8 per cent, the highest rate in India.[70] Coupled with this rising population has gone a decreasing share of plan resources, and even, during the second five-year-plan period, a drop in the absolute level of the outlay from that of the previous plan period.[71] Alongside this has developed a decline in the rate of growth of literacy, despite the boom in education.[72] Far from being a city that has grown 'without benefit of the industrial revolution', Calcutta, whose very founding is associated with the quickening of commerce and industry, seems to show rather a growth far more rapid than the growth of this commerce and industry, that in a bird's-eye view is apt to appear as a decline.[73]

---

and continues to be the chief centre of British capital and industry'.

[69] Nirmal Kumar Bose, 'Calcutta: A Premature Metropolis', in *Scientific American*, 213/3, Sept. 1965.

[70] Though the rate of growth of Calcutta's population was lower. Harold Lubell, 'Migration and Employment: The Case of Calcutta', p. 114.

[71] Rajajit Roy, *The Agony of West Bengal*, p. 30.

[72] Ibid., p. 31.

[73] See, for instance, the table of Bengal's foreign trade in N. K. Sinha, *The History of Bengal (1757–1905)*, p. 344.

Calcutta's position as the second city of Empire, second only to London, and the position of Bengal as the industrial (and intellectual?) leader of India in colonial times, has not been carried over in the post-independence period. By 1971 West Bengal had slipped behind Maharashtra in the number of factory establishments and the quantum of capital deployed, though the number of workers employed in the state was still the highest in India.[74] The rate of growth of industry was lower than in many other states, partly because of the relatively larger amount of capital already deployed, but partly also due to the decreasing attractiveness of investing in West Bengal on account of power shortages and trade-union power. Despite this overall relative decline, the state income between 1951–2 and 1967–8 rose by about 4 per cent annually, registering rates of growth higher than the all-India average in each of the three five-year-plan periods until then, and particularly higher during the second five-year-plan.[75] Per capita income, however, did not grow quite as rapidly. During the first two five-year plans per capita income in West Bengal grew by 0.6 per cent and 1.6 per cent, compared to an all-India average of about 1.8 per cent for both periods. During the third five-year plan, though, the growth of per capita income in the state was higher than the all-India figure.[76]

The analysis of this growth of state income, and the standard of living of workers, indicates however the most striking aspect of the industrial growth (or decline) of West Bengal.

Table 1

Percentage Breakdown of State Income of West Bengal
1951–2 to 1967–8[77]

	At current prices		At 1951–2 prices
Agriculture of which tea	39.43 to 50.04	of which animal	39.43 to 31.49
	2.61 to 1.84	husbandry	0.18 to 0.33

(Continued)

[74] *Statistical Abstract India*, 1970, Table 42, pp. 128–9.
[75] *Estimates of State Income And Its Regional Differentials West Bengal*, Bureau of Applied Economics and Statistics, Government of West Bengal, 1969, p. 1.
[76] Ibid., p. i.
[77] Ibid. Table 2.2 and 3.2, pp. 7 and 9.

Table   (*Continued*)

	At current prices	At 1951–2 prices
Mining, manufacturing	21.17 to 24.20	21.17 to 29.68
and small enterprises of which factory establishments	14.10 to 19.77	14.10 to 23.71
Commerce and transport	17.9 to 10.89	17.9 to 17.32
Others	21.50 to l4.87	21.50 to 22.11

The most striking feature of Table 1, the great inflation of the prices of agricultural goods in comparison to all other prices, and particularly industrial goods, is further borne out by the investigation of the expenses of workers (Table 2).

Table 2

Standard of Living of Labour[78]
(Percentage shares of expenses of workers)

	1939	1960	1973 (estimate)
Food including *pan*, tobacco, etc.	52.5	68.1	68.8
Fuel and light	7.5	4.7	4.2
Clothing	7.0	6.2	5.1
Housing	14.0	8.4	7.1
Miscellaneous	19.0	12.6	14.8

With this analysis it is easy to see the way in which it is possible to speak of Calcutta as pre-industrial, despite the relatively large development of industry both in the metropolis and along the Hooghly industrial belt. The proliferation of this industry is not such as to enable it to pay for the agricultural commodities, principally food-grains, necessary for its sustained growth. Far from being industrialized too little, however, the situation could well be construed as that of being too industrialized in comparison with the backwardness of the agriculture that must

[78] *Labour in West Bengal, 1973*, Deptt. of Labour, Government of West Bengal (no date of publication given), p. 235.

support such an industrialization. In what follows I shall have more to say about this situation as it reaches critical proportions in the prelude to the Naxalite events. Here it is only necessary to mention that in this disproportion lie concealed the paradoxes of the perspectives of development in much of the Third World, particularly where this is pursued within the perspectives of a nation-state. In the case of India and West Bengal these national perspectives are further complicated by the distribution of powers, revenues and controls between the state and the centre.

The insistence on the economic dimensions of the decline is a commonplace of Marxist and leftist rhetoric and scholarship in West Bengal. The political decline that has accompanied it is challenged, if only obliquely, by Marxist scholarship in Bengal today, as well as by CPI(M) rhetoric. Political decline has been traced to economic causes by no less a person than Nehru,[79] whereas economic decline has been traced to political causes.[80] At a distance from such partisan theorizing, Myron Weiner has traced the decline to 'the existence of hierarchical and generally authoritarian patterns within all institutions, from the family to schools, universities, administration and government, which serve to inhibit development of innovating individuals'.[81] Whatever the explanation cited, however, or whichever aspect they choose to emphasize, all informed observers tend to agree on the fact of decline. Political decline, though, does seem to pre-date economic decline, even if with Nehru we were to see the root of this decline in economic causes.

Culture and Calcutta

The decline itself is a total cultural event, and exists as such an awareness in the sensibility of informed Bengalis. Whether they seek to remedy this by political intervention, or seek in the drift of political-economy explanations or scapegoats to render it bearable and in some sense intelligible, educated Bengalis cannot escape a sense of diminished stature in comparing themselves with times past. In retrospect, though, even the Bengali Renaissance appears cold comfort. Challenged by the literate ideology of the Naxalites, the aim of this Renaissance seems to have

---

[79] See footnote 68, above.
[80] As in Ranajit Roy, *The Agony of West Bengal.*
[81] Myron Weiner, 'Notes on Political Development in West Bengal'.

been to appropriate the Western idea of freedom, only to transform it into a harmless Indian tradition (Young Bengal notwithstanding). The cutting edge, in so far as there was one, of this enlightenment was turned against Indian—particularly Hindu—society. The opposition to British rule arose as nationalism, when it did, only by a reassertion of Hindu elements that served to drive the wedge between Hindus and Muslims far enough to split them.

The internal challenge to this bhadralok society, hovering between a Hindu heritage with a secular face and an enlightened Westernism with an orthodox commitment, came from three different directions from the mid-sixties onwards. That of the Naxalites we shall be concerned with at much greater length. Another challenge, that to the eroticism of the culture and its repressed character, came from the Hungry Generation. This challenge has been codified and absorbed in the evolution of risqué Shyambazar theatre and the importation of sexually daring films from Kerala (that other bastion of Indian communism). The most successful, though not for that reason the most significant, threat to bhadralok culture came from the communism of the CPI(M). In succeeding, the CPI(M) has accommodated its ideology to the demands of the bhadralok and has emerged in an even more fundamental sense as a party of the bhadralok.

Stronghold of the bhadralok, Calcutta celebrated the end of imperial domination with communal carnage, and the awareness of its decline and the irrelevance of its heroes with the Naxalite terror. Throughout these, it was a sharp feature of the city-scape that provided the barometer of the seriousness of events. Divided as it is into *kothabari* and *busteebari*,[82] it is the activation of the *bustee*s that to the keepers of law signals the onset of danger, and proclaims the seriousness of the political party that undertakes such.[83] For the bustees, the teeming slums of Calcutta, form its greatest unknown, even though they are so shamelessly on display.[84]

[82] M. K. A. Siddiqui, 'The Neighbourhood in Calcutta', in M. K. A. Siddiqui, *Aspects of Society and Culture in Calcutta*, Calcutta, Anthropological Survey, 1982, p.154.

[83] This was perhaps the perceived threat of the CPI(M) in its early days. See the discussion of *mastans* in 'Urban Guerrilla', unsigned article in *Economic and Political Weekly*, 10 July 1971, p. 1380, which would argue for an institutionalization of the political mobilization of the bustees.

[84] 'In Calcutta, Prof. Sen's socio-economic survey of three rounds during 1954–58 reveals that approximately 28 per cent of the sample households lived in "bustees"'. A. R. Desai and S. D. Pillai, *A Profile of An Indian Slum*, University of Bombay, 1972, p. 20.

Chapter Four

The Naxalites in Perspective

The Communist Party of India (Marxist-Leninist) is still around, not as a single party, but as a number of sects, each claiming for itself continuity with the original founding group.[1] But certainly, no matter how sincere their protestations of sincerity, none of them practises the terrorist line that the leadership of the party adopted between 1970 and 1972, though one of these groups, at least, subscribes to the same theory of revolution sketched out by the leader of the party, Charu Mazumdar, in its terrorist phase. The party, or rather the various sects that still lay claim to its name, has lost the sense of urgency that could lead Charu Mazumdar to exclaim 'Make the seventies the decade of liberation', and with it the willingness to adopt the extreme measures that the party was once identified with, as also its place in the public eye. Not old enough to have entered the history books and not recent enough to be fresh in everyone's memory, the Naxalites, while having had an impact on the political scene and the moral constitution of the Indian sensibility, have become a group that most Indians have become aware of without clarity as to what they stand and stood for and the events that sprung them into the limelight.

The Naxalites take their name from an uprising of workers in tea gardens in the north Bengal countryside near Naxalbari *thana* in early 1967. The uprising was not a disorganized outburst of peasant anger but the result of political agitation by a group of communist organizers, though certainly not limited to the actions of these communist organizers. Second, the uprising was not a sharp, short event, soon ignited and soon put out, but a lingering and fairly long drawn-out struggle between the forces organized by revolutionaries and the groups opposed to them. The leadership of this uprising provided a focus around which organizers of communist revolutionary activity from different parts of the

---

[1] All references to incidents other than the thought of Charu Mazumdar are culled from copies of *The Statesman Overseas Weekly*, published every Saturday.

country coalesced to form first the All-India Co-ordination Committee of Communist Revolutionaries in November of 1967, and considerably later, in mid 1969, the Communist Party of India (Marxist-Leninist). Not all revolutionary communist groups of the time came under the umbrella of the CPI(M-L). Some stayed out on argued theoretical grounds, whereas others not formally affiliated swore allegiance, if not to the party at least to the line or aspiration it seemed to represent. The term Naxalite in its everyday usage encompassed all of these, though certainly for the purposes of this book and the desires of the leadership of the CPI(M-L) a Naxalite is a member of the CPI(M-L).

The CPI(M-L), as the AICCCR before it, represented the coalescence of many different independent groups, and some of the groups who were expected to form organizing nuclei of these chose to stay out of the organizations. But despite their independence of each other, most of those revolutionary groups were breakaways from the Communist Party of India (Marxist), which had itself split away from the Communist Party of India in 1964, In the popular mythology of the left in India the split of the CPI(M) from the CPI is seen to have been caused by the Sino-Indian war of 1962. But whatever role the Sino-Indian war may have had in sharpening discontent with the leadership in the CPI, it was certainly not the precipitant of the split, as the split itself did not come until two years later, with the dissidents fully capable of organizing themselves into an alternative party. Nevertheless, as many of the same ideological discontents were influential in provoking the formation of breakaway groups to the left of the CPI(M) as were instrumental in the generation of the split between the CPI and the CPI(M). Theoretically, the chief points of difference of the CPI(M) from the CPI were the characterization of the 'stage' of the Indian revolution with its corollaries—the class-nature of the Indian state and the alliance of classes necessary to overthrow it, and of course a stand on the issues of international communism made pressing by the split between China and the Soviet Union, which seemed to be taking the shape of a confrontation. It was this latter that led the press and the party in power, no less than the public, to identify the CPI(M) at its formation as a Maoist party. More, however, was entailed by the categorization 'Maoist' than alignment with the camps of international communism. There was the political dimension of the nature of the work the party was called upon to do, and the cultural dimension of the response to the West and westernization. Both of these figured importantly in the discontent felt by various sections of the CPI(M) with the nature of the solution that the CPI(M) leadership had chosen. But in both the split of the CPI(M) from the CPI and the subsequent split of some of the CPI(M) cadre from it the urgency of the matter brought home by the example of the Chinese success was summed up in the question, 'Why is it that the Indian revolution has not yet succeeded?' It led the CPI(M) to accuse the CPI of 'revisionism' and, subsequently, radicals within the CPI(M) to accuse it itself of revisionism.

At its formation, however, the CPI(M) was seen by the popular, and particularly the conservative press, as a revolutionary danger. In the old guard of the ruling Congress party the danger was viewed as a subversive Chinese-inspired threat, which the Home Minister cited as grounds for throwing large numbers of communists of the new party into prison. It was in prison in 1965 that Charu Mazumdar, a middle-ranking leader of the CPI(M) in West Bengal, wrote nine essays, subsequently famous in the CPI(M-L) as the Nine Deeds, detailing the failures and future course of the communist movement in India, together with a brief consideration of the historical process of international communism. He wrote these to be discussed by other party members. And if a definite starting point is to be ascribed to the formation of the CPI(M-L), this would probably qualify as the first initiative in that direction. In the essays Charu Mazumdar poetically called the Great Proletarian Cultural Revolution of China an exploding moral atom bomb from which splinters flew out to various parts of the world to start conflagrations wherever they landed. The poetry however is not purely metaphor, being quite close to Charu Mazumdar's view of the course of history, as reference to other, later writings will serve to make clear. The Soviet Union was seen as the chief revisionist force which came to the aid of a US Imperialism with its back to the wall in the post-War era. The Indian Communist movement he saw as a process of repeated revolutionary assaults by a communist cadre, followed by repeated betrayals by a revisionist leadership. The hallmark of this revisionism was to avoid making preparations for an armed assault on the state, in addition to compromising such attempts by the cadre before they could truly get off the ground. The chief defect of Indian communism was its inability to cope with the conditions of illegality foisted on it by the ruling powers as soon as it became a viable threat. And the heartland of this Indian revolution was the countryside, where both oppression and the hatred of it were at their most extreme. From all this flowed the necessity of building a secret rural party that would prepare for armed revolution with propaganda and the stockpiling of weapons, as the country was certainly ripe for revolution.

Despite the persecution of the CPI(M) (about which the press gleefully reported the Soviet Union did not protest), the party occupied positions of eminence in the Kerala and Bengal legislatures. In Kerala the communist coalition had been ousted from power by the imposition of President's Rule, whereas in Bengal the CPI(M) led the Opposition. In both these states the communists tried to draw attention to the grievances of urban dwellers, their low wages and salaries, and particularly the drastic food, i.e. grain, shortages. This perhaps seemed more of a real threat to the ruling Congress Party than the question of a national language, which occupied centre stage in the national political scene at the time. That it was so construed by the ruling powers seems reasonable on considering that the country was divided on the language issue, whereas what the communists were drawing attention to had at least the potential of uniting opposition to the Congress. The first large agitation in West Bengal in 1965, was, however, not organized overtly by the CPI(M). The first inkling of the depth of discontent surfaced with large-scale protests by secondary-school teachers over pay. The meetings they held in Calcutta were, however, addressed by the then leader of the Opposition, the CPI(M) leader Jyoti Basu.

The CPI(M)'s effort to mobilize social protest against the government did not get off the ground in West Bengal until July. The occasion was provided by a rise in tram fares and the papers recalled the demonstrations on the same issue in 1953, when tram fares had been raised by a single paisa. But in these demonstrations the most active role was played by students, a harbinger of the more active and more widespread involvement of students in politics to follow. Obviously the protest over the hike in tram fares was an expression of protest that touched on causes that lay much deeper—most importantly on the inability of pay to keep pace with inflation, and particularly the inflation in the price of foodgrains, which were already rationed in Calcutta. By 5 August the CP1(M) and its allies, the so-called leftist parties, were prepared to tackle these problems head-on and called for a general strike, a *hartal,* on that date. The reasons cited for the hartal were the hike in tram fares, high food prices, and police action, attempting to link directly economic discontent with political–administrative issues. As was to be expected, the hartal was far more successful in Calcutta than in the districts, though unlike the pattern that was to follow the hartal passed fairly peacefully, even in Calcutta. The threat was construed as an important one by the government at the centre, perhaps particularly since right through the year relations with Pakistan had been strained to a degree that could be construed as crisis, though that may have been at this stage merely the club with which the centre chose to beat the communist movement on the head.

Within a scant two weeks after the hartal in West Bengal, the Home Ministry undertook a study of 'incidents' in Bihar, West Bengal, Mysore, Hyderabad, UP and 'several other states' with a view to establishing the thesis of communist subversive conspiracy. In this view of communist conspiracy the CPI, the Soviet-line party, was entirely exonerated, for as the anti-communist press reported it had troubles of its own coping with the threat of the fledgling CPI(M) in drawing away its cadre and in encouraging dissidence within the party. As a matter of course the CPI(M) leaders of the hartal in West Bengal were arrested.

On 1 September 1965 open hostilities between India and Pakistan broke out on the western borders of India. Fighting continued until the 16th, and in the conflict the Chinese government stood by its ally, Pakistan. The strange alliance did not touch the mood or the theory of the radicals within the CPI(M) who were later to split away from, or be thrown out of it. They continued in their adoration of the potential of the Chinese revolution as mirrored in its everyday contemporary policy. But the CPI(M) leadership proper did not abide by this 'dereliction' of communist principles by the Chinese government, and made the first of the many steps that was to distance them from the Chinese line in international communist politics, and Maoism as the face of the impending world revolution. The CPI(M) offered support to the Indian government in the confrontation with Pakistan and proposed all-party civil defense committees to cope with the situation. With this offer of cooperation the fears of the central government about the CPI(M) were allayed somewhat, and certainly the local government in West Bengal was won over to a view of releasing all political prisoners. The chief minister of the state, P. C. Sen, made this demand of the centre on that date, and by the 18th it was almost certain that the CPI(M) leaders then in custody would be released. It is difficult to gauge, however, what impact on this decision was caused by the knowledge of the threat to the rationing system in food-grains in Calcutta because of the large influx of people from outside Calcutta (from as far away as Bihar and Orissa) and the racket in smuggling the cheap ration grain out of Calcutta. No doubt it was hoped that in this matter, as in that of national defence, the CPI(M) would be on the side of the forces of 'law and order', though it is entirely possible that the centre had decided on giving the CPI(M) enough rope to hang itself with. But by December of the year the food situation had reached crisis proportions with a drought. The headlines proclaimed that India was faced with its worst food crisis in the century, and this at a time when the Home Minister, Gulzarilal Nanda, seemed to be more concerned with problems of administrative inefficiency and made a statement to the effect that all government departments were overstaffed.

During the course of the coming year, however, the staff of these overstaffed departments got wage rises to counter inflation; something that could not be said for industrial workers, especially in West Bengal. *Their* protests were soon to add a new word to the Indian vocabulary— 'gherao'—the detention by encirclement of people in positions of authority until the demands of those encircling were met, or at least their legitimacy recognized. The movement of thousands and hundreds of thousands was still some way away though, and *The Statesman* at the turn of the year preened itself at the low crime statistics of Calcutta, lower than the districts, and far lower than the other great cities of the world.

The beginning of 1966 brought peace between India and Pakistan and a diplomatic victory for the Soviet Union when the leaders of India and Pakistan signed a treaty ending hostilities in Tashkent on 10 January. The Indian Prime Minister, Lal Bahadur Shastri, did not enjoy the acclaim of his people for it, as he died in Tashkent not long after signing the Declaration. His body was flown back to Delhi, cremated with state honours, and he was posthumously awarded the Bharat Ratna. At his death the Home Minister, G. L. Nanda, was temporarily sworn in as acting PM until the Congress Parliamentary Party chose a new leader for itself. Contenders for the office were Indira Gandhi and Morarji Desai, fated to remain rivals for a long time to come. In the election Indira Gandhi won with 355 votes to Desai's 169, the first sign of a fissure in the monolithic unanimity that had characterized the post-independence Congress Party. By 23 January Mrs Gandhi had chosen and announced her cabinet, and started making the motions of coping with the food problem that the war with Pakistan had temporarily eclipsed.

The first stirrings against the food shortages came not from West Bengal but from the other communist stronghold, Kerala. Although E. M. S. Namboodiripad, the General Secretary of the CPI(M), was arrested on 1 February on his return to Kerala from a visit to West Bengal, student activists agitating against cuts in rice rations sparked off state-wide incidents of violence. Police parties were attacked, telephone lines were cut, railway tracks disrupted, trains and buses stoned in various parts of the state. More than 200 arrests were made, including among them many CPI(M) and student leaders, though the hartal was also espoused by the dissident Kerala Congress which announced plans to intensify the agitation. That the events did not occur in West Bengal, or rather Calcutta, was simply because rations there were not reduced. The scale of events made it abundantly clear that immediate attention and action were required and on 5 February an agreement was signed with the USA for the supply of 3 million tons of foodgrains under rupee payment, while the government appealed for aid to all those who were in a position to give it. The problem figured, along with the question of the lifting of the emergency proclaimed during hostilities with Pakistan, in the considerations of the chief ministers of the various states held in Delhi on the 13th. With little to contribute to the solution of the food problem, the chief ministers agreed that it was not yet time to lift the emergency—as the Chinese threat still existed! They also discussed the continuance of the Defence of India Rules and not surprisingly agreed that these too should continue, modifying this somewhat by suggesting that they should be resorted to only in exceptional circumstances, relying on the ordinary law of the land where that sufficed. Response to India's appeal for aid was reasonably great, though, and on 3 March the government announced in New Delhi that at least twenty-three nations and international agencies besides the US had offered food aid. Not without irony, the Lok Sabha had spent ten minutes debating on 25 February the definition of a beggar, and the Press Trust of India estimated that the total number of communist detenus in the country was 1185.

If not the first to engage in hostilities over the food issue, West Bengal was only a step behind, though characteristically the CPI(M) and its allies did not restrict their demands merely to a review of the food policy of the government. There had been incidents earlier in the 24 Parganas and Nadia districts in which the police had opened fire. So on 10 March the CPI(M) and its leftist allies in the Opposition called for a Bengal

Bandh to protest both against the government's food policy and its refusal to institute a judicial inquiry into the police firing. The demonstrators attacked trains and railway property. The police fired on crowds at five places in the districts and four in Calcutta proper, killing thirteen people. In places where 'disturbances' started after dusk—parts of the city, the Rishra–Konnagar area and the Asansol industrial belt—the army was called out to maintain peace, and a dusk-to-dawn curfew was imposed in north Calcutta, at Rishra, Barrackpore, Jadavpur, Behala, Metiabruz, ten other municipal areas in Hooghly district and in Asansol town. The Chief Minister, P. C. Sen, said violence in the districts was associated with known communist strongholds and insisted that the whole outburst was political gimmickry, threatening to impose punitive taxes on the disturbed areas. In the legislature he appealed to the Opposition for the peace necessary for the success of the government's food policy, challenging them that they really had no better alternative to offer.

The Left United Front drew up an 11-point charter of demands as a reply to this, to which the Chief Minister replied, not exactly to the Opposition's satisfaction, but at any rate enough to make it possible for the two to meet and discuss matters on the 18th in more subdued circumstances than the heat of street agitations. The central government had already by then appointed a five-man committee to review the working of the food zones created for the movement of food-grains, as a possible source of solution of the food problem, barring of course the possibility of the absolute shortfall in the quantity of food-grains actually needed. Mrs Gandhi, like P. C. Sen, felt that the whole food agitation was only being conducted with an eye to the elections in 1967. After peaceful negotiations with the government for a few days the United Left Front and the Rashtriya Sangram Samity, at separate meetings, decided to call another hartal on 6 April, threatening that if the government used repressive measures again the hartal would be extended to 7 April, and as a preparation for the hartal 29 March would be observed as protest day. The chief minister for his part felt he had done all in his powers to meet the demands of the Opposition, and taken all steps necessary to ensure an adequate supply of food-grains in the various categories of rationing areas in the state.

The Prime Minister in the mean while left for the US on 24 March on a state visit, and on the 30th issued a joint communique with President Johnson. To the Indian press Indira Gandhi confessed that the quantum of aid received was insufficient for development needs and a concerted effort to expand trade was the only way to mobilize the necessary resources for the five-year plan.

In West Bengal the promised hartal passed generally peacefully, with a few stray cases of violence on 6 April despite the chief minister's claims that he had met the demands of the Opposition and was prepared to go even further. The central government on the other hand was pressing ahead with its review of food zones, no doubt egged on by the report of the UN Food and Agriculture Organization that the system of food zones was responsible for the rice crisis. And as if to drive home the point the Federation of All-India Food Grain Dealers urged abolition of these zones, and finally on 18 April the government did announce a new food- zone policy. Lending weight to this was the picture of large government stocks and scarcity. At the end of May the Congress leader K. Kamaraj called on all socialists to join the Congress.

Despite the crucial importance of this matter, events were afoot that in the press at least dwarfed this as news. Close on the heels of the Prime Minister's visit to the US, the Planning Minister arrived in New York to assess foreign aid for the fourth five-year plan. Knowledgeable sources already felt that the value of the rupee was in doubt, but politician to the end Asoka Mehta maintained that he had not come 10,000 miles to discuss the value of the rupee; it was not in his brief; 'What we do with the rupee is a matter for us to decide.' And on 5 June, some six weeks or so after this brave face, the rupee was devalued by 36.5 per cent. Politicians, statesmen-manqué and members of parliament made much of it, calling it a 'humiliating necessity'. And Rajagopalachari, founder-leader of the right-wing Swatantra Party, wanted to have it both ways—hailing devaluation as a courageous step at the same time that he called it a 'capital offence' for which the electorate should throw the Congress out of power. The Left, though, did not have much to contribute to the furore about devaluation and were particularly silent in West Bengal, having their eyes perhaps on the cases of looting of grain in various parts of Midnapore district in May. India's foreign debts prior to devaluation totalled some Rs 7000 crores. The Prime Minister did not lose her cool, insisting to Congress workers in Madhya Pradesh that India could not be bought over, explaining that most of the US aid was for the private sector and most Soviet aid for the public sector, and that 'Ours is a mixed economy. We want both sectors to progress.' Four Gulf states, however, did not accept devaluation. Qatar, Abu Dhabi, Dubai and Sharjah continued to trade rupees at the pre-devaluation rate of Rs 13.33 to the pound.

The next few months were relatively quiet. On 26 June statutory censorship was imposed on the country for the first time since independence, and on 7 July the Prime Minister left for a ten day tour of the UAR, Yugoslavia, and the Soviet Union. On 28 August the Education Commission released its report opposing the adoption of Hindi as the medium of instruction in higher education in all parts of India. Congress leaders in West Bengal accused the CPI(M) of being out to retard progress, and the Union Home Ministry accused it of having finalized a strategy of deliberate sabotage at the meeting of its Central Committee at Tenali in June. The CPI(M) meanwhile entered into an understanding with thirteen other opposition parties to form a coalition to challenge the Congress electorally in the coming elections and to provide an alternative government to that of the Congress.

In September, however, there was a large demonstration in Delhi, outside the Parliament, demanding a ban on cow slaughter, a movement that gained momentum in the coming few weeks and led to the resignation of Home Minister Gulzarilal Nanda on 9 November, after seven deaths had taken place during violence in the course of the demonstration of more than 1,000,000 people for the banning of cow slaughter on the 7th. The agitation was also significant for the fact of causing the arrest of a Hindu religious leader, the Jagadguru Sankaracharya of Puri, while he was on a hunger strike to press the demand for the banning of cow slaughter on 20 November. In West Bengal in September the Bengal Engineering College of Sibpore was closed for a while when over 2000 of its students went on hunger strike, protesting against police action in disturbances which started with a few students trying to prevent black-marketing in cinema tickets. Apart from this the central government, and the Prime Minister particularly, were seriously worried about the mounting signs of discontent and alienation in West Bengal, despite the fact that in July a Congress Party spokesman had ventured that it was Kerala that was the main source of worry to the Congress. In September the Prime Minister sent three senior officials to Calcutta to consult with the Chief Minister of Bengal and senior police officers. In the same month members of the CPI and CPI(M) clashed violently at a meeting of the West Bengal Federation of Engineering and Metal Workers' Union, showing the hostility latent between them despite having come to some kind of understanding on the electoral front. But the most striking feature of the end of the year in Calcutta was the closure of Calcutta University for sixty-nine days because of student action, incorporating violent encounters with the police and the violent confrontation with authority. The police fired on others as well in Metiabruz where there were violent disturbances in November. The first rumblings of the industrial crisis were felt with the West Bengal Cotton Mills facing closure. In December the Tramway Workers went on strike. As though to set the seal on the year, the Chief Ministers' Conference in New Delhi on 16 November decided to continue single-state food zones, and the Lok Sabha passed a bill extending the Preventive Detention Act for another three years.

The general elections of 1967 were fast approaching and all the indications were that the popularity of the Congress was waning, and particularly so in West Bengal. A poll conducted by the Indian Institute of Public Opinion in July 1966 had shown a 19 per cent drop in the Congress vote. More tellingly in August, the press had reported a drop in the demand for Congress tickets in West Bengal. On 8 February, a scant week before polling began, stones were thrown at the Prime Minister in Bhubaneswar on an election tour, injuring her on the nose and upper lip seriously enough for her to need an operation on the 10th. While not quite in the same league as the ex-Home Minister in her fear of Communists, the Prime Minister nevertheless accused the CPI(M) of trying to create a rift in the armed forces. In West Bengal the shape of things to come was indicated by an irate mob setting fire to the Eden Garden Cricket Stadium on New Year's Day. More to the point, by 11 February thirty-one clashes in connection with the impending general election had been reported in West Bengal alone. The revolutionaries still within the CPI(M) or already expelled from it, of course, did not set any great store by the general election. Nothing was to be achieved by it except a perpetuation of the status quo, and the first public indication of their views came again, not from West Bengal but Kerala. During election week wall newspapers published in the name of 'Kerala Red Guards' appeared at several places in Kerala denouncing the CPI(M) leader E. M. S. Namboodiripad as a bourgeois agent and as a No. 1 revisionist in league with the revisionists of the CPI who fondly believed that communism could be achieved by the ballot box and democratic means. The newspapers held up O. J. Joseph, recently subjected to disciplinary action in the CPI(M), and Kunnikkal Narayanan, expelled from it about a month earlier, as true Communists, and emphasized the inevitability of armed revolution for the achievement of Communism, exhorting people to be prepared for it.

The elections were held between 15 and 22 February. The Congress put up its poorest showing since independence, failing miserably in four states (Kerala, Madras, Bihar and Orissa) and losing its absolute majority in a further four (West Bengal, UP, Rajasthan and Punjab). In Kerala the CPI(M)-led United Front won an absolute majority. In West Bengal the CPI(M) did not do as well as it had hoped, winning a little over a quarter of the seats it had contested, and the CPI, despite the CPI(M)'s polemics against it, increased its strength. On 2 March Ajoy Mukherjee of the Bangla Congress, heading the United Front—on which the CPI and CPI(M) were members—, was sworn in as Chief Minister of West Bengal. And on the very day of his swearing-in the first 'incident' was reported from Naxalbari. In Delhi of course the Congress still had a majority, and after a brief threat to contest the Congress Parliamentary Party's leadership Morarji Desai withdrew, leaving Indira Gandhi to be elected unanimously. Her cabinet, with Morarji Desai as Deputy Prime Minister, was sworn in on 13 March. Whether from considerations of the victory of non-Congress powers in the states or not is difficult to say, but almost the first significant act of the new government was the announcement on 18 March by the Home Minister, Chavan, that the emergency would be lifted from 1 July 'except where conditions warrant its continuance'.

The food situation continued to be difficult. There were conditions of famine in Bihar urgently needing some kind of relief programme. The West Bengal government on its part announced a new food policy, abolishing inter-district and intra-district cordons and the levy system, and announcing a higher rate of procurement for rice and paddy. Despite this higher rate the policy envisaged the maintenance of current prices of rationed articles. On the industrial front the United Front government was called upon to do something about gheraos. In the brief period from its assumption of power to 14 April there had been 28 gheraos in the districts and 23 in Calcutta, varying in duration from 41/2 hours to seven days. Police help had been provided to rescue the victims, but the Chief Minister held lock-outs, retrenchments, lay-offs, management's failure to implement tribunal awards and non-payment of workers' legitimate dues by employers to be the precipitating cause of gheraos.

Turning attention away from the turbulent situation in the states, policemen in Delhi were involved in attempts to organize themselves and fell afoul of the law. Seven members of the police had been dismissed from the force for inciting others to agitate in contravention of the police rules, and in their support nearly 2000 policemen demonstrated outside Parliament on 14 April, in open defiance of the government ban on demonstrations and processions; 931 policemen were arrested in all in the course of the agitation.

The Kerala government headed by the CPI(M) leader E. M. S. Namboodiripad, almost as though to confirm the accusations of the revolutionaries, was lauded by the press for its blend of a Marxist commitment and bourgeois pragmatism that, despite ritual noises in the Assembly, made private capital—particularly US investment—completely secure in the state. The CPI(M) in West Bengal was not having as easy a time, and the Central Committee called for a campaign against US imperialism that was suppressing freedom in Vietnam and was a threat to the freedom of India. More obviously and immediately the CPI(M) came into a confrontation with All-India Radio, which refused to permit one of its leaders' speeches over the radio, claiming it was objection-able. Incidents of conflict also developed between the CPI(M) and the police, until now on opposite sides of the fence. Despite these troubles the CPI(M) organized a massive May Day rally in Calcutta, declared a holiday by the UF government. Among other speeches and cultural events speakers at the rally suggested that the economic crisis facing India was mainly caused by dependence on 'the so-called imperialist aid and PL 480 and foreign collaboration agreements which have ruined our economy and brought devaluation at the dictate of the World Bank.' To improve matters speakers recommended nationalization of banks, foreign oil companies, general insurance and foreign trade; a moratorium on foreign-debt payment; a ban on the remittance of profits; nationalization of foreign capital; break-up of land monopoly; and a moratorium on peasants'-debt payment. Under the unsettled conditions of the polity other disturbances also surfaced, including a communal riot in Calcutta in April when 11 were killed and 100 injured. The army was called out to restore order, there were riots in the CIT Road area of Calcutta in June, allegedly sparked off by underworld feuds in which 5 were killed, 2 as a result of police firing. In the districts, particularly West Dinajpur, Nadia and 24 Parganas, there were many incidents of 'People's Committees' seizing and distributing hoarded rice, and even stopping trucks carrying grain illicitly, seizing it and surrendering it to the authorities.

At the end of May Naxalbari, smouldering on a slow fuse all these months but relatively ignored by the government both of the state and of the centre as an administrative matter, exploded into big news, with the death of a police officer and nine tribals, five of them women. There had been an unequal encounter between the tribals, armed with bows and arrows and spears, and the police, armed with guns. From now on Naxalbari and the Naxalites figured prominently in the news. Through June there were forty incidents reported from Naxalbari. In mid month six state ministers visited the area, appealing to the peasants to abandon their 'misguided' movement. At the time the ministers were issuing their appeal a gun duel was in progress between attackers and the owner of a house, and the ministers came away with the impression that even larger-scale police operations might be necessary to control the situation. The Lok Sabha discussed the issue and the Home Minister agreed readily to members' suggestions to send a parliamentary delegation to the area. This, however, did not find favour with the state government as it considered the Naxalbari movement a 'law and order' problem and thus within the jurisdiction of the state ministry. In Calcutta, meanwhile, a meeting held, under the auspices of several students' and workers' organizations condemned the police firing, supported the peasant movement there, and warned the ministers on tour that they would be considered reactionaries if it was true that they had authorized the police to fire on the peasants.

The CPI(M), to begin with, characterized the Naxalbari events, along with communal flare-ups and other violent incidents, as part of a conspiracy to discredit and dislodge the UF government, but later through Harekrishna Konar, the Land Revenue Minister, attempted to persuade the revolutionaries to withdraw their movement. The revolutionaries he met assured him they would discuss the matter with their colleagues before coming to a decision, but the press seemed somewhat doubtful of the outcome as landlords in the region had begun to organize armed resistance groups to counter the revolutionary threat. Radio Peking hailed the Naxalbari events as the 'Spring Thunder' of revolution in India, offering encouragement to the revolutionaries by this recognition of their authenticity. The Home Minister warned that Maoism was rearing its ugly head in Naxalbari. On 5 July, after an acrimonious six-hour meeting, the West Bengal cabinet agreed as to its policy with regard to the Naxalbari uprising. It would attempt to isolate the extremists by speeding up the work of land reform and by setting up distribution committees, while at the same time stepping up the police operations against them and perpetrators of violence. The revolutionaries on their part responded to the government's appeals to surrender by cutting off some of the roads connecting their strongholds, called in the police jargon 'pole zones'. The committees of peasants set up by the revolutionaries marked out various landlords' lands which they regarded as rightfully theirs, and in the heartlands of the rebellion the peasant committees' decisions were law.

The Jana Sangh, suspecting the motives of the communists in the legislature perhaps, urged the Chief Minister to take the Naxalbari matter into his own hands and deal firmly with the revolutionaries. The government in Delhi decided to take a hand in the matter and on 11 July passed an order banning the carrying of bows, arrows and spears in the Naxalbari area. The order caused a rift in the West Bengal government between the Chief Minister, who considered it entirely in order, and some of his colleagues, among them the CPI(M) leader Jyoti Basu, who construed the order as illegitimate intervention by the Centre. In sum, with the vociferous intervention of both the CPI and CPI(M) in the legislature it was decided against implementing the ban as it would frustrate the Cabinet's policy of isolating the extremists and alienate the tribals. On 12 July, meanwhile, the police arrested seventy-five revolutionaries from their hideouts deep in the disturbed areas in pre-dawn raids; bows, arrows and spears were seized from their caches, loudspeakers and amplifiers confiscated, and not a shot was fired. With other such raids and continuous patrolling, the police felt by 21 July that they had sufficiently isolated the extremists and brought the situation under control, though none of the top leaders had been arrested. But the violence continued and so did the writ of peasants' committees and the activities of the revolutionaries, and in August *The Statesman's* correspondent felt that peace in Naxalbari was not possible without the arrest of the leaders, despite mass surrenders at Kharibari on 25 July.

While all this was going on, much had changed in Calcutta. On 1 June a new governor of the state, strongman Dharma Vira, was sworn in. Increasingly dissatisfied with its role in the UF, and the functioning of the coalition, the CPI(M) began to press for midterm elections in the state. The CPI thought this was premature. Late in June a meeting organized by the university to decide ways of resuming the postponed examinations ended in pandemonium when fighting broke out between two groups of students. Gheraos were rife and there was even one in the state legislature. Despite various concessions to industrialists by the state government, they seemed chary of committing themselves to a course of investment and expansion, no doubt on the look-out for better terms and a more sympathetic government. Demonstrations were organized in support of Naxalbari, one in front of the Assembly building. There was a cut in the quantum of rice supply from the Centre to the states. On 19 July the West Bengal government took over the British owned Calcutta Tramways Company. The All India Congress Committee, showing its socialist swing, decided on 22 June to abolish privy purses, and approved the social control of banks. By mid-July the issue of privy purses was debated in the Lok Sabha and it was clear that their abolition would be a popular step. Like the states' legislatures, which witnessed many disorders, disorders leading to adjournments occurred in the Lok Sabha as well. In Calcutta in mid July some Congressmen kidnapped an MLA of the Bangla Congress (the senior partner in the ruling coalition) offering him a ministership if he would leave the Bangla Congress and join the Congress.

By August the food shortage in the state was becoming acute. Unable to raise enough internally the state government appealed to the Centre to grant more, and some ministers decided on a sit-down strike in front of Parliament to draw attention to the issue. And on the 25th the government in power organized a general strike in the state. The bandh paralysed activity, particularly in Calcutta. But this was almost the last occasion on which the United Front acted in a concerted manner. Rifts which had been hastily patched up all along began to loom larger and larger, with the CPI(M) keenest for a mid-term election and calling out against the conspiracy to topple the UF government.

The industrial scene was no less troubled. Between March and August 1967, 915 gheraos had been recorded, and by October, the Puja season, there was a sharp rise in the number of bonus disputes. The cabinet set up a tripartite review of labour disputes to be conducted by a cabinet sub-committee, while the Chief Minister bewailed the fact that the labour problem had got mixed up with the law-and-order problem. But the committee was ineffectual as rifts between the UF partners deepened. By late October the MP Humayun Kabir of the BKD was calling for President's Rule in West Bengal. In early November a polemical pamphlet issued by the revolutionaries appeared crowing over the 'jam' the CPI(M) had got itself into, and to cap it they were ousted from the leadership of the Kisan Sabha by the CPI(M). By early November the crisis in the UF cabinet materialized with the resignation of the Food

Minister, P. C. Ghosh, and the decision of fifteen other MLAs not to support the UF. The CPI(M) sensed the danger of the situation. Some of their leaders, addressing a huge rally on the Brigade Parade Ground in Calcutta, warned them to be prepared for moves to topple the UF. It was in this situation that the formation of the All-India Co-ordination Committee of Communist Revolutionaries was announced, drawing together revolutionaries from all parts of India who professed a belief in the Naxalbari model of revolution, as well as in the countryside encircling the cities through People's War. This was done with an eye to the future constitution of a party. Among those present at its first meeting were Charu Mazumdar, Shiv Kumar Misra (recently expelled from the Central Committee of the CPI(M)), S. Tiwari (formerly a member of the CPI(M)'s UP Committee), and Satyanarain Sinha from Bihar. In this troubled atmosphere the CPI staged a mock trial in front of the USIS in Calcutta condemning President Johnson of the USA to death for his crimes in Vietnam.

On 21 November, on his personal assessment that the UF ministry had lost the support of the majority, after it had failed to heed his advice to hold an early session of the Assembly for a trial of strength the governor, Dharma Vira, dismissed the UF government. Governments in Haryana and Punjab also toppled, though not through fiat, as in West Bengal. In place of the UF a Progressive Democratic Front Ministry with Congress support headed by P. C. Ghosh was set up. Widespread riots followed the dismissal of the UF, sparked off by a call for a forty-eight hour hartal in the state by the dismissed UF. Various extremist leaders, including Charu Mazumdar (though none of the active leaders of Naxalbari) were arrested. Successively, three hartals were called by the UF and its supporters, the last by the Rashtriya Sangram Samity on 21 November. The legislature, convened for a trial of strength, was adjourned by the Independent Speaker sine die, as he refused to recognize the P. C. Ghosh ministry. There were two pitched battles between students and police on the flimsiest of causes on 4 and 5 December. The UF began a campaign to dislodge the P. C. Ghosh ministry and its leaders were subjected to arrests and indignities. And, as though to put the seal of approval on the Congress hegemony and terror tactics, the Lok Sabha, in a session from which the whole opposition except the Swatantra Party and the Jana Sangh walked out, passed the Unlawful Activities (Prevention) Bill on 19 December. Overtly the Bill was directed against disrupters of the sovereignty and territorial integrity of the country, and specifically those who preached cession or secession. But what it said and what the Opposition understood were clearly two different things.

The P. C. Ghosh ministry did not stay long in power in spite of the attempts of the more conservative sections of the press to build up Ghosh. On 18 February 1968, a scant twelve days after the High Court in Calcutta had upheld the legitimacy of the dismissal of the UF government and of his appointment, he resigned. Two days later President's Rule was proclaimed in the state. There was speculation in early March that mid-term elections would be held in November or December, as well as speculation on the possibility of a showdown between extremists and the party mainliners at the All-India party plenum of the CPI(M) to be held in West Bengal between 6 and 12 April. At the party plenum there was indeed a confrontation between extremists and mainliners, but not violent or indeed of any great depth or scope. The extremist position characterizing the Soviet Union (in line with Chinese opinions on the matter) as a social-imperialist power was rejected in favour of seeing the Soviet leadership as revisionist but not imperialist. Soon after *Deshabrati*, one of the organs of communist revolutionaries outside the CPI(M) and later to become a mouth-piece of the CPI(M-L), called on revolutionaries within the CPI(M) to quit that party and come forward to build an alternative truly revolutionary party. That there was serious intent for this cannot be doubted as Sushital Roy Chowdhury, the editor of the paper, had a series of meetings with dissident Andhra delegates to the CPI(M)'s Central Committee plenum at Burdwan. On 13 and 14 April the CPI(M) dominated Central Kisan Council met as well and noted the spread and intensification of peasant unrest and feudal exploitation, particularly in West Bengal, Bihar, Assam, Tripura, Andhra, Uttar Pradesh and Kerala. Kisan leaders from Andhra who had attended the Central Committee plenum advocated preparations for armed resistance and presented accounts of the peasants' resistance to the police and landlords. In a resolution, the CKC congratulated 'the fighting peasants' and attacked 'the feudal terror let loose by Congress governments in Tripura and the Champaran district of Bihar and Srikakulam district of Andhra'.

It was thus that Srikakulam first appeared in the large national dailies. The struggle between peasants and landlords and between peasants and the police had been going on there for some time; 516 Girijans (native tribal people) had been arrested and 83 country-made guns seized, along with other traditional weapons. Vempatapu Satyanarayanan, the leader of the movement for eight years, had never been arrested. Roughly 100 villages spread over 200 mountainous square miles were under Marxist sway. And with the coming into prominence of Communist agrarian activities, Naxalbari too was recalled, as was its absconding leadership. The West Bengal Police suspected Kanu Sanyal, the chief Naxalbari leader, of training Communist cadres in Nepal.

The West Bengal political scene was in utter disarray, with neither of the two contenders, the Congress or the UF, having set its own house in order. The walls of Calcutta blossomed with the slogans of the various Communist factions, chiefly the Maoists and particularly in Tollygunge. But if the CPI(M) replies to the revolutionaries were small and few in Tollygunge, in Calcutta University there were reasoned replies of six or seven lines each to the revolutionaries' impetuosity. One of these of course was that the revolution would not come until the people of the country had lost faith in elections. But the Maoist invasion of the university was not too far off. On 7 May, for the second time in five days, the Vice-Chancellor was gheraoed by students shouting Maoist slogans and demanding the further postponement of the BA and BSc examinations. And as if orchestrated into the Marxist-Maoist drift of politics, Surajit Lahiri (former Chief Justice of the Calcutta High Court, Chairman of the Commission of Inquiry set up by the P. C. Sen ministry after the widespread food riots, violent demonstrations and police firings early in 1966) observed in his report, 'the food policy pursued by the state of West Bengal in 1965 and 1966 succeeded in converting the entire population of the State into a race of criminals'.

With most of the preparations of the Congress and the UF proceeding behind closed doors or pitched at the level of details, more interesting news about the revolutionaries was available in the press, some of it mere rumour-mongering. At the end of May Naxalites were reported to be trying to extend their activities into Jalpaiguri district and even to the border between Cooch Bihar and Bhutan. But in Siliguri the anniversary of the police firing in Prasadhu Jote where ten died was commemorated at an open meeting organized by the Naxalbari Krishak Sangram Sahayak Samiti.

Late in June a difference of opinion surfaced in the All-India Co-ordination Committee of Communist Revolutionaries between the Nagi Reddy group and others over the characterization of the Soviet state as imperialist. The mainliners believed it, whereas Nagi Reddy had reservations. Promode Das Gupta, secretary of the West Bengal's

CPI(M) unit, remained unperturbed by the revolutionaries' goings-on, maintaining that extremism arose from frustrations arising from immaturity and lack of faith in the mass movement. In Kerala meanwhile an MLA expelled from the CPI(M), Das, claimed that he and six other MLAs now subscribed to the views held by the 'brave Naxalites' regarding the futility of parliamentary democracty and the need for armed revolution.

All this made for exciting news in the face of the industrial doldrums West Bengal was in. Investors preferred the west coast, where a rabid Shiv Sena had brought the Communists to heel, to the uncertainties of turbulent West Bengal. Kerala too was a trouble spot and it was claimed that the Naxalites there committed systematic sabotage on the Idikki project on 15 June. Jangal Santhal, one of the local leaders of the Naxalbari uprising, arrested some little while earlier, was convicted for committing armed dacoity and was sentenced to five years' rigorous imprisonment, to run concurrently with another sentence for seven years. And the collapse of the revolutionary scenario seemed to be heralded with the breakaway of Nagi Reddy from the AICCCR in the quest of forming an independent revolutionary party.

At the Centre the Indian princes appealed to protect their privy purses but were turned down by the central government. More importantly, the Deputy Prime Minister, Morarji Desai, erstwhile defender of free trade, moved a bill in Parliament on 1 August for the social control of banks which was duly passed by the Lok Sabha on the 6th. And almost as important, employees (non-journalist) of the six major newspapers and allied publications went on strike for fifty-nine days, demanding implementation of the pay-scales recommended by the Wage Board appointed for the purpose. At the end of the strike the employers promised 70 per cent of the recommendations and agreed to arbitration for the rest. Sections of the central government employees too went on a one-day token strike on 19 September, for which there were mass arrests; 2400 being released from Tihar Jail, Delhi on the 22nd, but the government withdrew recognition of a number of railway and postal staff unions as a result. By the 29th, the strike a failure, postal work in Delhi went back to normal.

In October West Bengal was visited by natural calamity, to add to all its other troubles. From the 3rd to the 13th there was incessant rain, and floods engulfed most areas in north Bengal. Jalpaiguri town was inundated, the estimated death toll there alone being of the order of 2000 to

3000. An area estimated at 2000 square miles was affected and between 400,000 and 700,000 were made homeless. The damage to property was not even computed. In view of the calamity and the relief operations it necessitated, eleven political parties asked that the projected November election be postponed, and so it was. The new date set for the West Bengal elections was February 1969. As information trickled in it was estimated that 5,000,000 were hit by the floods.

That same month, as part of its snowballing feud with the Centre, the CPI(M) in Kerala called for a general strike and the-picketing of union government offices. The hartal turned violent, resulting in at lest one death and injury to several others. But the response was not everything the CPI(M) might have envisaged.

On 31 October, after months of being hunted, the Naxalite leader Kanu Sanyal, chief organizer of the Naxalbari revolt, was arrested in his hideout at Birsinghjote in the Phansidewa thana area of Darjeeling district, along with four others, including another Naxalbari leader, Keshab Sarkar. They did not offer any resistance but demanded a higher classification in prison, a demand rejected by the presiding magistrate. Presented with the news, Charu Mazumdar was confident Kanu Sanyal would soon be out, though he was shocked at the arrest. *The Statesman* also quoted Charu Mazumdar as saying that Kanu should not have given up without a fight, an allegation later denied by Charu Mazumdar in *Deshabrati* as a gross fabrication. But if with Kanu Sanyal's arrest one phase of the revolutionaries' activity in West Bengal had come to an end, another phase, equally dramatic though not as long-lasting, was beginning in Kerala. On 22 November Naxalites attacked the Tellichery police station in Cannanore district, and again on the 24th the same or other Naxalites attacked the police wireless station at Pulpalli in Wynad district. This was, of course, not at all the same kind of thing as the Naxalbari movement, which had mobilized the peasantry to grab land and attack the police with whatever they had. They subscribed nevetheless to a philosophy of armed revolution and were willing to put their platitudes to the test with their lives. There were at this time several groups in Kerala and south India, generally without co-ordination with each other or with the revolutionaries of West Bengal, whose vocabulary nevertheless was largely the same. Apart from Negi Reddy, who had struck off to form a revolutionary party of his own, there was another group in Kerala which on 24 November announced the formation of a third, revolutionary, Communist party. But all these were mere flashes in the pan compared with what was to happen in Andhra and West Bengal under the aegis of the CPI(M-L). But with the attacks on the police stations the centre was alarmed, and on 15 December the Deputy Prime Minister Morarji Desai warned the Kerala government that if it did not tackle the Naxalites the centre would intervene. As far as many Congressmen (and some others) were concerned, there seemed to be too much resemblance between the CPI(M) and the Naxalites, and indeed the CPI(M) seemed to have provided the breeding ground for them.

In Calcutta meanwhile, the arrival of the World Bank President, McNamara, was the occasion for fresh clashes between students and policemen. Three trams were burnt. At least 70 people, including 25 policemen, were injured. More than 80 were arrested. McNamara, nevertheless, was optimistic about the prospects for India's development, believing at the same time that in India both the country and development agencies like the World Bank were on trial. He went on record as saying, 'If India cannot be developed, mainly by her own efforts but with such external assistance as she requires and as other nations of the world can provide, then I think world development plans cannot succeed anywhere.'

Rather ominously though the Lok Sabha passed the Industrial Security Force Bill, empowering the government to set up a centralized watch and ward unit for public-sector undertakings.

The ill-fated Kerala revolutionaries did not seem to get off the ground though, for even before the Deputy PM's warning to the Kerala government, Kunnikkal Narayanan, believed to have master-minded both raids in Kerala, surrendered himself at the Trichur police station.

The West Bengal Naxalites, however, particularly in Calcutta, were thriving despite Promode Das Gupta's view that the Naxalite movement was disintegrating. But over the impending elections there seemed to be some difference of opinion amongst them, the hard-liners pressing for a boycott, the soft-liners pleading for another chance to be given to the UF to fail.

At the beginning of 1969 *The Statesman* estimated that in Andhra 6000 (or nearly one-sixth of their membership) had defected from the CPI(M), in Kerala about 4000, in West Bengal about 5000. It estimated the Naxalite strength in Bihar at about 1000, in UP around 700, a couple of hundred each in MP and Rajasthan, and rumours of some in Kashmir. But after these defections the CPI(M) seemed to be firm in its rejection of the extremists' views, as proved by the rejection of Maoist theses in political resolutions at the Party Congress on 2 January. The

CPI(M) also considered the Kerala government a means for mass struggle against the Centre, as the Chief Minister E. M. S. Namboodiripad told a public meeting at Trivandrum on the 8th. Nevertheless the Central government gave concurrence to the Kerala Land Reform (Amendment) Bill.

The mid-term elections in three states—Punjab, Bihar and UP—were held on 9 February. By 1 February in West Bengal there had been about 60 'election clashes' involving rival groups of campaigners—about 56 in the districts and 6 or so in Calcutta. The United Front was returned to power in West Bengal with, 218 seats out of 280. The large bulk of Naxalites in the state had, of course, campaigned to boycott the elections, but strangely enough 'boycott election' posters appeared in Gorakhpur in UP describing elections as 'purposeless' and a 'fraud'. The newly instated UF government lost no time in issuing a warning to industrialists and landlords, urging them to take note of the changed political situation in West Bengal and act accordingly. This was in the course of addressing a vast gathering on the Brigade Parade Ground on 22 February. The speakers were Ajoy Mukherjee, elected leader of the UF legislature party, and Jyoti Basu of the CPI(M), his deputy.

The Naxalites had by now made inroads in the universities. Some of them gheraoed the Vice-Chancellor on 5 March in the afternoon in his office. He was rescued by teachers the next day at 7:30 a.m. The overt cause for the gherao was the demand to dissolve the students' union, which allegedly was not functioning properly, and to hold fresh elections. The students' union office was ransacked and papers set on fire. Pro-Congress Chhatra Parishad students also participated in this, according to a university source. The Vice-Chancellor was gheraoed again on the 13th for seven hours, to be rescued by UF volunteers and students belonging to both wings of the Students' Federation. The Naxalite students prevented reporters and photographers from entering the University. The gherao was a sequel to a 48-hour ultimatum demanding an apology from the Vice-Chancellor and the teachers who had rescued him on the previous occasion. There were two other gheraos at the university. Already in embryo the Naxalites and the CPI(M) were beginning to face each other as opponents. But as before, the shape of the future appeared in Kerala, where two prominent leaders of the Kerala State Coordination Committee were attacked and injured by about fifty people, said to belong to the CPI(M). Jyoti Basu, on his part, hailed the rescue of the Vice-Chancellor as a historic achievement, criticized the

Naxalites as 'adventurists' and asked 'progressive people' to unite and fight the Congress-Naxalite conspiracy against the UF.

On 8 April, in a clash of unknown origin between management and workers at the Cossipore Gun and Shell Factory in Calcutta, the police fired, killing five and injuring eight. In a protest against this the ruling UF called a state-wide bandh on the 10th which, but for an incident where the police fired in Kanchrapara, Nadia, passed off peacefully, and the UF congratulated themselves on their success. It was perhaps one of the last successes of the UF in concert.

On 18 April the Administrative Reforms Commission presented its report on personnel and administration to the Prime Minister, in which it urged that central government employees should not have the right to strike and recommended that this ban be extended to state government employees as well. And, on the 22nd, the government decided to bring half the country, comprising eight states and three union territories, into a single wheat zone.

But in Calcutta on the 6th a mysterious scandal occurred. At an event in Rabindra Sarobar Stadium rowdies allegedly ran amuck and molested women there. Rumours were rife. An investigation committee was appointed. Women demonstrated, holding Jyoti Basu responsible for what had happened.

On 9 April, unrepentant, Kanu Sanyal was released from prison. He held 'people's pressure' and the attempt of the UF to create confusion in the people's ranks to be responsible for his release. News appeared in the press of killings and dacoities by the revolutionaries in Srikakulam. And on 1 May, at a huge May Day Rally at the foot of the Ochterlony Monument, Kanu Sanyal announced the formation of a third, a 'truly revolutionary' party—the Communist Party of India (Marxist-Leninist). He made it abundantly clear that Charu Mazumdar was the principal inspiration behind the formation of the party. The party would be a party of agrarian revolution, with peasants as its main power base. Speakers made repeated reference to the 'organized and planned attack by Mr Jyoti Basu's police and goondas'. Both CPI and CPI(M) circles pooh-poohed the formation of the new party, saying that it made no significant difference. A correspondent estimated that at its formation the CPI(M-L) had 6000 members in Andhra, 5000 in West Bengal, 4000 in Kerala, 1000 in Bihar, 700 in UP, and 200 each in MP and Rajasthan. At that very May Day meeting supporters of the Naxalites clashed with supporters of the UF holding a rival rally close by. Bombs were used and police had to use tear gas to bring the situation under control. At a rough estimate about a hundred people were injured. The formation of the CPI(M-L) drew from the then Home Minister, Chavan, the warning that violent Naxalite activity would be dealt with firmly.

With the death of President Zakir Hussain on 3 May, Vice-President Giri was sworn in as the acting president.

Jyoti Basu ridiculed Kanu Sanyal's claim that he had been released by history by saying it was he, Jyoti Basu, who had done so and history had nothing to do with it. But with the formation of the CPI(M-L) and the benevolence of the UF government at that moment, the Naxalites made many gains in Bengal. They organized an open poster exhibition in the steel town of Durgapur which drew large crowds, and if the UF was not afraid the Centre was certainly wary. Incidents of violence continued to be reported from Andhra, but for the time being Naxalites were not the main perpetrators of violence in West Bengal. The constituents of the UF had begun to fight amongst themselves—not in the legislature, but at cadre level on the streets and in the villages. Paradoxically Kanu Sanyal in mid May was touring the Naxalbari area on a cycle, mobilizing support for his movement, demanding 15 *bigha*s (2 hectares) of *khas* (government) land for cultivators. But with the consciousness of a link between the Srikakulam revolutionaries and the CPI(M-L), a high-powered state-level committee was set up to investigate the movement in Srikakulam.

Clashes between the constituents of the UF began to be more and more everyday occurrences. So too did gheraos. The underworld capitalized on this street fighting and the making of home-made bombs became a lucrative trade, at the same time that being gheraoed turned from a harrowing experience into some kind of a status symbol. West Bengal was fast approaching the collapse of civilized politics.

Late in May, voices began to be raised against the rising trend of 'political' murders—which had nothing to do with the Naxalites or their activities. Not that the occasional incident *of a jotedar* being hacked to death was not reported, but certainly not with the frequency of the far more organized inter-party clashes. Whereas the Bangla Congress leaders expressed concern, the State CPI(M) thought of raising a volunteer force, feeling itself under attack and claiming that the CIA was involved. The clashes between the various parties were all-embracing, CPI(M) and PSP, CPI(M) and CPI, RSP and CPI(M) and among the others as well. The CPI(M) certainly felt a sense of fragility and pressure, and their leader Jyoti Basu, exhorting the unions to make hay while the sun shone, urged them to strengthen themselves for the coming struggles while the UF was still in power. Students, too, were on the rampage, and not merely Naxalites among them. The Stock Exchange was ransacked by students—belonging to the Bengal Province Students' Federation and the Pashchim Banga Yuba Sangh—who, after demonstrating in front of Writers' Building, demanded, unemployment allowance and 'a reply to Durgapur'. But the CPI(M-L) students, too, were quite obviously actively involved in some of the violence, as when they set fire to a tram on College Street protesting against the police firing in Durgapur. The ultimate symbol of the chaos that had been let loose and turned things topsy-turvy came when several hundred policemen in uniform stormed into the Assembly house, then in session, broke microphone stands, overturned tables, tore up papers and assaulted at least one minister and several MLAs. The Speaker promptly adjourned the House and hurriedly left. The policemen had come in procession from Anderson House, carrying the body of a constable killed by some political party.

If near pandemonium reigned in the politics of West Bengal, the Centre was not without its crisis, admittedly infinitely more civilized, though perhaps almost as disconcerting for the participants. From 10 to 13 July the AICC met in Bangalore for three days, taking certain decisions on economic policy and changes in the Congress Party constitution. On the 16th the Prime Minister took away the finance portfolio from her Deputy, Morarji Desai, who submitted his resignation from the Union cabinet. On the 19th Desai's resignation was accepted, and within an hour of this the Prime Minister announced the decision to nationalize fourteen major commercial banks. An ordinance to this effect was promulgated by the acting president, V. V. Giri. On the 25th the Bank Nationalization Bill was presented in the Lok Sabha. President Nixon of the US arrived on a state visit at this delicate juncture. It would be interesting to know what he discussed with the Prime Minister. On 9 August, with the president's assent, bank nationalization passed into law. The impending election of a new president was the final blow to split the Congress Party. The Congress Party nominee for the job was Sanjiva Reddy, though Indira Gandhi favoured V. V. Giri. The Prime Minister insisted on member's freedom to vote in the presidential election, and the Party was divided on the issue. On 18 August the Congress President, Nijalingappa, served a show cause notice on Mrs Gandhi and several others for anti-party activities. On the 20th V. V. Giri was elected

President against the Congress nominee N. Sanjiva Reddy, and on the 24th duly sworn in. On 7 September the Prime Minister conferred with Kosygin of the Soviet Union in Delhi. On the 8th the Supreme Court issued a limited stay order on the Bank Nationalization Act. On 9 October the Congress President Nijalingappa rejected the demand of the Prime Minister's group to convene a session of the All-India Congress Committee. On 1 November the Indira Gandhi group decided to convene an AICC session in Delhi to rival the session convened by the group headed by the Congress President Nijalingappa. Both sessions were held in Delhi at the same time.

On 7 November conciliatory talks between Mrs Gandhi and Nijalingappa failed and by the 9th factional fighting in the Congress had come to a stalemate. On the 12th the Congress Working Committee expelled Indira Gandhi from the party and the Congress Party was formally split into the Congress(R) headed by Mrs Gandhi and the Congress(O) with President Nijalingappa. On the 13th the Congress Parliamentary Party reaffirmed their faith in the Prime Minister, whereas the Congress MPs who supported Nijalingappa formed a new party in Parliament. On the 17th this new party named itself the 'Congress Party in Parliament—Opposition' under the chairmanship of Morarji Desai. On the 22nd, as a sort of ritual gesture, the AICC members of the Prime Minister's group expelled Nijalingappa from the presidency and elected C. Subramaniam president. On the 25th, as a sort of bonus from the crisis, perhaps from fear to having it used against themselves in states where they were weak, the government decided not to extend the Preventive Detention Act when it expired and advised the states to make their own laws on the issues concerning them. On 30 November the Congress(O) expelled fourteen state leaders. On 1 December Jagjivan Ram was chosen President of the Congress(R). Finally, on 17 December, for the first time since independence, a duly recognized opposition came into being in Parliament, having the requisite strength to qualify as an Opposition.

While this crisis played itself out at the Centre, beleaguered, strifetorn West Bengal acquired on 19 September a more liberal governor, S. S. Dhavan. As though crisis was endemic or contagious, the Kerala UF headed by E. M. S. Namboodiripad resigned in late October. The Naxalites, after a period of relative quiescence in the Bengal countryside, launched movements in Gopiballanpur and Debra in August and October respectively. With violence rife in the state and finding himself helpless as Chief Minister, Ajoy Mukherjee began a three-day fast on

1 December to appeal to the public against the prevalence of violence in the politics of West Bengal. As expected, the enquiry instituted into the Rabindra Sarobar incident reported on 15 December that there had been no molestation of women during the incident—comfort for some at any rate. But certainly the Naxalbari movement had drawn the agrarian problem to the fore as chief ministers of states met for a two-day conference in Delhi to discuss land reforms on 27 and 28 November. Setting the seal on a year of parliamentary crisis and the evolution of political violence into a fine art on 31 December, the Preventive Detention Act expired.

The defeated presidential candidate, N. Sanjiva Reddy, felt that only a mahatma or a de Gaulle could save Indian democracy. But many people in Bengal felt that it was mainly the CPI(M) that was to blame for the chaos in the state's politics. Leaders of the Congress, the Forward Bloc, the SSP all condemned the CPI(M) for its role in fostering violence and instability in West Bengal. But in addition to inter-party violence, the peasant unrest and labour militancy continued as well, and certainly the Naxalites were active—more so in the rural areas yet than in Calcutta, where their main activity seemed to be painting slogans on walls. The CPI(M) for its part was ready to take its struggle and message into the unions. The CPI Chairman accused the CPI(M) of trying to precipitate a split in the AITUC (the Communist trade union congress), but the CPI(M) vehemently denied the allegation, rounding instead on the CPI itself, accusing it of treating the AITUC as its 'pocket borough'. To two petitioners, victims of a 'people's court', the Chief Minister of Bengal was quoted as saying, 'Organize yourselves for your defence. Are you cowards? You should know that this Government is unable to give you protection.' Relations between the Bangla Congress and the CPI(M) were particularly bad, and the CPI(M) fuelled the fears of the Bangla Congress when Promode Das Gupta, General Secretary of the CPI(M), and Harekrishna Konar told a rally that trade-union volunteers would soon have to undertake the task of a revolutionary army, as the NLF was doing in Vietnam. Conciliatory attempts between the parties, however, continued to be made.

At the Centre the government launched a scheme to give bank credits and other facilities to small farmers. The Supreme Court however struck down the Banking Companies (Requisition and Transfer of Undertakings) Act, 1966, which had provided for the nationalization of the fourteen major banks. At this the President of India promulgated an ordinance re-nationalizing the fourteen major commercial banks with retrospective effect from 19 July 1969.

The CPI(M-L) could hardly be expected to lag behind in such a situation. In February 1970 the mouth-piece of the party, *Liberation,* carried an article by Charu Mazumdar entitled 'A Few Words About Guerrilla Actions' which immediately achieved notoriety as a 'murder manual' (which indeed it seemed to be). The article on how to conduct guerilla operations advised activists, after conducting propaganda, to form a squad of those who hated the class enemy the most by whispering in their ears 'How would it be if we killed such and such?' Then, after arranging hide-outs, they were advised to kill the enemy by stealth and disappear to their hide-outs while the news of their action spread, returning when things cooled down. They could then generate further enthusiasm among the poor. The tactics would strike terror into the hearts of the privileged and separate the wheat from the chaff as the opinion went around that—'he who has not dipped his hand in the blood of class enemies can hardly be called a communist.' The document became the basis for the 'campaign of annihilation' that marked the evolution of the CPI(M-L) into a full-fledged terror group. Students and youth in Calcutta, relatively quiescent until now, entered the arena of violent activities outside their universities in the city. On 3 March seven cinema houses were attacked by Naxalite youth and damaged. The cinemas were screening a film called *Prem Pujari* (Worshipper of Love) which the Naxalites found objectionable because it depicted China in a bad light. From now on the violence perpetrated by the CPI(M-L) escalated fairly rapidly. In this situation of all against all, hoodlums openly defied the law.

By 6 March the Bangla Congress had had enough and advised Ajoy Mukherjee to resign as Chief Minister by the 16th, which he duly did, and President's Rule was imposed for the second time in West Bengal with a suspension of the Assembly.

The CPI(M) entered vigorously into the attempt to wrest the leadership of the AITUC, and on 31 March Jyoti Basu was shot at in Patna, showing West Bengal to be not the only violent state, just the extremest case.

Throughout April and May there were repeated and large-scale clashes between the police and Naxalites in the universities of Calcutta. The students and youth avowing allegiance to the CPI(M-L) also began to implement the annihilation campaign in Calcutta. More prominently, they began to attack and deface or mutilate statues of Bengali heroes of the Renaissance and the nationalist movement. Seeing this the government put up a permanent police guard around the statue of Mahatma Gandhi at the head of Park Street. The fear of Naxalite activities however was more widespread than their actual occurrence. The Home Minister, Y. B. Chavan, told the Lok Sabha in April that the Naxalites had extended their activities to Assam, Nagaland and Mizo areas. It is difficult to decide on what evidence he came to this conclusion, but if anything was designed to agitate the Congressmen in Parliament, this extension to sensitive areas where the state was already challenged certainly would. Right on cue, the Assam government issued a state-wide alert to district authorities on Naxalite plans for launching long drawn-out guerilla warfare from their bases on the border.

The crisis in the centre was however deepening rather than coming to some kind of a resolution. The day-to-day running of government went on and Jagjivan Ram, the Food and Agriculture minister, announced on 4 April that the whole of the country was one food zone for wheat, except for the statutorily rationed areas of West Bengal and Maharashtra. The president's election was challenged in court. On 20 April, for the first time in history, a president appeared in court as a respondent witness when Giri gave evidence in the petition challenging his election. On 11 May the Supreme Court upheld his election as entirely lawful.

On 20 May the AITUC split formally and the CPI(M) organized its own Centre for Indian Trades Unions (CITU).

In June both factions of the Congress held committee sessions in Delhi and a major reshuffle of the cabinet was announced. In May, too, the CPI(M-L) organized its first congress in Calcutta. Despite the fact that many of the leaders were wanted men, the Congress conducted its deliberations successfully, and this was seen by Charu Mazumdar as a great victory, as sign of the high tide of the revolution, an opinion to which the crest the CPI(M-L) was riding on in Calcutta seemed to lend added weight. Vempatapu Satyanarayan, the Srikakulam leader, attended these deliberations, and the CPI(M-L) cadre in the city celebrated the event with a huge procession in open defiance of the police. Satyanarayan was killed shortly after in July, allegedly in an encounter with the police in the Bori Hills in Parvatipuram subdivision. From the time of the imposition of President's Rule in West Bengal, 1200 Naxalites had been held. July, too, saw the setting up of a Working Group by the Information and Broadcasting ministry to prepare a multimedia campaign against communalism and political violence. The Prime Minister maintained her cool, however, claiming that the Naxalite problem was being exaggerated. As though to tease her particularly, there were bomb attacks on police pickets in Jadavpur and police lathi-charged students, teachers and staff indiscriminately. And the CPI(M), until now supercilious of the CPI(M-L), publicly warned Naxalites through Jyoti Basu's pronouncements that the CPI(M) would retaliate, indicating the dimensions the problem was assuming and the threat felt by the CPI(M).

Finally in September and November 1970 special laws were brought into force to cope with the Naxalites. On 10 September the West Bengal government extended the scope of the Bengal Suppression of Terrorist Outrages Acts 1932 to suppress them, and in November President V. V. Giri approved the West Bengal Maintenance of Public Order Bill. But in November, too, opposition to the terroristic line in the cities surfaced within the ranks of the CPI(M-L). Sushital Roy Chowdhury questioned the revolutionary potential of smashing statues and their legitimacy, as also the extension of the 'annihilation campaign' to the cities. His complaint was that this extension had been undertaken without any discussion in the Central Committee. Charu Mazumdar wrote replies defending both aspects, and again without any discussion in the Central Committee Sushital Roy Chowdhury was boycotted by the lower rungs of the party and died not long after in complete obscurity.

If the Prime Minister thought the Naxalite problem was being exaggerated it was probably only because she had her hands full in Delhi without bothering too much about West Bengal. In September the Lok Sabha adopted the 24th Constitutional Amendment Bill (Abolition of Privy Purses and Princely Privileges) by 339 votes to 154. The Bill failed to get the required two-thirds majority in the Rajya Sabha, and once again on the 7th a presidential order derecognizing the ex-rulers was issued. On the 14th however the Supreme Court admitted the ex-rulers' petition challenging the presidential derecognition order, and on 15 December a special bench of the Supreme Court declared the presidential order derecognizing the princes *ultra-vires* of the Constitution. Despite this constitutional crisis, to aggravate the organizational crisis of the Congress Party itself, the government did manage to transact some business, such as appointing a Central Land Reform Committee to recommend measures to expedite land reforms in the states. But the Prime Minister obviously felt herself blocked and thwarted at each step, and on her advice the president dissolved the fourth Lok Sabha a year before its tenure was due to end, so that the government could seek a fresh mandate. Indira Gandhi was asked to head the caretaker government. The pathetic senselessness of the times and its challenge was underlined when on 20 December the Vice-Chancellor of Jadavpur University was murdered, probably by Naxalites.

Violent incidents continued to be characteristic of the political situation in West Bengal throughout the next year—inter-party violence, of which some Naxalite violence was a part, Naxalite killings, and criminal or underworld violence, without the possibility of the police in any way bringing them under control. Yet in late February 1971 the governor of West Bengal told a visiting team of Asian and African journalists in Calcutta that the city was safer for a woman moving alone than the streets of Delhi; what violence there was, was restricted to political parties, and that too to some of them; and if the press did not play them up, ordinary people going about their lives would know nothing of violent incidents in the city. The press certainly was active and some sections were vociferous in demanding a clean-up of the city. Police continued to make arrests but to little avail.

The year 1971 began, however, with preparations for the elections. The two Congresses disputed each other for the election symbol, the two yoked bullocks of the United Congress Party. The Supreme Court disallowed both from using it and the Congress(R) went into the elections with a cow and a calf as its symbol, the Congress(O) with a woman spinning at a charkha. Polling was held between 1 and 7 March and the Congress(R) led by Indira Gandhi won more than two-thirds of the seats, 350 out of 518; Indira Gandhi was thus assured of a decisive majority in the Fifth Lok Sabha. It was perhaps a personal victory for her as she had in the election campaign appealed to the electorate to strengthen her hands to implement socialist policies, or at any rate policies beneficial to the poor.

Elections to the West Bengal Assembly were also held on 10 March and no party secured an absolute majority. After a delay of more than two weeks Ajoy Mukherjee managed to scrape together the support for a non-Marxist Democratic Front ministry which took office on 2 April, putting an end to President's Rule. But it was beyond the capacity of this ministry to cope with chaotic conditions in the state. Having done little, the ministry resigned a little over two months later on 28 June, inaugurating another period of President's Rule from the 29th: but President's Rule this time with a difference, for the Congress leader Siddhartha Shankar Ray was appointed Special Advisor to deal with the state's problems. The parties made ritual protests about this but to little avail, and Ray emerged as the most powerful man in West Bengal. On 21 August a new governor was appointed to West Bengal, A. L. Dias, but the governor had lost the eminence and power enjoyed by Dharma Vira, despite the still unsettled conditions of West Bengal politics.

But by far the most important events of 1971 took place not in India but in neighbouring East Pakistan, later Bangladesh. In a slow escalation of hostilities from the beginning of the year onwards the liberation movement in East Pakistan gained momentum, with India a sympathetic bystander, not committing itself to open support of the liberation fighters until war with Pakistan became inescapable. Relations between India and Pakistan had been deteriorating since the beginning of the year when a Fokker Friendship aircraft of the Indian Airlines was hijacked, taken to Lahore and blown up, in full view of the authorities, and broadcast on television. And despite sections of her own party clamouring for her to support the Bangladeshi struggle, Indira Gandhi maintained a reticent course until Pakistan attacked on 3 December 1971, when Indian forces swiftly retaliated. Pakistan declared war on India on the 4th, and Indian troops moved in to support the Mukti Bahini in Bangladesh. Within a matter of days the fighting was settled and on 16 December Indira Gandhi announced in the Lok Sabha that General A. A. K. Niazi, commanding the Pakistani forces in Bangladesh, had surrendered unconditionally to the GOC-in-C of the Indian and Bangladesh forces on the Eastern Front, Lt.-Gen. J. S. Aurora, at 4:31 p.m. The victory did almost as much to consolidate Indira Gandhi's position as the election had done.

If the War had been a godsend for the Indian Prime Minister, it spelt the beginning of the end for the CPI(M-L). No longer substantially involved in the countryside but ferociously active in urban centres and particularly in Calcutta, the cadre of the CPI(M-L), with its customary respect for China and the Chinese leadership, was thrown completely out of step by the Chinese stand on the issue. The Chinese repeatedly emphasized that what was happening in East Pakistan was the internal affair of the Pakistani government and warned India to keep out of it. With the sympathy there was among leftists for the Bangladeshi cause, and particularly among Bengalis, this sounded very much like opportunist support for the reactionary Yahya regime. Large sections of the CPI(M-L) were disillusioned or demoralized. But the dispute which took place within the CPI(M-L) did not give any voice to *this* sentiment.

The battle lines within the party were between Charu Mazumdar—who maintained that revolutionaries in India should support and join hands with communist revolutionaries (led by Md. Toha) in East Pakistan to utilize the liberation movement to gain leadership of the mass movement—and the doctrinaire disciple Ashim Chatterjee (leader in Gopiballavpur and Debra) who maintained, following the Chinese leadership, that Indians should not interfere in the internal affairs of Pakistan. The dispute, though largely academic, since most of the strength of the Naxalites was by this time concentrated in Calcutta anyway, served to express the disintegrative forces at work within the CPI(M-L) and demoralize it further. Confusion was just round the corner.

The resistance to the CPI(M-L) too achieved organized form under Siddhartha Shankar Ray's leadership. The Congress began to organize 'volunteer' squads of hoodlums to fight the Naxalites. What the police had failed to do and despaired of doing (in fact on 30 May policemen's wives and relations protesting against lack of protection for the police in their encounter with Naxalites had turned violently on the authorities) the Congress volunteers accomplished, perhaps aided by the demoralization and exhaustion of the movement. On 12 and 13 August a band of these Congress volunteers cordoned off one of the Naxalite strongholds in Cossipore-Baranagar and ran amuck, massacring all known Naxalites, threatening and beating or killing sympathizers. CPI(M-L) sympathizers of course claimed that people from the CPI(M) and police and the para-military were involved as well, but the facts of the matter were never settled. If the police did not actively collude, it is certain at any rate that they did nothing to check the Congress volunteers. After the incident the Leftist parties vociferously demanded an enquiry into the matter, but this was not undertaken. A similar incident was reported somewhat later in the same vague detail in Barasat; that too remained unilluminated. Most were content to leave well enough alone. It is quite certain that similar incidents must have occurred all over Calcutta and in the other urban centres of West Bengal, for by October there were 16,000 organized Congress resistance groups in West Bengal with 300,000 members, of whom 12,000 groups were in Calcutta. Certainly the formula for bringing the Naxalites to heel had been found, with the Naxalites themselves in a situation where they bad lost much credibility or at least active support.

The new year opened with some good news even for the Leftists. India discontinued the imports of grain from the USA under the PL

480 agreement which it had been buying since August 1956. It was also officially announced that, with record rice production in 1970–1, India was now self-sufficient in rice. An easing of the situation certainly seemed to be on the cards. And ending an era, the government issued orders on 4 February, stopping the payment of privy purses to the ex-rulers of princely states to be effective from January 1972.

On 5 March 1972 general elections began for sixteen state assemblies and two union territories. West Bengal was, after all, not the only state to have been politically unstable over these years. Before the polling in West Bengal the Inspector General of the West Bengal police claimed law and order in the state was back to normal. How credible this statement was is difficult to gauge. Certainly the Congress volunteer squads were still active, but looting and lawlessness in the countryside seemed to have ended, as also attacks on politicians in the city. On 14 March the results of the polling were declared. The Congress had won absolute majorities in fourteen states and the union territory of Delhi, including West Bengal. The Congress in West Bengal was jubilant and claimed that an 'Indira Wave' in the wake of her socialist policies and brilliant conduct of affairs regarding Bangladesh had done the trick. The CPI(M) was scornful of these claims and accused the Congress of having rigged its victory with false voting, intimidation, and hanky-panky with ballot boxes. They presented some evidence for this, but in the nature of the case all that was inconclusive. More impressively the CPI(M) attempted to demonstrate from the returns that there had been no 'Indira Wave' toppling the Left. Whatever may be the case, on 20 March Siddhartha Shankar Ray was sworn in as Chief Minister for West Bengal with a solid Congress majority to support him.

The Naxalites were by now entirely subdued. But the coping stone had still to be laid, for Charu Mazumdar continued to write articles of the revolutionary upsurge that he was sure was just-around the corner. On 8 June two prominent leaders of the CPI(M-L)—Santosh Rana and Professor Paresh Chatterjee of the Indian Institute of Management— were arrested in Calcutta. And, finally, on 16 July, Charu Mazumdar himself was arrested. But his health was failing at the time, and he was sent to hospital under armed guard. He died a scant eleven days later, on 27 July. Did they kill him? With that the terrorist days of the CPI(M-L) were well and truly done. By the end of 1972 a police spokesman of West Bengal called it 'one of the most peaceful states in India'.

Chapter Five

The Communist Party of India (Marxist–Leninist)

Both in Delhi and in Bengal the political crises of the late 1960s encompassed issues of socialism. Whereas in Delhi these issues concerned the expropriation of erstwhile princes and banks, in Bengal they concerned the viability and legitimacy of communist participation in coalition governments. To be sure, the ideological issue did not gain any measure of clarity in Delhi, even though the government's adoption of a socialist stance precipitated a constitutional crisis and led to a confrontation between Parliament and the Supreme Court. Related to this issue, the vote for the president split the Congress Party and created the first constituted Opposition in Parliament. In Bengal, a much more violent arena altogether, ideological issues connected with socialism and communism were more explicitly posed. In the case of the relationship between the CPI(M) and its partners in power, this issue came to revolve around the question of violence, posed on a wider scale by the adoption of gherao tactics by trade unions, and later elevated to a point of principle by the CPI(M-L). In the case of the confrontation between the CPI(M) and the CPI(M-L) this issue of violence was again central, though rather posed as the question of participation in elections. But, paradoxically, though the ideological issues were more clearly defined in Bengal, no actual socialist programme or measure was at stake. Thus, in Delhi where socialist measures were mooted and enacted, no point of socialist principle ever gained the importance of such matters for Communists in Bengal, as yet only concerned with strategies for achieving power rather than exercising it.

This socialist crisis was essentially perceived and enacted by the participants as a crisis of the spirit. It was as questions of morals and values that the opposing viewpoints were pitted against each other, and as morals and values that they were perceived. The underlying awareness, the world-view in terms of which these morals and values were formulated and expressed, never surfaced as an explicit object of discourse.

True, all contenders had an elaborated metaphysic, their literate ideology, by which they sought to 'seek' solutions and justify their actions. How far this metaphysic can be from the immediate awareness of the self, at least in the case of the Naxalites, it has been my aim in this study to describe. And yet it is in the terms of the elaborated literate ideology that this crisis of the spirit manifests itself—and in action. Indeed, the distance between the literate ideology and the existential ideology is a constitutive element of the crisis.

In its literary manifestation this crisis presents itself as a political crisis. But the horizons of politics, whether construed narrowly as the business of government, or generally as the issue of power, cannot do justice to the scope of the confrontation or the implications of the conflict. The political rhetoric in which the crisis is couched points inwards to the beleaguered expanse of the totality in which the problem of identity is posed. It is certainly possible to contend that the spirit as this totality is essentially political in character, but that does not do justice either to the multiform variety of the culture in which this spirit is imbedded, or indeed to the self-awareness of the participants for whom the crisis was a crisis. That they encoded this awareness of crisis in a political discourse has to do with the status of politics in Indian culture, and more fundamentally, is constitutive of the crisis itself.

The crisis of the spirit has a manifest external form. The Marxist rhetoric, in which the issue of socialism has been 'elevated' to a material principle, regards this externality to be determinant and fundamentally economic. This rhetoric is centrally implicated in our concern here, in that the Naxalites claimed to be Marxist-Leninists. Whatever the rigour or lack of rigour of these Naxalites in elaborating an economic explanation, it is necessary therefore not to overlook this economic dimension.

Caught up in the political crisis both at the Centre and in Bengal were a fiscal squeeze for the governments in Delhi and Calcutta and the working population, and the difficulties of an adequate supply of foodgrains to the cities. The emergence and qualified resolution of these problems coincided with the emergence and resolution of the political crisis. At Delhi the fiscal squeeze, brought to the forefront by the devaluation of the rupee, was intimately associated with the dependence of the national government on the USA for foodgrains. In Bengal the problems of foodgrains and finance nevertheless coalesced about the problems of the price for grain and the meeting of procurement quotas. (Historic parallels, if historic parallels are to be sought, can be found in the 'scissors crisis' of the post-revolutionary Bolshevik government in the Soviet Union.) Clearly, in this economic backdrop, 'imperialism' and 'feudalism', the motifs of the Marxist discourse in India, were both overtly implicated. But the resolution of the crisis leaves them relatively untouched. Both at the Centre and in Bengal, Indian socialism as an economic praxis defined itself as an attack on native Indian finance, merchant and industrial capital. Its achievement was the organization of the distribution of agrarian produce in the cities, and the amelioration of the situation of the waged (white-collar and blue-collar workers) with respect to general inflation.

In retrospect the economic form of the appearance and resolution of the crisis has a different shape than that which appears in the rhetoric of the contenders when the crisis is posed. The very economic categories, semi-feudalism semi-colonialism for instance, in which the Naxalites formulate their horizons, remain at a distance from the way in which economic issues arise and are resolved, moving untouched through the vicissitudes of the crisis in which they rise to awareness. This fact, if no other, should alert us to what is being argued here—that the constitution of the crisis, though posed in a politico-economic verbiage, is essentially spiritual and cultural. The reclamation of this ground of meaningfulness—of even the economic categories—is the intent of the account which follows.

The Emergence of the Naxalites

Though obviously not effective as a direct cause, the Sino-Soviet dispute in international communism provided the terms of reference for contending points of view in post-independence Indian communism. Indeed before this dispute became a dispute the Bolshevik and Chinese revolutions stood out as alternative models for Indian communist revolutionaries.[1] The most significant change initiated by the Sino-Soviet split, however, was to expand this counterposition of strategies (i.e. whether the revolution in India would be urban or agrarian) into a more wide-ranging ideological confusion. For those who believed the Soviet interpretations of Marxism, of course, no such confusion resulted. For those less sure of the Soviet claim to orthodoxy and perhaps, more importantly, less satisfied with the performance of the communist movement in

[1] Gene D. Overstreet and Marshall Windmiller, *Communism in India*, Berkeley and Los Angeles, University of California Press, 1959, p. 286 *et seq.*

India, for one reason or another, not only did the Sino-Soviet split raise important issues concerning the movement as a whole, but it provided the occasion to begin to discuss these. And with the Sino-Indian war of 1962 dissidence within the communist movement became overt and explicit. The strategic question, relatively quiescent since the brief revolutionary flurry in the aftermath of independence, became a salient one again, though not in the form that it had had at that time. What was at stake in 1962 was rather the legitimacy of the Indian government's war with China, the nature of the government that waged this war, and the question of communist support for such a government.

But the dissidence within the movement was not restricted to these issues, nor indeed exhausted by them. It is even questionable if these were the central issues at stake, though in what followed the differences between the CPI and the CPI(M) coalesced about these points of reference. What was thrown into sharp relief was the resentment of a middle rank against the leadership, the leadership's attempts to control and then conciliate this resentment, and an inchoate awareness of solidarity about which the battle lines were drawn.[2] There had been disputes in the party before, and particularly in the aftermath of independence. But whereas then the dispute had concerned a clearly defined question, namely the strategy of the party, the questions at issue now were a mass of petty and important considerations spanning the gamut from ideology to organization.[3] In the two years before the CPI(M) finally split away, the dissident press within the party gained in volume and sharpness of tone. The split when it finally came in 1964 centred about a scandal that challenged the revolutionary bona fides of the leader of the party, S. A. Dange. Letters had purportedly been discovered in which he pledged his support to the government in exchange for his release from jail. It was about this question that the Communist Party of India finally split, and the Communist Party of India (Marxist) was constituted.

Whatever else it was, and there is certainly much else, the split in the communist movement was thus provoked by a lack of confidence in the leadership—not in its theoretical or strategic capabilities or perspectives,

[2] On the entrenched character of the leadership of the communist movement in India see Ashish Kumar Roy, *The Spring Thunder and After*, Calcutta, Minerva Associates, 1975, p. 37, though this observation is probably truer of the breakaway of the Naxalites from the CPI(M).

[3] See the periodicals of the period cited in *Spring Thunder and After*, p. 77.

but its *morality*. It is a feature of communism that has strangely gone unremarked until the present, particularly because of the very limited communist expressions of the sentiment, but a great deal of communist fervour (as perhaps fervour of any kind) is premised on the sense of moral superiority. In India this sense of moral superiority is coupled with a sense of theoretical superiority—not merely in the sense of a belief in the superiority of their doctrine (though there is that as well) but a belief in their greater ability to deal with issues of knowledge despite their relatively lower academic accomplishments.[4] In the split in Indian communism, however, it is Dange's revolutionary morality *per se* that was thrown into question. Contrived or not, it thus delineates a ground where amity is impossible.

In the fact of raising the question of the leader's commitment can be glimpsed the vaster sense of the betrayal of the movement as a whole. In the way in which it is posed, what is at stake is not even an overt theoretical renegacy of the kind with which Lenin accused Kautsky, but a covert capitulation under gestures of defiance, and this not as metaphor but as fact. The 'discovery' of Dange's personal 'betrayal' however only provides a focus for a sense of the betrayal by the movement as a whole. There were sections of the dissidents that felt this sharply, and none more so than those who later constituted the CPI(M-L). But at the time of the split this awareness is not explicit, perhaps because it raised issues too difficult to disentangle, though, nevertheless, it is present as an undertow that dictates a split and complete dissociation from the betrayers.

The formation of the CPI(M), however, left the theoretical—strategic and moral—issues unresolved. Indeed the moral issues, or rather the theoretical issues in moral garb, had not yet been posed. The strategic issues nevertheless needed to be defined and resolved, if nothing else, as matters of principle, in keeping with communist precedents; and this to the satisfaction of the dissident press, cut loose from supervision by the CPI leadership by those who later came to lead the CPI(M), and from the supervision of these latter by their imprisonment. The leadership of the CPI(M) resolved on the minimum programme, likely to draw the whole dissident movement into it, of opposition to the Congress regime at the centre. This strategic pragmatism, which was content to leave aside the theoretical questions posed both by the Sino-Soviet split, and the question of revolution, sufficed to unite the dissidents for a time

[4] Marcus F. Franda, *Radical Politics in West Bengal*, MIT Press, 1971, p. 19.

under its leadership without, however, fundamentally resolving the issues—and resentments—that had led to the split. Kerala, Bengal and Andhra were the CPI(M) strongholds, but strongholds that were held together fairly weakly.

But if the CPI(M) as a whole was fairly unsure of its perspectives beyond its opposition to the Congress, the Congress was fairly definite about its hostility to the CPI(M) and prepared to do something about it. With help from the press, which stigmatized the CPI(M) as pro-Chinese, Maoist and revolutionary, the government at Delhi imprisoned the leaders for as long as it could. It was in such imprisonments and out of them that the attitudes of both the CPI(M) leadership, and those of the dissidents who later parted from it, took form.

Charu Mazumdar's earliest forays into the theoretical realm, beginning some time in 1965, have sweeping rhetoric and a rhetorical concept-universe. One is aware immediately of the attempt to find an adequate and all-embracing explanation for the one truly cosmic event crying out for explanation—the 'failure' of the communist revolution in India. True it is not as a failure that this lack of success actually occurred, or indeed is theorized. But the whole poignancy of the question 'Why is it that the Indian revolution has not succeeded as yet?' lies in the belief in the possibility, if not indeed inevitability, of this success, as a promise that has been betrayed by the actual course of events. And it is only as a betrayal by the leadership that Mazumdar can find an adequate explanation for this. The form of this betrayal is not the covert renegacy of a Dange, but the deliberate misconstrual by the leadership of the character of the forces to which they are opposed. Assuming the benignness of sections of the powers that be, this leadership is unable to cope with the adverse conditions that the hostility of the powers that be imposes, and in its deliberate disavowal of making preparations for such conditions of adversity with secrecy and the stockpiling of arms it can be seen to have betrayed its revolutionary potential. Characteristic of Mazumdar's thought, even at this early stage, the essence of politics—as in this the crucial question of the distinction between a revisionist and a revolutionary politics—is seen to lie in a question *of technique.*

But if technique is how the crucial political question presents itself to the communist organizer, the process of which it forms a part, the metaphysical universe of the emergence and development of Revolution is an even more fundamental concern of the communist theoretician. This metaphysic, in Mazumdar's elaboration of it, is composed of two separate but interrelated aspects—the national and the international. Nationally, the revolutionary forces of the people, as adequately represented by the rank and file of the communist organization, have time and again pressed forward for the realization of their revolutionary potential, only to be betrayed by a revisionist leadership. The whole sequence, of Indian communist history is thus to be construed as successive revolutionary initiatives from below betrayed by subsequent revisionist compromises by the leadership.

Damning as this indictment of the national leadership is, it still falls short of the condemnation of Soviet revisionism on the international scene. In the post-War era, imperialism, particularly US imperialism, is seen to have been on its last legs, and just when the people of the world had cornered it and it had its back to the wall, Soviet social-imperialism, which was the overt expression of Soviet revisionism, came to its rescue.

No precise date for this turn to revisionism is proferred. On the national scene it has presumably been a feature of the organization ever since it was founded, though how then it could ever have been founded becomes something of a mystery. On the international scene, in consonance with Chinese communist thought of the time, it is logical to suppose that the victory of revisionism in the Soviet Union dates from Khruschev's denunciation of Stalin. Such an attempt at precise dating plays hob with the overall scenario, but these elements of Mazumdar's 'world-view' are neither elaborated with an eye to detail nor desirous of an attention to detail that would be considered academic and barren. The central point of the metaphysic has been grasped when the world is construed as the arena for the clash of the forces of Revolution and Counter-revolution, with Revisionism, a late comer (and the specific problem of the contemporary problematic), representing the forces of Counter-revolution in the guise of revolutionary leadership. The spiritual atom bomb that explodes all the myths of Revisionism is seen to be the Chinese Revolution, and more specifically the Great Proletarian Cultural Revolution in China. In metaphor at the very least, if not as a symptom of the distinctive features of this world-view, sparks are seen to fly out from the explosion of this bomb to start conflagrations wherever they land, as for example in Vietnam. Dates again get obviously confused, but the gist of the matter is clear. A sequence of worlds-historic events consisting of the Paris Commune, the Bolshevik Revolution, the Chinese Revolution and the Great Proletarian Revolution in China is established as the relevant orientation for revolutionaries. And to the roster of the great communist leaders—indeed revolutionary authorities—of Marx, Engels and Lenin, is added the name of Mao-Tse-Tung, elevated to the position of greatest living authority on Marxism-Leninism, and the genius who has creatively developed it to the new, higher, stage of Mao-Tse-Tung Thought.

Thus a reduction of the questions of politics on the one hand to technique, is elaborated on the other hand as their significance as symbol. And it is fundamentally as such a symbolic weapon, rooted in technique, that Mao-Tse-Tung Thought is extolled as the Marxism-Leninism of our time and the attack on Revisionism. The elaboration of this fundamental locus of theory, attempting to reconcile its dichotomies, on the one hand in the oral discourse of the organizers as the doctrine of partisanship, on the other in the thought of Mazumdar as the concepts of 'class character' and 'integration', is part of the subsequent history of the Naxalites which I shall later consider. At this early phase the question of the relevance of Mao-Tse-Tung Thought is only that of exposing and overthrowing the revisionist leadership and making preparations for armed agrarian revolution, with the Chinese as the model. Nor at this early phase is the concern with building a truly revolutionary party or (even later) true revolutionaries central to Mazumdar's thought. Taking the organizational givens of the situation as satisfactory enough, Mazumdar proposes ah area-wise seizure of power, capable of being put into action with little ado.

Such were Mazumdar's first attempts at theory, elaborated over a period of some two years, in nine brief essays, later to be hallowed in the CPI(M-L) as the Nine Deeds.[5] They formed a small intervention in the fairly more widespread soul-searching and theoretical endeavours of the dissenting communist radicals of the time. This dissent, largely Maoist in inspiration, was directed mainly at considering political questions, as politics was then understood and codified in communist circles, in a plainly informal spirit.[6] But the authorship and readership of this literature was restricted to communist organizers and intellectuals of middle

---

[5] In all the literature about the Naxalites, reference is made only to *Eight Essays*. If I recall correctly, there are nine.

[6] A large number of periodicals were published at this time, of which perhaps the best known was *Chinta*. See also Ashish Roy, *The Spring Thunder and After*, p. 77 for other periodicals.

and lower ranks, though, of course, it is impossible to rule out the perusal of such by people not familiar with its concerns or rhetoric. It is impossible to say what degree of attention the CPI(M) leadership paid to these endeavours of its dissidents, but though dissenting they clearly did not challenge or question its claim to leadership. Yet Mazumdar's writings, not all of which were published at the time (and indeed have not been published since then either) were circulated as loose sheets among the Communist cadre, drawing censure from a member of the State leadership for the breach of party discipline entailed in doing so without the permission of the Provincial Committee, and for the adventurist character of their drift.[7] They did, however, impress Sushital Roy Chowdhury, then a member of the Provincial Committee and later to edit *Deshabrati*, the official organ of the CPI(M-L) for some time, who wrote to Mazumdar supporting his views.[8]

More important than the circulation of his writings at the time, though, were his successful attempts to create a circle of disciples in and around his native town of Siliguri, to carry out the activities his ideas entailed. In this he was aided by the fact that he was a communist of long standing and a well-known leader of the district. He drew to him older organizers who had known him for some time and also younger people just out of university or still students. The urge to action *per se* did not, however, distinguish Mazumdar's thought. That had indeed been a bedrock sentiment of communist organizers throughout the period of their history, the sense of superiority on which their contempt of other ideas was based. It was what gave the theorizing of the dissidents its urgency and poignancy, in that holding fast to the priority of praxis they had thus been forced into considerations of thought and theory not unequivocally related to a praxis.[9] What distinguished Mazumdar's thought was rather the technicist (perhaps one should say also mechanical) reduction that made it possible to arrive at a line of action from concerns that were principally symbolic. In having arrived at the interpretation of Revolution as technique, he had cut through the

[7] Amiya Kumar Samanta, 'The Terai Upsurge', *The Calcutta Historical Journal*, vol. VI, no. 1, 1981, p. 77.

[8] Ibid.

[9] It is significant that one of the most influential of the dissident magazines was called *Chinta*—meaning 'thought'. I have never seen copies of *Chinta*. It was mentioned to me by a seller of radical literature in Calcutta when I visited in 1983.

confusions with which the leadership of the CPI(M), and indeed the dissidents as well, were having to grapple. The oversimplification from which action ensued precipitated clarifications through which policy hardened.

Other dissidents, closer to the rush of events in which the CPI(M) was involved at this time, lacked the distance from the headlong rush of these to be able to evolve, let alone pursue, an independent course of action. Committed as they were in thought, and more importantly sensibility, to a theory in the service of action, they lacked both the theoretical and moral ground to dissociate themselves from the action (in plenty) that was accruing with the deepening of the political-economic crisis. Nor indeed did they wish to. The large-scale mobilizations for its demonstrations that the leadership of the CPI(M) was able to effect, not to mention their latent *and* overt violence, was sufficient to allay any doubts about the revolutionary direction in which these events were moving. The two years through which Charu Mazumdar formulated and pursued his ideas were simultaneously years in which the fledgling CPI(M) advanced on a more aggressive social mobilization, established a closer consensus among its leaders, and turned ever and ever more ferociously on the parent CPI. Its successes fuelled its aggressiveness, and so served effectively to contain the enthusiasm of the dissidents for ever increased 'militancy' as an indicator of the revolutionary character of the movements and the leadership. The most successful of these movements from the point of view of the CPI(M), and the dissidents within it—i.e. from the point of view of propaganda, numbers mobilized (and violence precipitated!)—was the so-called 'Food Movement' of early 1966.

It would seem to contradict the major thrust of my argument that this event of crucial significance is fundamentally concerned with food, a vehement assertion, if such were needed, of man's materiality, and bears it emblazoned on its name. True, this name is current coin only in the leftist circles where it has been gathered up into mythologized histories of the period, but that does not detract from its appositeness, as testified to by the reference to the same events as food riots, and violence connected with the food policy of the government in the official enquiry that reported on them in 1968. But far from refuting my contentions, these events illustrate the necessity of some such thesis as mine. For it is not primarily as the physical object of hunger that food comes to figure so prominently in this narrative, but rather as a metaphysical entity, symbolical and revelatory. Indeed it is as such a metaphysical power that references to materiality are invoked to attack metaphysics. What these events demonstrate, and that fairly clearly, is that both for the organizers of the movement and for those who participated in it, 'food' has the quality of a metaphysical cipher in the sense of Jaspers, though differently for the organizers and the participants.[10] For the organizers the food issue is the occasion to organize, simultaneously, the symbol they uphold to demonstrate their truth and the untruth of their opponents as well as the possibility on which their hopes (of success) are founded. For the participants the food issue is the revelation of the unrighteousness of the powers that be (whether as the illegitimacy of the regime or, more commonly, merely its corruption) and the legitimation of their recourse to protest, and even violence. For the violent, common looters or more sophisticated students, food is the formal validation of the reality of revelatory—and cleansing—violence. Clearly, the physical reality of food, its function as an object of hunger, is not denied, but it is not as such a reality that it provokes such events. The hunger of 'rioters' has a metaphysical voracity that food cannot fill.

The 'Food Movement' had no tangible outcome. It did not overturn policy or effectively transform it. And yet its psychological and social-psychological consequences were crucial. It established the legitimacy of the leftist alliance that challenged the existing regime, and cemented this alliance. It transformed the mundane issues of everyday politics into counters in a strategic game geared to the perspectives of power. It initiated the process of the popular initiative for the recognition of resentments that would culminate in the paralysis of power. But most of all it introduced the perspectives of political agitation into the university milieu, it 'radicalized' the students. Students in large numbers participated in the movement, and through this the student movement itself gained an autonomous dynamic and a leftward (if not, indeed, outright communist) slant. This radicalization had been hovering in the wings since the split in the communist movement, which had introduced the issues of communist politics into the ranks of student-intellectuals. Offering, as it did an arena for the co-operation of the contending parties in the split, apart from all those not party to it whom it also drew in, the 'Food Movement' initiated into organized politics not only large

---

[10] Karl Jaspers, *Philosophy*, vol. 3, trans. E. B. Ashton, Chicago and London, University of Chicago Press, 1971, pp. 7–8.

sections of the student population but the important sections of it which were ideologically informed. Most significantly it introduced ideology and the concept of ideology, in its Maoist sense, into the ambit of student politics.

The general election when it came almost ten months later in February 1967 found no one unprepared. All parties had been equally alive to its prospect, not least the Congress which had dismissed the whole 'Food Movement' as an election stunt. But besides the parties and the parties' hopefuls, the elections, certainly in Bengal if not equally in some other parts of India, had announced their importance to sections of the population usually relatively unconcerned with politics. For this reason as much as any other, the relatively lethargic and conservative (Congress fared worse than it had ever done in independent India.

The only section for whom the very prospect of the elections posed a problem, soon to achieve ideological dimensions, were the dissidents within the CPI(M), and among them Charu Mazumdar. For these the commitment to Revolution, somehow at odds with the process of seeking and legitimation by votes by which the Congress party maintained itself in power, produced a latent sense of discomfort with the parliamentary path which the CPI(M) seemed to have chosen. In Kerala, where the dissidents had adopted, so far, more extreme postures, inviting on themselves the disciplinary wrath of the CPI(M) leadership, this discomfort surfaced as an open hostility to the CPI(M) leadership for its participation in the electoral process, and an agreement with the revolutionary dissidents it had expelled. Posters appeared and slogans were painted on walls. In Bengal, however, the rift had not yet taken on the aspect of a split. Jangal Santhal, one of the revolutionary peasant leaders from the Naxalbari district, where organizers under Charu Mazumdar's directions were preaching and organizing an uprising, stood as a candidate in the elections. True, he utilized the resources put at his disposal for this by the CPI(M) to preach revolution and spread the message that little was to be expected from the outcome of elections.[11] Nevertheless the confusion on this issue among the dissidents of Bengal, and the ambivalence of even their most radical sections, is indicated by the fact that Jangal Santhal *did* stand as a candidate in the elections. It is perhaps a working out of the logic of Charu Mazumdar's original revolutionary perspectives that he found himself pressed into denying the validity of

---

[11] Amiya Kumar Samanta, 'Terai Upsurge', p. 78.

the electoral action he had undertaken. Not surprisingly, Santhal lost in the election.

On the very day on which the newly elected government of West Bengal, in which the CPI(M) was a partner, took office, the first 'incident' from Naxalbari was reported in the press. The unfurling of events could not have been more dramatic. Biplab Das Gupta has seen in this no more than a desire on the part of the dissidents led by Charu Mazumdar to embarrass the leadership of the CPI(M), forgetting the pressure on the dissidents to distinguish themselves from the CPI(M) in this its hour of electoral victory.[12] It is impossible to discount the impetus provided by the elections in precipitating the revolutionary outbreak. As to whether the press had cavalierly overlooked earlier 'incidents' and chose to play up the revolutionary threat now that the erstwhile Opposition, with the CPI(M) a leading member of it, was in power, must remain a matter of speculation. What is certain is that the attention events in Naxalbari drew, both from the press and the government in Delhi, had not a little to do with the fact that Bengal was ruled by a non-Congress government in which communists participated. Events in Srikakulam in Andhra, equally disturbing and much larger in scope, remained unpublicized until those revolutionaries chose to throw in their lot with the organizers of Naxalbari. Despite the unsureness indicated by the actions of a Jangal Santhal, Mazumdar, and with him by now Sushital Roy Chowdhury, was fairly convinced of the necessity of keeping away from the elections and the electoral process. But as in much else in the sequence of events we are considering this sureness did not manifest itself until after the event, when the certainty had firmed and had had occasion to confirm itself.

The elections themselves and the preparations for them present graphically the disintegration of an older order and ethos and the emergence of a new, dictated largely in this, its formative phase, by pragmatic considerations. Not the least of the events leading up to this emergence of a new order, as yet still nascent, is the schism in the West Bengal Congress party itself, parallelling and overshadowing the schism in the communist ranks, if not in the amount of publicity it drew, certainly in its implications. As in communist circles, the schism had a fundamentally moral orientation and moral outlooks were principally involved in bringing it about. And

[12] Biplab Das Gupta, *The Naxalite Movement*, Bombay, Allied Publishers, 1974, p. 224.

as in the case of the communist schism, this emergence of 'new' moral standpoints was inextricably connected with the emergence of personalities and organizations. I shall not here go into the details of this schism, but merely glance at its significant turning points.

The schism surfaced in July 1965 as the opposition between Atulya Ghosh, the strongman of Congress politics in Bengal, and Ajoy Mukherjee, its titular leader.[13] The opposition implicated issues of Gandhian ideology, but formed around the politics of the persons of these, the leaders of the opposing factions. Nirmalendu De, a close associate of Ghosh who had moved a resolution censuring Mukherjee, was expelled from the post of Secretary-General by him. A new no-confidence motion in the party against Mukherjee succeeded on 20 January 1966, and he was ousted from the leadership by 296 votes to 40 but refused to resign. He was then formally expelled from the party. In the following months Ajoy Mukherjee toured West Bengal, exposing the perfidy and duplicity of the Congress in Bengal, and drew support for his position. From 15 June 1966 onwards he promoted his own conception of the Congress for Bengal, the Bangla Congress. The Bangla Congress it was that emerged as the leader of the United Front government that brought nineteen years of Congress rule to an end in the state of West Bengal.

Early attempts at and negotiations towards a grand alliance directed against the Congress failed because of the 'intransigence' of the Bangla Congress and the 'exaggerated claims' of the CPI(M).[14] Two distinct anti-Congress blocs fought the elections, the one led by an alliance between the CPI and Bangla Congress called the People's United Leftist Front (PULF), the other by the CPI(M) called the United Leftist Front (ULF). The elections gave neither of these fronts the capacity to form a ministry. Indeed, the largest single party in the legislature was still the Congress, but this was cold comfort in a situation where this majority counted for nothing, least of all the capacity to organize a ministry, as the majority in any case was opposed to the Congress. After the elections, however, the two left fronts and various independents united to form the United Democratic Front (UDF), electing Ajoy Mukherjee their leader, and as the leader of this majority in the legislature Mukherjee

[13] Sohail Jawaid, *The Naxalite Movement in India*, New Delhi, Associated Publishing House, 1979, p. 69.
[14] Ibid., pp. 70–1.

announced his capacity to form a ministry to the then governor, Padmaja Naidu, and was invited to do so. 'Of the 14 parties in the United Front only five' were 'prepared to try constitutional methods. The rest all "swore" by revolution and work[ed] for it'.[15]

One of the earliest acts of the newly formed United Front government was to call a public rally on the Maidan in Calcutta on 1 March. At the large rally various public 'populist' measures were announced. Police guards for ministers were to be dispensed with. The salaries of ministers in the cabinet were reduced, that of the Chief Minister from Rs 1150 per month to Rs 700 per month, and those of the others from Rs 900 per month to Rs 500 per month. Air-conditioning in Writers' Building (the secretariat) was to be switched off as a gesture of 'solidarity with poor people'. In addition, the official charter of the government's plan of action, the 18-point programme, was approved.

It is easy to dismiss the populist measures as gimmicks geared to gaining popularity. But newly installed in power, the United Front had little need for such gimmickry except to re-establish the very credibility of democratic government forfeited by the outgoing Congress government. More important even perhaps than this relatively external rationale for populism is the internal crisis of conscience that this expedient indicates of those in government and politics generally. Whether as Gandhian measure or Marxist imperative, the swing to populism was not merely necessary to retain the legitimacy of the democratic process, but also dictated by the crisis in the consciousness of politics and its direction among its leading exponents. For certainly the new United Front government took both its mandate and its responsibilities seriously. Within the 'first fifty days' of its assumption of power the government announced a number of radical measures at complete variance with the policies, and even more with the attitudes of the outgoing Congress government—

reduction of taxes on slums, non-realization of cess [on agricultural produce] in the drought-stricken areas, holding of all elections in 25 superseded municipal areas, increase in the purchase price of paddy, giving of land up to 3 cottahs (20 cottahs = 3 acres) to landless labourers and poor peasants, enhancement of dearness allowance to Government officials and teachers, confirmation of temporary Government servants, reinstatement of victimized public servants, lapsing of the State Security Act, granting of trade union rights to workers, and most

[15] C. R. Irani, *Bengal the Communist Challenge*, Bombay etc., Lalvani, 1968, p. 8.

importantly, directions to the police administration in not interfering in legitimate trade union movement.[16]

Though lacking a unified or indeed (in the case of both the leading members of the coalition, the Bangla Congress and the CPI(M)) a coherent view of their social perspectives and ideological moorings, the parties in power found little difficulty in arriving at pragmatic measures to cope with the situation. But equally certainly in the attitudes underlying these measures there was a sharp difference in the leading members of the coalition—the Bangla Congress and the CPI(M)— which revealed itself clearly almost two years later about the question of violence in politics. The revolutionary inclinations of the CPI(M) made an ill fit with the ameliorative intents of the Bangla Congress. But the two, for all their discomfort at their alliance, could find grounds of agreement.

Their agreement was not shaken by the spate of gheraos in industrial districts that blossomed in the wake of their trade union policy. All parties to the coalition (rightly, if later investigations are to be believed) held the policy of lock-outs and closures by the employers to be at the root of this, though obviously gheraos were a much more prevalent occurrence than lock-outs or closures.[17] Certainly the industrial climate as a whole was influenced by these lock-outs and closures and equally certainly by the trade-union policy of the new government itself. Nor was the agreement between the partners to the coalition shaken by their shift in perspective on the matter of foodgrains (the most important single issue, perhaps, underlying their victory), now that they were in power. An amusing comment on this shift is provided by Irani:

The Communist Party of India (Marxist) did one better. Before the elections they refused to accept that there was any shortage of foodgrains at all. In a policy document published just before the elections they assumed the State's population at 40 millions (allowing for the known rate of increase in the years following the 1961 Census) and sought to prove with figures that 'without even a ton of

[16] Dr J. C. Johari, *Naxalite Politics in India*, Institute of Constitutional and Parliamentary Studies, 1972, p. 2.

[17] Debabrata Banerjee, 'A Decadal Survey of the Labour Scene in West Bengal', in *Problems of the Economy and Planning in West Bengal: Proceedings of a Symposium 24–27 February, 1974*, Calcutta, Centre for Studies in Social Sciences, June 1975, pp. 243–51.

foodgrains from the Central store a surplus of 10.53 lakh (1.05 million) tons remains'. The root of the crisis therefore lay in the machinations of 'anti-social vultures'. Yet within days of the formation of the United Front Government every senior Minister except the Food Minister had accused the Central Government of withholding essential foodgrains from the people of West Bengal and half-a-dozen of them journeyed to Delhi in August and threatened the Prime Minister with dharna (a polite form of the gherao) if the Centre did not immediately concede the demand for 15 lakhs (1.5 million) tons of foodgrains to supplement West Bengal's own production. One wonders what happened suddenly to the 'surplus of 10.53 lakh tons'! The Communists can claim that they merely copied a good example of Congress double-talk. Was it not the then Chief Minister P. C. Sen, they must recall, who thundered: 'No Government worth the name can allow laissez-faire conditions to continue to any significant extent so far as rice and wheat are concerned', and then proceeded to drop all procurement in November 1966 in the interests of seeking a few more votes for his party in the general elections only three months away?[18]

Illuminating as this comment is of the oppositional essence of the CPI(M)'s political postures, and by extension of those of the United Front as a whole, however, it conceals the complexities of the situation with regard to foodgrains. My earlier comments have already indicated the metaphysical status of the whole agitation. Here it is necessary to add to that the comment of the enquiry of 1968 that the government policies of 1965 and 1966 with regard to foodgrains served to transform 'the entire population of the State into a race of criminals',[19] and even more tellingly Irani's own earlier observations on the matter:

A disturbing feature, by no means uncommon in the rest of the country is the falling level of market arrivals of foodgrains compared to total production. Of the total production of 5.34 million tons of rice in 1963-4 only 163,250 tons were offered in the twenty-seven leading rice markets in the State. In 1964-5, the market arrivals dropped to 131,040 tons although the crop that year had increased to 5.76 million tons. This trend has become more accentuated in the later years.[20]

Disagreement among the governing parties, when it first surfaced on 5 July, was about the policy to adopt with regard to the events in

[18] C. R. Irani, pp. 15–16.
[19] See above, chapter 4.
[20] C. R. Irani, p. 15.

Naxalbari. An earlier threat by a minister belonging to the SSP to withdraw from the ministry if a minister belonging to the scheduled castes was not included in the cabinet had been easily staved off by acceding to his demand.[21] Disagreement over the policy to adopt in Naxalbari was more serious than this. It arose out of the failure of most of the wanted revolutionaries of the region to surrender themselves by the deadline proclaimed by the government. Only 20 out of 650 surrendered. But the disagreement, paradoxically, produced the compromise that could be most expected to succeed in the circumstances. Johari writes:

The views of U.F. cabinet ministers ran into three directions—the non-communists insisted on conferring more powers on the police and civil officers to round up all wanted elements; the Communists (like Biswanath Mukherjee who was a member of the CPI and also president of the Kisan Sabhas and H. K. Konar who was a member of the CPM and also secretary of the Kisan Sabhas) laid stress on further extension of the period of grace keeping in view the fear of the loss of their leadership over the agitating Kisan Sabhas in the event of any drastic police action taken against their extremist leaders; and others recommended increase in the number of police patrols to ensure safety and prevention of violent clashes. After a heated discussion, the cabinet decided with a unanimous vote to adopt three measures: (i) expediting the work of land distribution committees and land reforms, (ii) setting up and organization of police patrol camps to ensure strict enforcement of prohibitory orders and prevention of clashes, and (iii) encouraging surrender policy and investigation of cases involving serious offences on both sides to continue. This decision of the West Bengal cabinet highlighted its policy of isolating the extremists and restoring normalcy in the Naxalbari areas.[22]

Despite the hesitations of a Biswanath Mukherjee or an H. K. Konar, however, the opposition between the CPI(M) and the dissidents within it was by now an accomplished fact and Naxalbari part of revolutionary myth.

The opposition to the CPI(M) had of course become clear to some dissident leaders as early as March. At that time a Krishak Samiti convention was held, where the official state leadership was not represented, and a decision taken by the majority to adopt revolutionary methods. Charu Mazumdar and Sushital Roy Chowdhury circulated a document demanding that the CPI(M) not take part in elections.[23] Party membership of the CPI(M) declined from 22,000 to 17,000 by the end of May,[24] and Krishak Samiti membership rose from 5,000 to 40,000.[25] The opposition was certainly clear to Charu Mazumdar by May when he persuaded Kanu Sanyal to renege on the promises of co-operation Sanyal had given Konar when they met on the 17th of that month.[26]

As for Naxalbari itself, Irani's earlier estimate of 180 serious cases reported between March and June[27] is raised by Samanta's later investigation to 219, including dacoity, gun-snatching, looting, arson, assault, mischief, theft, occupation of and ploughing land by force, intimidation, 4 murders, 11 killed in police action and 1 policeman killed.[28] In the circle of dissidents collaborating in the Krishak Samiti convention the example was known and acted upon, though not widely publicized. In May–June violence of a similar though much more limited sort occurred in Sonarpur in the 24 Parganas districts and slogans were raised—'Naxalbari Lal Salaam' (Red Salute to Naxalbari) and 'Naxalbari's Way is our way'.[29] Similar slogans and an even more limited violence recurred in Santipur, Nabadvip, Ranaghat, and Chakdah divisions of Nadia district.[30] But these were not big news. Only Naxalbari was. On 5 June the Peking paper *People's Daily* attacked the leadership of the CPI(M) in its editorial, and on the 28th a Peking Radio broadcast applauded Naxalbari. These established the bona-fides of the Naxalbari group to a much wider circle of revolutionaries than the Krishak Samiti.

The CPI(M) faced by this opposton began hostilities with the dissidents. It had already dissolved the Darjeeling District Committee led by Charu Mazumdar. At the state committee meeting of 19–20 June, the CPI(M) acknowledged the far wider organization of the revolutionary dissidents, declared all of them outside the pale of the party and expelled nineteen members, including Sushital Roy Chowdhury, then

[23] Sohail Jawaid, p. 77.
[24] Ibid., pp. 77–8.
[25] Ibid., p. 78.
[26] Amiya Kumar Samanta, pp. 81–2.
[27] C. R. Irani, p. 23.
[28] Amiya Kumar Samanta, p. 85.
[29] C. R. Irani, pp. 34–6.
[30] Ibid., p. 36.

an editor of the party paper *Deshahitaishi*.[31] Promode Das Gupta, the CPI(M) leader, even alleged that the CIA had infiltrated the local leadership of Naxalbari.[32] Sushital Roy Chowdhury was not one to give in. On 28 June, the day of the Peking broadcast applauding Naxalbari, he and some of his followers conducted a raid on the offices of *Deshahitaishi*, trying to re-establish his claims as an editor, and the CPI(M) had to call on the police to help. This abandoning of dignity in favour of 'revolutionary' action on the part of Roy Chowdhury is indicative of a sentiment destined to grow more pervasive and profound. For the moment, recovering his dignity after the event, Roy Chowdhury with his editorial experience had by 6 July launched a rival to *Deshahitaishi*—*Deshabrati*, as a mouthpiece of the revolutionary dissidents, and declared open war with the CPI(M).[33]

The Growth of the Myth and the Following

With the Chinese support of the revolutionary dissidents and their criticism of the leadership of the CPI(M), the CPI(M) felt called upon to settle the matter of its Maoism. Between 18 and 27 August 1967 the Central Committee of the party met at Madurai and decided the nature of its differences with the CPC. These concerned (i) 'the programmatic aspect i.e. the class character of the present Indian state and government, the character and role of the different sections of the Indian bourgeoisie and its attitude to imperialism etc.', (ii) 'the actual assessment of the economic-political situation in the country, the degree of development of the class contradictions and class-consciousness among the proletariat and toiling peasantry, and the concrete tactics and forms of struggle adopted to the requirement of the mass struggles', and (iii) the 'political-organizational principles governing the fraternal relations between two Communist Parties i.e. our party and the CPC'.[34] With the first two sets of considerations the CPI(M) distanced itself from both aspects of the Maoism that the revolutionary dissidents upheld, i.e. the viability of the Chinese model of revolution in India, and the imminence

[31] Ibid., p. 33.
[32] Ibid.
[33] Ibid., p. 38.
[34] *Divergent Views Between Our Party And the CPC on Certain Fundamental Issues of Programme and Policy, adopted at the Central Committee of the CPI(M) at its Madurai Session from August 18 to 27, 1967*, p. 2.

and necessity of this revolution. With the third the leaders of the party undertook to level a criticism against the CPC for their public criticism, principally the broadcasts, of the leadership of the CPI(M). This, of course, only hardened the attitude of the revolutionary dissidents against the CPI(M) and its leadership, but what is even more significant than this hardening of attitude, which was in some sense predictable, is the form this hardening took, driving a deeper wedge between the two factions and making reconciliation impossible. Though, certainly, the dissidents disagreed with the CPI(M) about matters such as the class character of the state, etc., these did not become the focus of investigation and dispute. The crucial difference, which became the nub of verbal confrontations, was that the dissidents considered the time 'ripe' for revolution, and the CPI(M) leadership did not, apart from all considerations as to how this revolution would actually come to pass. And it is about this article of revolutionary belief that a clear line of demarcation was established between the revolutionary dissidents and the CPI(M). The passages concerned with the issue in the Central Committee document read:

As correctly observed by the Sixth Congress of the C.I. (Communist International) in its theses on the Revolutionary Movement in Colonies and Semi-Colonies, there exists an 'excessively marked lack of correspondence between the objective revolutionary situation and the weakness of the subjective factors', and it persists even today, in several countries.[35]

and

The single biggest weakness in the whole situation is the deplorable state of the, political level of the proletariat, its class consciousness, its organization, and its unity with the other toiling masses and particularly the peasantry.[36]

In thus making the difference of opinion hinge about a 'subjective' issue, the CPI(M) in fact only recognized what was the actual state of affairs, namely that matters of communist strategy were in fact decided about such subjective evaluations. It opened the way for the revolutionary dissidents to point to Naxalbari as the objective fact that upheld their contention of the time being ripe for revolution, and established the basis for Charu Mazumdar's emergence into authority as a person with insight into the subjectivity of the revolutionary masses. And for the rest

[35] Ibid., p. 8.
[36] Ibid., p. 13.

the very causes that provoked the CPI(M) to distance itself from the CPC—their partisanship with Naxalbari and their criticism of the CPI(M)—were cause enough for partisans of Naxalbari to affirm more vehemently than ever before 'China's Chairman is our Chairman, China's path is our path'.

While Naxalbari had not as yet been reduced to its pure idea, an original myth forming the basis of distinction as the Paris Commune and Bolshevik Revolution in the Communist orthodoxy and the Chinese revolution in the Maoist, the ground for this distillation had already been laid. Certainly to Charu Mazumdar himself Naxalbari at this point stood as an indicator of the state of affairs, the vindication of his own earlier ideas and the pointer to the requirements of the future. The need for alternative forms of organization that had surfaced in the creation of the Naxalbari Krishak Sangram Sahayak Samitis in the towns, principally in Calcutta and Siliguri, was the one felt most acutely by Mazumdar in the following months, and formulated by him into a call to build a new party (other than the CPI(M)) in the first issue of the English-language mouthpiece of the Naxalites, *Liberation,* in November. The call for a new party as it occurs in that issue is a Utopian one, rhetorical and plaintive:

But revolution can never succeed without a revolutionary party: a party which is firmly rooted in the thought of Chairman Mao Tsetung, a party composed of millions of workers, peasants and middle-class youths inspired by the ideal of self-sacrifice: a party that guarantees full inner-party democratic right to criticism and self-criticism and whose members freely and voluntarily abide by its discipline: a party that allows its members to act not only under orders from the [*sic*] above but to judge each directive with full freedom and even to defy wrong directives in the interest of the revolution: a party which ensures voluntary job-division to every member who attaches equal importance to all sorts of jobs ranging from high to low: a party whose members put into practice the Marxist-Leninist ideal in their own lives and, by practising the ideas themselves, inspire the masses to make greater self-sacrifices and to take greater initiative in revolutionary activities; a party whose members never despair under any circumstances and are not cowed by any predicament but resolutely march forward to overcome it. Only a party like this can build a united front of people of different classes holding different views in this country. Only a revolutionary party like this can lead the Indian revolution to success.[37]

---

[37] Charu Mazumdar, 'It Is Time to Build a Revolutionary Party', *Liberation,* November 1967.

In this delineation of the shape of the new party, two points stand out glaringly emphasized. The first is the insistence on self-sacrifice, mentioned explicitly twice and touched obliquely in the reference to practising Marxist-Leninist ideals 'in their own lives'. This indeed lays bare one of the most important existential determinants of the critique of Revisionism—the denunciation of it as a hypocrisy that permits self-seeking under the garb of service to the Revolution, the radical turning away from 'Kathedersocialismus'.[38] Equally important in the concept is the element of sacrifice, certainly marked in the popular perception of the communist as saint, a perception not restricted to India, though gaining a peculiar potency in it. This aspect of the matter will be discussed again in the elucidation of the existential ideology of the Naxalites.

The second point is the emphasis placed on inner-party democracy, the party as an institution that permits freedom of thought. This is interesting in two respects. The first, that of the origin of this aspiration, points unequivocally to the CPI(M)'s dismissive treatment of the revolutionary dissidents, a treatment that is somehow implicated in the accusation of revisionism with which Mazumdar brands it. The second, that of its fate, as in the advice Mazumdar was to give young men later not to bother their heads about party policy, points equally unequivocally to the rhetorical-Utopian character of this aspiration, as rooted solely in the circumstances from which it seeks to escape.[39] The authoritarianism that is criticized, in other words, is solely the authoritarianism that is not exercised by the persons making that criticism.

It is as the origination of the myth of Naxalbari that the All India Coordination Committee of Communist Revolutionaries was founded. Overtly intended to co-ordinate the activities of revolutionaries all over the country, it is only with the focus of Naxalbari as an inspiration that the grounds for the consensus on leadership could be laid. Though many others still occupied prominent positions in this leadership, pride of place went to the leaders of Naxalbari, and particularly Charu Mazumdar.

In November 1967 the United Front government of West Bengal was dismissed and, whatever its implications for the growth of the

[38] Socialism of the chair, a term attributed to German academics and bureaucrats concerned with 'the social question'. Marianne Weber, *Max Weber. A Biography* (1926). Trans. Harry Zohn, New York, John Wiley, 1975.
[39] Charu Mazumdar, 'A Few Words to the Revolutionary Students and Youth', *Liberation*, March 1970.

revolutionary movement as a whole, the event made no significant impact on the revolutionary leadership. Concerning as it did the parliamentary process, the significance of the event for the fate of the parliamentary system as a whole was disdained by the leadership of the Co-ordination Committee, already tacitly committed to the non-parliamentary, if not yet anti-parliamentary, perspectives of Mazumdar. Even to have taken the event into account in their strategic calculations would have seemed to this leadership a betrayal of the tenets on which Naxalbari had been founded. In this dogmatic distancing from the facts of the political environment lay the seeds both of the possibility of the growth of the Naxalite movement in which the myth could be developed as myth, and its final collapse. A more immediate encounter with the facts of the political case would immediately have indicated to the revolutionary leadership the tremendous revolutionary potential of the dismissal of the UF government, evident in the movements organized by the CPI(M) and other parties that followed this dismissal, and the location of this revolutionary potential in the urban areas. Already themselves constituted of urban representatives, the revolutionary nuclei rather expected deliverance to proceed from the countryside. It is as a peculiar mingling of this rural perspective with urban activism that such people—and there were many—as were drawn to the support of Naxalbari in the course of the CPI(M) organized movements against the dismissal of the UF were affected. For the already swelling supporters of the Naxalite movement, these movements became arenas of independent initiative ignored by the official leadership.

Supporters of the Naxalbari uprising thus encountered the CPI(M) in a theoretical vacuum. Much as in the case with the relation of the CPI(M) to the CPC earlier, pragmatic criteria, i.e. criteria unformulated as principle, dictated the course of this relation, with one significant difference. Whereas the CPI(M) earlier had not been committed to Chinese approval of its policy, though it would have preferred it, the tacit assumptions about the course of organization among the revolutionaries indicated the existing communist organizations, and principally the CPI(M), as the source of fresh converts to the cause. With their own experience of a prior dissidence from within only later followed by explicit repudiation and the assertion of independence, the fledgling revolutionaries hoped to repeat the coup until the whole of the CPI(M), if not the entire communist movement, or at least the majority of their membership, were won over. Mazumdar's call for a new party notwithstanding, it was in the older parties that the revolutionaries hoped to find the material for this new party. The facts of Naxalbari, despite the pre-eminence of that event in the rhetoric of the revolutionaries, remained in relative obscurity, while oral appeals were made to the significant change in communist activity that it represented. And most of all, in the confrontation with the CPI(M), Naxalbari represented the opposition to the parliamentary and thus 'peaceful' perspectives of that party, at the same time that the intention of the vast mass of its cadre were presumed to be revolutionary or violent. The emergence of a theoretical attitude to the CPI(M), coinciding with this attempt to woo cadres, was thus rendered impossible, as the revolutionaries refused to acknowledge the ideological solidarity of that party. So long as the revolutionaries encountered members of the CPI(M) sympathetic to the Naxalite cause, the subtle distinction between leadership and cadre could have been expected to maintain the semblance of co-existence. With a staunch supporter of the CPI(M), however, no relations except those of outright hostility were possible, for that party, along with the whole history of the communist movement, had been damned as revisionist.

The pragmatic avoidance of theorizing the Naxalites' relation to the CPI(M) had its greatest success in April 1968, and the theory of the revolutionaries its first public defeat when the Cental Committee of the CPI(M) and the Central Kisan Council dominated by that party met in West Bengal. At the former the view that characterized the Soviet Union as social-imperialist was defeated in favour of the view that saw it as revisionist but not imperialist, and in both the delegation from Andhra came out clearly in favour of the revolutionaries. *Deshabrati* called on the revolutionaries in the CPI(M) to quit that party in favour of building a truly revolutionary party. With this major inroad into the ranks of the CPI(M), however, Charu Mazumdar turned his face away from the established communist parties as grounds for conversion and recruitment.

So, if we rely on the revolutionary force inside the party [i.e. the CPI(M)] we shall never be able to build up a revolutionary party. We must lay our main stress on the hundreds of thousands of young people outside the party. Only then can we build up a genuinely revolutionary party and establish revolutionary bases of armed struggle.[40]

[40] Charu Mazumdar, 'The Indian People's Democratic Revolution', *Liberation*, June 1968.

—he wrote in the June 1968 issue of *Liberation*. Appearing as it did in *Liberation*, the injunction had almost the weight of an official line, but in actual fact the matter never formed the substance of official deliberations, though it obviously preyed on the minds of the revolutionaries and was the subject of repeated 'unofficial' discussions. For Mazumdar's pronouncement did not settle the issue once and for all. Until the end, the question of the revolutionaries' relation to the CPI(M) remained a vexed and ambiguous matter, despite the fact of open hostilities between the two, and despite or perhaps abetted by official silence on the matter on the part of the revolutionary leadership.

In the same issue of *Liberation* (June 1968) appeared Charu Mazumdar's attempt to elevate the Naxalbari uprising into an instating and instated myth. In 'One year of Naxalbari Struggle', supposedly written on 23 May, he wrote:

This [i.e. Naxalbari] is the first time that peasants have struggled not for their partial demands but for the seizure of state power. If the Naxalbari peasant struggle has any lesson for us, it is this: militant struggles must be carried on not for land, crops, etc., but for the seizure of state power. It is precisely this that gives the Naxalbari struggle its uniqueness.[41]

The pressures to provoke such a declaration at this time are easy to see. In the face of the large Andhra influx into the organizing leadership inspired by Naxalbari, and the attempt to present a bold and simple message to the 'hundreds of thousands of young people outside the party', some formulation more direct than the complicated history of the birth of the uprising seemed called for, one which would, in line with Maoist rhetoric, play down the role of the intelligentsia in favour of the peasants. But this pressure is largely an external one. More important for Mazumdar, perhaps, was the attempt to comprehend the 'uniqueness' of the Naxalbari struggle, attested to by the burgeoning support in its favour, long after it had petered out. Mazumdar must have felt called upon to render this uniqueness intrinsic to the Naxalbari events themselves—rather than the (for him) accidental and peripheral interest in the issue in the ranks of urban radicals. And characteristically, he located this uniqueness in a fact of psychology—for it is only thus that the contention that the Naxalbari peasants fought for the seizure of power could have held water, even at the time—and a fact of psychology

[41] Charu Mazumdar, 'One Year of Naxalbari Struggle', *Liberation*, June 1968.

to which the awareness of the participants is not central! It is only thus that one can maintain the reality of the struggle for state power in the absence of organs of this power. It is as such a psychological pundit that Mazumdar was later elevated to his role of the 'revolutionary authority' of the party—as one possessing insight into *sreni-charitra*—class character, with the word character referring ambiguously to ontology and psychology. At this time Mazumdar's formulation stood out as a bold and clear rendering of the Naxalbari uprising, allowing it to be used as an originating myth.

What weight was attached to this pronouncement is hard to gauge. Certainly in Kanu Sanyal's 'Report on the Peasant Movement in the Terai Region' which appeared in Bengali on 24 October 1968 (more than a year after the event) in *Deshabrati* shortly before his arrest, and then in English in the November issue of *Liberation* shortly after, such emphasis is placed on the distinctively political character of the Naxalbari struggle. He might however have presumed this emphasis from his readers, considering the earlier publication of Mazumdar's views, and rather have been concerned with fleshing out its more overt features in his report. With Sanyal's report, written in the style of Mao's celebrated 'Hunan Report', and meant to be its Indian equivalent, the myth of Naxalbari is well launched. Indications of what Mazumdar sought to explain in calling the struggle one for the seizure of state power are found in the phenomenal rise of Kisan Sabha enrolment after the launching of the struggle—from 5000 to 40,000, a figure which Samanta is inclined to doubt.[42] Sanyal's own emphasis with regard to the question of the struggle for state power falls on the question of arms. That the peasants armed themselves is seen as evidence of their desire to contest political power. Certainly when weapons are brandished some notion of power is at stake, but not necessarily political power in the sense in which we, or indeed the communists, understand it today.[43]

The drift away from Naxalbari and its leadership, however, began prior to the publication of these two most important articles in the formation of the myth of Naxalbari, and may indeed have been part of the dynamic that provoked them. The dissidents among the dissidents, now revolutionaries, took issue not with questions pertaining to Naxalbari, but the overall theoretical view of the Naxalites. It was over the question

[42] Amiya Kumar Samanta, p. 94.
[43] For a detailed discussion of the issue of state power, see ibid.

of the imperialist character of the Soviet Union, already defeated in the CPI(M) when broached there, that Nagi Reddy chose to voice his reservations concerning the correctness of the Naxalbari leadership, in June. This provoked the Naxalbari leadership to establish independent ties with the Srikakulam group, who were inclined to the Naxalite view in any case, by-passing Nagi Reddy and finally expelling him from the All-India Co-ordination Committee of Communist Revolutionaries. The drift of Nagi Reddy and his followers, however, was far from being the trend, as news of Naxalbari spread and drew allegiance from distant parts, only vaguely acquainted with the events and the theory. What appealed most of all, perhaps, was the call to armed revolution and the announcement that it had begun.

This forms the main emphasis of Charu Mazumdar's article on 'The United Front and the Revolutionary Party' which appeared in *Liberation* in July 1968, where Mazumdar seems to stand out as a leader of a (non-existent) armed struggle and not just its most passionate advocate.

A united front can be successfully built up only by directing successfully an armed struggle. The principal thing about a united front is that it is the united front of the working class and the peasantry…. And in the present era the sole criterion to judge whether a party is revolutionary or not is whether the party is directing an armed struggle or not.[44]

The emphasis is mainly directed against the revolutionary pretensions of the CPI(M), which at this time could have been seen to constitute an obstacle to the formation of a new, 'truly revolutionary' party, and almost certainly so by Mazumdar. But, besides this, it throws a fresh and more acceptable light on the Naxalbari events, as precisely such an armed struggle that distinguished it from the struggles waged by the CPI(M). The question of arms in Naxalbari did, indeed, come in for some discussion both at the Centre and in the West Bengal legislature at the time of the events, but that is more in the nature of a joke from the point of view of the present discussion. In the profounder sense, in which 'armed struggle' refers to violent extra-parliamentary politics, the Naxalbari agitators did indeed draw a sharp and unmistakable line between themselves and the CPI(M), a line which was to get blurred again in the months that followed, but not unrecognizably. Indeed, the

---

[44] Charu Mazumdar, 'United Front and the Revolutionary Party', *Liberation*, July 1968.

consciousness of this line was one of the few recognizable landmarks of the Naxalite horizon.

The first public pronouncement to characterize the CPI(M) as revisionist occurred in the October 1968 issue *of Liberation,* significantly in a context devaluing the role of the intelligentsia, of which the supporters of Naxalbari formed a part. In 'Undertake the Work of Building a Revolutionary Party' Mazumdar wrote:

Publishing Party newspapers and periodicals became the sole occupation of the Party leaders. And what good are these Party publications in our country where the overwhelming majority of the people are unable to read or write? These serve only the petty-bourgeois intellectuals. It is in no way possible to educate our workers and peasants politically through the Party papers. That is why the Seventh Congress of the Party [the Congress at which the CPI split] gave birth to a revisionist party and not a revolutionary party.[45]

The concern with revisionism was a concern throughout the birth and life of the party, but this is one of the few occasions in which the concern with being an 'intellectual', so central to the sensibility of the party (the CPI(M-L)) comes to the fore, and significantly, the attack on 'intellectuals' and on the CPI(M) is indistinguishable. In this attack lurk the pathos and predicament of the Naxalite revolt, doomed to being a movement of 'intellectuals' in its attack upon intellectuals, and that of Mazumdar himself, fulminating against reading and writing in a situation in which he could be little other than a writer of articles and pamphlets.

It was not, however, in this self-conscious form that this criticism of the CPI(M) rose to awareness. It was overtly a rallying cry to muster the working class and, more particularly, the peasantry. Even, and particularly here, the difference from the revisionists and the CPI(M) stood out:

The revolutionary tactics for developing peasant movements in the rural areas can never be the same as the revisionist tactics…. Revisionism works in peasant movements with a view to keeping the Party's activities open and relies for the movements on the Party's leaders who belong to the intelligentsia…. The foremost duty of the revolutionaries is to spread and propagate the thought of Chairman Mao and to try to intensify the peasants' class struggle. Consequently, the Party organisation must organise propaganda by means of secret meetings.

[45] Charu Mazumdar, 'Undertake the Work of Building a Revolutionary Party', *Liberation,* October 1968.

It may be that the peasants, acting under the influence of their old method of working, will ask for meetings and demonstrations. In such cases, the Party organization may help organise one or two such meetings or demonstrations.[46]

The emphasis on secrecy, which was a characteristic of Mazumdar's thought from the outset, receives here special importance without any clarity as to what it is necessary to be secret about. Propaganda is the blanket term under which the secret organization permeates the society, rather than the other way about.

All this has the air of shadow-boxing, in which the opponent is real enough but where the protagonist himself is a thing of air, a creature of the imagination. No actual conflicts are at issue, no real goals at stake. An opponent is being defined for the sake of bringing sharper clarity to the lineaments of the self. The enemy is thus internal, an internalized ghost with which one must settle accounts if one is to get about the business of being revolutionary. Nowhere is this more so the case than when Mazumdar is advising the young, and others, in a conflict that he has satisfactorily resolved for himself. Offering his thoughts 'To the Young and the Student Community' in the 2 May 1968 issue of *Deshabrati*, Mazumdar opines:

In our experience good representatives of the student movement and even boys who have manned barricades for some student or political demand later take the IAS examination becoming hakims, meaning they have contributed directly to the counterrevolutionary camp.

The political organisation of the students and the young must necessarily be a *Red Guard* [in English] organization. And their work will be to propagate Chairman's quotations in as wide an area as possible.[47]

Already aware of the choices that the as-yet indistinct future is likely to impose on the young people he is advising, he brings this future to bear as a criterion of judgement on their present. In this is betrayed an element of the urgency of the motivation of the likes of Mazumdar—committed to *being* revolutionary in the face of a universal slide to revisionism!

---

[46] Charu Mazumdar, 'Develop Peasants' Class Struggle Through Class Analysis, Investigation and Study', *Liberation*, November 1968.
[47] Charu Mazumdar, 'To the Young and the Student Community', *Deshabrati*, 2 May 1968. My translation.

Occasion for a real encounter with this revisionism was not too far off, if only to the revolutionaries on the unreal ground of revisionist politics itself, in the shape of the mid-term elections in February 1969. Mazumdar expressed himself on the issue as early as December 1968:

In the present era when imperialism is heading towards total collapse, revolutionary struggle in every country has taken the form of armed struggle; Soviet revisionism, unable to retain its mask of socialism, has been forced to adopt imperialist tactics; world revolution has entered a new higher phase; and socialism is marching irrepressibly forward to victory—in such an era, to take to the parliamentary road means stopping this onward march of world revolution. Today, the revolutionary Marxist-Leninists cannot opt for the parliamentary road. This is true not only for the colonial and semi-colonial countries, but for the capitalist countries as well…. So the slogans 'boycott elections' and 'establish rural bases and create areas of armed struggle' which the revolutionary Marxist-Leninists have advanced remain valid for the entire era.[48]

Clearly, he accords enormous theoretical and strategic importance to the question. It is rooted in the technical-symbolic world of his theory as a significant event.

In the light of this the following report in *The Statesman*, which I shall quote at length, seems amusing.

NAXALITES DIVIDED ON POLL ISSUE

by a staff reporter

A section of the Naxalite students appear to be in favour of modifying their stand that the mid-term elections should be boycotted. A spokesman of this section told this reporter that during person-to-person campaigns, they have been telling the people that boycotting was the best method; but if they decide to vote, they should vote for the United Front.

Explaining this stand, the spokesman said that many people still had illusions about the United Front. To shatter this illusion, the UF should be given 'another chance to fail'.

According to him, it would not do if the people were merely dissuaded from working. That would be a negative approach. The people should be encouraged actively to take part in the Naxalbari brand of politics. If they were not 'mature'

---

[48] Charu Mazumdar, 'Boycott Elections! International Significance of the Slogan', *Liberation*, December 1968.

enough for this, they should at least be encouraged to come out of their houses and vote because 'Naxalbari politics was not the politics of sitting at home'.

He said if the 'progressive' section of the people were discouraged from voting, then there was every chance that the Congress would win. According to him, if the Congress won, it would let loose a 'reign of terror' and the United Front would 'cash in' on this to grab power at the next elections. He was sure that if the UF won, it would continue its 'misrule' because no good can be done to the people 'under the present system'. This misrule, he said, would prove the other Naxalite slogan that the 'two fronts of imperialism are the Congress and the United Front'.

Some other students this reporter spoke to said, however, that those who advocated such views were probably in collusion with the CPI(M). They said the majority of the Naxalites were firmly of the view that the elections should be boycotted and that they were campaigning to this effect. They said all the Naxalite papers were advocating this and there had been no deviation from the boycott stand.[49]

It is difficult to decide whether the reporter's attempts to see a rift, or the naive sophistications of the 'spokesman' of the rift, are more amusing. The report nevertheless serves to establish two important aspects of the Naxalites' politics at this stages—first, that it was a power to contend with on the university scene, and second, the peculiar ambivalence towards the CPI(M) that was characteristic of this scene.

In the period leading up to the elections political violence became an established fact of the West Bengal political scene. Still restricted to the somewhat nebulous 'election clashes' of newspaper reportage, it did not yet have the assassinatory edge it was to acquire later, or even the pre-ponderance of a particular party that would permit the raising of an accusatory finger. The CPI(M) certainly was intimately involved in this violence, and later accusations—by the Bangla Congress and the CPI particularly—held it to be greatly or solely responsible. At this distance, with the lack of adequate evidence, it is impossible to be sure about the rights and wrongs of particular cases. Indubitable is the hostility between constituents of the UF and the Congress that could quite easily break out into violence, and the pressure on the CPI(M) driving it to 'militancy' that the emergence of a revolutionary group must have created. Coterminous with this violence there must also have proceeded the large-scale induction of the *mastan*, the *bustee* tough, into organized politics. This trend had been established somewhat earlier, perhaps in

[49] *The Statesman Overseas Weekly*, 21 December 1968.

the 1967 election, but this election saw a far greater involvement of mastans in electoral politics.[50]

The UF won the elections in February 1969 with an increased majority. Obviously, Charu Mazumdar's call to boycott elections could not be implemented seriously. But nevertheless, sympathy for the partisans of Naxalbari had made large and significant inroads into the university scene, and most prominently into the politics of Presidency College, the premier college of Calcutta. And corresponding to the ambivalence of the Naxalite students regarding the CPI(M), there was a deep undertow of sympathy for the Naxalite cause among those who had heard of it but were otherwise drawn to the CPI(M).

If the formation of the first UF had precipitated, in some small measure, the outbreak in Naxalbari itself, the second can be seen as contributing to the formation of the CPI(M-L), the party of Naxalbari. Certainly the UF immediately after coming to power released all the Naxalite prisoners, particularly Kanu Sanyal, perhaps in an attempt to preserve its revolutionary bona-fides. Politically, conditions were favourable to the formation of a revolutionary party. The populist rhetoric of the UF that had sprung it to power could not afford to publicly disclaim revolutionary initiatives. But it was not this reason that Mazumdar invoked in his exhortation 'Why Must We Form the Party Now?' in the March issue of *Liberation*. His comments rather centred on the internal necessity of creating a revolutionary party: 'Unless we build up a revolutionary party, discipline will remain slack and as a result, we shall not be resolute enough to make supreme sacrifices, shall be unable to surmount the obstacles to attain victory'.[51] The emphasis on sacrifice is characteristic, and its coupling with discipline odd. It is significant that among the causes for the formation of perhaps the most indisciplined party on the Indian scene discipline should have received such prominence. It stems partly from Mazumdar's schooling in the communist rhetoric and style of work, but even more importantly, perhaps, from the need to impose on himself the garb of duty for pursuing the revolutionary course that came to him naturally, from the need to find tangible legitimation for his own pronouncements. More obscurely and perhaps problematically,

[50] Unsigned article (claimed by Ranajit Gupta in my interview), 'Urban Güerrillas', *Economic and Political Weekly*, 10 July 1971, p. 130.
[51] Charu Mazumdar, 'Why Must We Form the Party Now?', *Liberation*, March 1969.

the emphasis on discipline and its coupling with sacrifice draws from the imperative to find a coherent form for his aspiration which has recognizable lineaments.

There was hardly anything disciplined about the formation and announcement of the formation of the CPI(M-L). The whole affair was handled with a stagey secrecy that was later to infect the whole character of its politics. Secretly formed on Lenin's birthday, 22 April, the formation was announced at a May Day rally in Calcutta by the recently released Sanyal, where Asit Sen, who was chairing the rally, had no inkling that such an announcement was in the offing, still less that the even itself had taken place. At the rally where the formation of the CPI(M-L) was announced, the first public clash between the Naxalites and supporters of the CPI(M) took place.

The Party and Terror

The formation of the party had the effect of bringing together the leadership of the Naxalbari-type politics and the numerous urban supporters it had gathered, largely students, though not solely these, into a tight organization. The tightness of the organization pertained to its ideological solidarity rather than to any code of discipline. Such discipline as there was pertained to its ideological solidarity rather than to any code of discipline. This 'discipline' pertained to the defence of ideological positions already deemed self-evident, and the straining to implement the 'revolutionary line' as the membership was aware of it. It was, for all this looseness, a constituted organization, with a membership, financial transactions, publications, and communications between its various tiers.

Mazumdar's view of the role of young people and students was that of propagandist auxiliaries in the main thrust of revolutionary work. Writing of their tasks in April he said: 'The political organization of the youth and the students must necessarily be a Red Guard organization, and they should undertake the task of spreading the Quotations of Chairman Mao as widely as possible in different areas.'[52] By September, however, he had returned to the question of commitment of which he had treated earlier. This time it was not so much as a question of their subsequent fate after their period as students that concerned him but rather the form of their revolutionary commitment as students itself.

[52] Charu Mazumdar, 'To the Youth and Students', *Liberation*, April 1969.

As in the case of his thought on Naxalbari, the question of the authenticity of commitment was bound up inextricably with the form of its expression, with the technique of revolutionary activity. In 'Party's Call to the Youth and Students', he wrote:

In their attempts to kill this revolutionary potentiality in our youth and students before it can develop, the imperialists and reactionary ruling classes have held out before them the bait of college unions.... What the college unions hold out and advocate before the revolutionary students is basically a viewpoint based on economism. Thus, these unions destroy the revolutionary talent of the youth... preventing them from integrating themselves with the workers and peasants. Because of this, the union leadership, in most cases, is found to sink into the mire of opportunism and 'careerism' begins to develop among them, while the temptation of staying on in leadership drags them into all kinds of opportunist 'alliances' and thus destroys their revolutionary morality...

The task that now faces the students and youth is to study the Thought of Chairman Mao Tsetung, to repudiate the path of capitalism and to integrate themselves with the workers and peasants.[53]

Here, the task of 'integrating' is raised as an explicit injunction, and though in this context it has the fairly limited meaning of learning and propagating Mao's thought, it is a concept that was to grow in importance both for the leadership and the large number of young people who 'followed' it. I shall presently be concerned with a more detailed analysis of the concept; here it suffices to note the transformation of the frittering of students' revolutionary energies from an expression of the scheme of things into the result of an active policy of the imperialists and reactionaries. In this shift two aspects are of significance—first that the customary flow of revolutionary politics in the universities has been integrated into the overarching scheme of struggle between Revolution and Reaction, one moreover in which at the moment Reaction is dominant; and second that the emphasis is placed on the revolutionary potential of the young as the bedrock sentiment indicating the tendency of things. The young and students do seem to form a significant element, if not indeed the most significant element, of Mazumdar's hopes. And what emerges here, as in a great deal of Mazumdar's writings, is the exhortation implicit in these hopes, often made explicit, to commitment and what is synonymous with it, self-sacrifice.

[53] Charu Mazumdar, 'Party's Call to the Youth and Students', *Liberation*, September 1969.

The use of the words 'Red Guard' in the earlier quotation refers the process of the Indian Revolution to the precedent of the Great Proletarian Cultural Revolution in China. Red Guards, there, as they were made known in India, were youths who went about various regions of the countryside popularizing Mao's thought. It is quite clear that this was what Mazumdar had in mind, and, indeed, some bands of youths from the urban regions of Bengal and elsewhere did forage out into the countryside to preach Mao's thought, or the 'Lessons of Naxalbari'. For the most part, however, this Red Guard activity took the form of 'walling'—painting up appropriate slogans from the Red Book on the walls in cities and urban areas. The walls of Calcutta became at this time battlegrounds between the various parties as space to paint up the slogans they considered appropriate. Violence was by now an accepted part of the relations between the constituents of the UF and those between the UF and its opponents. It had not yet, however, entered the politics of young people and certainly not in the activities of 'walling'.

At the same time as the following of the CPI(M-L) became largely urban middle-class in its character, its rural perspective was reiterated by Mazumdar:

The task before the comrades, who belong to the petty-bourgeois intelligentsia and are inspired by the thought of Mao Tsetung which they have learned, is to educate the poor and landless peasants in the thought of Mao Tsetung. Dependence on the petty-bourgeois intelligentsia is the result of the influence of bourgeois ideology, and we must rid the party of this.[54]

The element of participation of the 'petty bourgeois intelligentsia', the by now main component of the party, was denigrated as 'bourgeois ideology' in the name of a revolution taking its springs supposedly in a source independent from them. But in the same essay as that in which this appeared was also included an exhortation to show independent initiative regardless of directives from the party leadership: 'every Party member must show initiative in whatever he does.... The practice of waiting for instructions to come from the Party leadership will rob this Party of its mobility and the Party will be unable to fulfil its revolutionary task'.[55] What this dual injunction prefigured for the course of the party at the

[54] Charu Mazumdar, 'Fight Against the Concrete Manifestations of Revisionism', *Liberation*, September 1969.
[55] Ibid.

time, no one could have said. But certainly, as summations of the feelings rife in the ranks of the party at the time—the feeling of helplessness at being 'petty-bourgeois intelligentsia', and the equally sharp feeling of the need to exercise initiative—these instructions encompass adequately the pass at which the Naxalites had arrived. Torn between their commitment, the need to express it, and the world view in which this commitment, essential and redeeming, was equally without consequence and peripheral, the party, shortly after its formation, had come to a crucial impasse.

As yet, however, the way out of this impasse, or at least the hope of it, was a promise of the line of agrarian revolution. As auxiliaries the 'petty bourgeois intelligentsia' to be mobilized in the cause of this revolution, propelling it to its inevitable culmination in victory. But in line with the 'political' reinterpretation of the Naxalbari struggle, this agrarian revolution itself was redefined more precisely as a guerrilla struggle rather than an 'economistic' one. Priorities, redefined to coincide with Mazumdar's general outlook and to establish a clear line of demarcation between the CPI(M-L) and the CPI(M), were part of the same essay which addressed the 'petty bourgeois intelligentsia':

We do not say that we shall never wage struggle for economic demands. What we say is that political propaganda and building Party organizations are the foremost and main task before us.

Economism in the peasant movement expresses itself in the form of rejecting the necessity for waging guerrilla warfare, thus concentrating the attention of the peasants on the question of seizing land and crops....

... Such ideas based on economism belittle the importance of setting up secret Party organizations among the revolutionary classes, thus preventing the members of these classes from entering into the Party.[56]

This speculation emerged at a time of political crisis in the West Bengal legislature, when the infighting amongst the parties was assuming fierce and bloody proportions. Policemen too had been killed. And on a grander though less violent scale the issues of socialism had been thrown onto the scales of legislation at the Centre. But these disturbing events did not enter, except perhaps peripherally, into the vision of the revolutionaries, which was dominated by the prospect of Revolution. It was almost as if all the material indicators of the prospects of this revolution were dismissed as so much superficial stage-managing in favour of a

[56] Ibid.

sight that enshrined the soul as the principal battleground and the visible world as its mere manifestation. Obviously, the political pandemonium of the times could not have escaped the Naxalites' notice, but it never became an important object of their concern—other than as a general indicator of the drift of events towards Revolution. At the very time when events were so pregnant with the possibility of political upheaval, Mazumdar addressed the faithful to 'Develop Revolutionary War to Eliminate the War of Aggression Against China'.[57] The remote possibility of a war against China, the heartland of the Revolution, the home of Chairman Mao, took precedence over much more immediate political events closer to home in the priorities governing the course of the Revolution. And in this Mazumdar was appealing quite directly to the large numbers of students attracted by the 'politics of Naxalbari', for whom world-revolutionary events were much more the food of everyday politics than the everyday business of politics itself. The injunction highlights another feature of this politics, crucial to its structure, and that is the location of the politics in a personal (person to person one may almost say) commitment to the particular leadership of the Revolution—the inculcation of a doctrine, in whatever bad faith it may have been practised, of necessary loyalty to a (presumably) infallible authority. The doctrine was to have an important outcome in the later development of the CPI(M-L). As yet nascent, it first expressed itself here as the tip of an iceberg of personalist loyalties—and hatreds.

The exhortation to guerrilla warfare had, of course, a relevance in the context of the struggle in Srikakulam, where fighting had escalated into direct confrontation between para-military detachments of the Indian armed forces and roving bands of guerrillas. The scale of events there had no parallel elsewhere in India, and at about this time it began to emerge in the slogans of the Naxalites, painted up on walls in Bengali towns and especially Calcutta, as the shining exemplar of Naxalbari politics. But the exhortation to guerrilla warface was not put forward solely as the solution to the situation in Srikakulam, but as a formal principle governing the activities of revolutionaries anywhere and everywhere. And it was as such a principle that revolutionaries from the universities of Calcutta and other towns attempted to put it into effect in Debra and Gopiballavpur, at about this time. In these regions they attempted peasant mobilizations directed against landlords, without

[57] *Liberation*, October 1969.

recourse to 'economic' programmes, aimed almost solely at unseating the landlords' power. Large-scale mobilizations were effected, for a time. Large numbers of peasants gathered to watch revolutionaries hurl abuse at particularly infamous landlords and, occasionally, 'execute' them. Stories were bruited about in Calcutta of peasants having 'played football' with the decapitated heads of such landlords. In the absence of escalating warfare such activities passed for guerrilla warfare.

Not, however, for Charu Mazumdar. For with the successes of Debra and Gopiballavpur, he was to caution: 'open mass movement and mass organizations are obstacles in the way of the development and expansion of guerrilla warfare.'[58] In the same article in which he thus decisively turned away from mass organizations, elements of the symbolical under-pinnings of his thought were reasserted: 'The only yardstick for a revolutionary is whether one follows the Communist Party of China, Chairman Mao and Vice-Chairman Lin Piao. Today China is the centre of world revolution and the base area of the revolutionary struggle of every country. So uniting with the Communist Party of China means uniting with the revolutionary people of the whole world.'[59] And with the literalness of the symbolism the intellectual horizons of revolution-aries were deliberately shrunk to conform to the peasant masses being addressed by Mao in the course of the Chinese revolution:

Therefore these [the 'Three Main Rules for Discipline' and 'Eight Points for Attention' written by Mao for the Red Army in China] are now the only things for the revolutionaries to read. So, the revolutionary intellectuals have the respon-sibility of making not only the peasant masses but also the other classes of revolutionary people conscious of the importance of these writings; they have also the responsibility of creating the urge for learning lessons from these writings.[60]

Clearly, in Mazumdar's mind guerrilla warfare was not only the need of the hour but the fact of the matter! Obviously to him the 'masses' were not only prepared for Revolution but ready to plunge into it at a moment's notice. There remained the problem of the 'integration' of the revolutionary intellectuals:

[58] Charu Mazumdar, 'March Forward by Summing Up the Experience of the Revolutionary Peasant Struggle of India', *Liberation* , December 1969.
[59] Ibid.
[60] Ibid.

The revolutionary intellectuals must fulfil another task—the task of propagating among the peasant masses the experience of the revolutionary war that is now going on in various countries of the world and task of spreading and propagating the lessons of the great Chinese revolution among the peasants. It is only by carrying out these tasks that the revolutionary intellectuals can integrate themselves with the poor and landless peasants.[61]

Here the task of *fomenting* revolution has been transformed into that of *integrating* oneself with it. And even more importantly for the revolutionary intellectuals themselves, that is how the task now appears to them. Even playing the most active roles in the instigation and exercise of revolutionary acts, they see themselves as merely engaged in the business of integrating themselves with a revolutionary mass. As yet there were still the regions of peasant activity under the party's leadership to give Mazumdar's detailing of what was entailed in 'integration' some coherence, i.e. the business of taking Mao's teachings to the countryside could still be construed as the proper description of the activity in which the revolutionaries were engaged. But this was soon to change, and through tendencies already present within the movement at this time.

Though the preparations and execution of the Naxalbari episode had taken place in relative obscurity, the events of Debra and Gopiballavpur, however much more obscure their significance and outcome, were played out in the full glare of the publicity of the student sects where the Naxalbari politics were recognized. Students sympathetic to the cause of the 'people' watched some of their erstwhile leaders prepare to 'integrate' themselves with it, and then actually engage in the business of doing so. The radical inversion of this process of 'declassing', the substitution of the imagined mores of an absent people for those with which one had been brought up, to which these former were *logically* opposed, became a commonplace of the conversation of the revolutionary sects. 'Declassing' acquired the trappings of fashion in a double sense—that of becoming fashionable, and even more profoundly and fundamentally of being construed in a way that related it essentially to fashion. Clothes, manner of spech, dress, manners, and the like became the counters in the game of declassification and 'integration'.

Enthusiasm, one way or the other, was almost universal in the student milieu. Partisanship with one or the other of the political sects

[61] Ibid.

vying for allegiance was the order of the day. In this womb of ferventness both the Revolution and the Counter-revolution were formed.

To Mazumdar, riding the crest of this enthusiasm, only the revolutionary potentialities were visible, and that too in the peculiar perspective which he brought to the consideration of Revolution. Writing in *Liberation* in February he exhorted the revolutionaries to 'Make the 1970s the Decade of Liberation'[62] and looking back over the immediately preceding period could see only an 'uncommon advance': 'How was this uncommon advance [i.e. in '69] possible? This advance was possible because the Indian revolutionaries received the guidance of Chairman Mao Tsetung's leadership every day through the radio broadcasts from Peking. This made it possible to arrive at a unanimity all over India regarding the general line and main task of the party.'[63] It is significant to note the importance Mazumdar ascribes to the Peking broadcasts. The fact of organization to which they draw attention is the pitiful inadequacy of the Indian revolutionaries at either conducting their own propaganda, or establishing unanimity amongst themselves as to a general course of action without the need for an authoritative voice. But the fact of sensibility which they emphasize is that of boundless and unquestioning obedience to a vested authority, paradoxically of Revolution! Despite this organizational inadequacy, if that is the right word, hinted at in these words, Mazumdar reaffirmed the pattern of the Chinese revolution and its imminence in India. 'The year 1970 has arrived with the promise of the birth of a disciplined people's army and the emergence of extensive liberated areas....'[64] How he could visualize such a disciplined assault seems difficult to imagine until one comes to grips with his theory of theory and organization hinted at in the same article. 'Once inspired with the revolutionary theory, that is, Mao Tsetung thought, men turn into spiritual atom bombs which are more powerful than thousands of atom bombs.'[65] Mazumdar's whole vision of the Revolution is premised on such 'atom bombs' and the spontaneous conflagration which their activity will unleash.

[62] Charu Mazumdar, 'Make the 1970's the Decade of Liberation', *Liberation*, February 1970.
[63] Ibid.
[64] Ibid.
[65] Ibid.

The February issue of *Liberation* also carried the infamous 'murder manual' discussed in the last chapter. This article reinforced the 'sponta-neist' organizational tendencies that we have just been considering. The vision emerged of the party as the spiritual instigator of an all-round conflagration that was presently contained but soon to burst its bounds. It is on this enthusiasm for Revolution, imagined to be fact, that the whole of Mazumdar's organizational theory is premised. And, indeed, those who did not feel this imminence as a significant factor in their horizon were peripheral, if not unimportant, actors in the events that ensued.

On 3 March 1970 urban violence by the CPI(M-L) was inaugurated with the attack on seven cinema houses screening the, film *Prem Pujari*. The legitimation bruited about by the young party activists was that the film formed part of the Anti-China War Plot, and that in thus disrupt-ing its screening they were striking a blow for China and for the Revolution. Within the circles of young party activists, however, the 'action' (a euphemism soon to encompass all and any planned violent activity) received an added dimension. The attack on the cinema houses was seen as a preparation for guerrilla attacks in the city of Calcutta. Within party circles, the boast was that much as a simultaneous attack on seven cinema houses had been carried out, so one could be carried out on the seven most significant civic and police institutions of the city, and the city paralysed. It was thus not as a 'cultural revolution', the sub-sequent justification, that the urban violence of the CPI(M-L) first began, however 'cultural' its targets may have been. To those who par-ticipated in it, it was part and parcel of the all-out guerrilla war that they believed peasants had unleashed in the countryside. And it continued to have this character to them, throughout the period of its proliferation and decline.

Shortly after, the Chief Minister of West Bengal, Ajoy Mukherjee, resigned on the advice of his Bangla Congress colleagues and followers. President's Rule was imposed, and the clashes between the parties lost even the mild check that participation in a coalition had imposed. If inter-party relations deteriorated sharply after this, this deterioration was most sharply marked in the relations between the CPI and the CPI(M). The two entered into acrimonious and sometimes violent struggle for the leadership of the trade union federation, the AITUC, not without an element of farce in the proceedings. It might be coinci-dence that from about this time the CPI began to veer towards greater sympathy for the Naxalites—their dedication rather than their meth-ods—though it is possible to read something profounder into it. Certainly in the period that followed the CPI(M)'s relations with both the CPI and the CPI(M-L) assumed the proportions of open confronta-tion. And though the CPI and the GPI(M-L) never made common cause against the CPI(M), and indeed the CPI(M-L) retained its aver-sion for the CPI as revisionist, the CPI turned more and more towards defence of the Naxalite behaviour as misguided idealism.

This is rather strange for it was now that the Naxalite movement blos-somed fulsomely as an exercise in terror. And the focus of the activity was the city of Calcutta. In the months that followed, 'annihilation', the murder of 'class-enemies' by secret groups of Naxalites appeared and pro-liferated in the city. As was later pointed out within party circles, the matter was not discussed in the Central Committee before its implemen-tation.[66] As in the case of the attack on the screening *of Prem Pujari,* the initiative came entirely from the lower echelons of the party. And these chose their targets, the so-called class-enemies, from the immediate circle of their life-world—petty tradesmen, oppositionists and, most impor-tantly, ordinary policemen on duty and rival CPI(M) activists.[67] The practice of political assassinations, as was pointed out later in the year by a CPI observer, had been part of the West Bengal scene for quite some time now, with no more active exponent than the CPI(M).[68] For this reason perhaps, the adoption of the tactic—soon to be proclaimed a strategy—went relatively unnoticed in its beginnings. But what could not be ignored was the invasion of state-run and vernacular-medium schools by the Naxalite ideology. It could not be ignored because in addi-tion to 'walling' (i. e. the painting of Naxalite slogans on walls) the schoolboy 'squads' defaced and mutilated statues and portraits, disrupted classes and destroyed or damaged property. Whereas 'annihilations' were relatively few and far between, this other violence spread rapidly through-out the city. Driven by enthusiasms most people found impossible to understand, schoolchildren in large numbers celebrated a spree of

---

[66] Purna [Pseudonym of Sushital Roy Chowdhury], 'On Statue Smashing' [Circulated document of the CPI(M-L).]
[67] Lists of class enemies annihilated are given in Ranajit Gupta, and in Biplab Das Gupta.
[68] Ranen Sen, 'What is Happening in West Bengal?' in *CPM Terror in West Bengal,* New Delhi, CPI Publications, October 1970, pp. 3–4.

vandalism. And this too appeared and proliferated without the conscious direction of the party leadership. Fired by a rhetoric and a myth from which they were distanced, almost to the point of unintelligibility, students and young people fleshed out the reality of Revolution as terror.

Terror, however, formed no part of the deliberations of the Central Committee when the CPI(M-L) met for its first Congress in May. The whole of this fundamental shift in the orientation of the membership of the CPI(M-L) was not deemed worthy of cognizance. The Party programme adopted at the Congress reiterated the original formulae, to wit:

11. ...Thus, instead of two mountains, British imperialism and feudalism, the Indian people are now weighed down under the four huge mountains, namely, imperialism headed by U.S. imperialism, Soviet social-imperialism, feudalism and comprador-bureaucrat capital....

16. In brief, out of all the major contradictions in our country, that is the contradiction between imperialism and social-imperialism on the one hand and our people on the other, the contradiction between feudalism and the broad masses of the people, the contradiction between capital and labour and the contradiction within the ruling classes, the one between the landlords and the peasantry, i.e. the contradiction between feudalism and the broad masses of the Indian people is the principal contradiction in the present phase.

17. The resolution of this contradiction will lead to the resolution of all other contradictions too.[69]

The perspective was still that of agrarian revolution, but within the broad rubric of this framework much had changed.

The Political–Organizational Report adopted at the Congress drew attention to the most devious of revisionist stratagems—centrism.

In order to achieve victory we must pay attention to the building of our Party— CPI(M-L). This task is the most important, most immediate and most sacred task of the revolutionary people of India. We must build up our Party among the landless and poor peasants and on this alone the revolutionary striking power of the Party and the revolutionary people depends. The working class and petty bourgeois cadres must integrate themselves with the landless and poor peasants and this task of integration cannot be overemphasized. The history of our inner-party struggles since the 20th Congress of the CPSU shows that the right-wing revisionist line was defeated by the left-wing revolutionary cadres

---

[69] 'Programme of the CPI(M-L)', Party Congress May 1970, *Lalkar Weekly*, Leamington Spa.

again and again but the victory of the left forces could not be consolidated, thanks to the subtle manoeuvre of the centrist elements. Thus, the history of our inner-party struggles shows that centrism is the vilest weapon of the revisionists and we must fight all signs of centrism. Centrism undermines the revolutionary politics and makes the fighter defenceless.[70]

As to what this centrism was or what its features were at that juncture, the Report did not make clear. It left it to the rank and file to determine for itself what centrism was, with perhaps the clue contained in the term *centrism* itself, or more obviously in the Bengali term, *madhyapantha*, of trying to keep to a middle position, or perhaps, equivocating. With the entry of this caution against the views current in the party itself, the door was opened to the infighting that later accrued. The occasion for the caution at this stage of affairs was perhaps the attempt of the leadership to raise 'the battle of annihilation' (i.e. the murder of 'class-enemies') from a tactical to a strategic plane. Hesitation was perhaps expected and the Report made it a point to state unequivocally that 'this battle of annihilation can solve all the problems facing us and lead the struggle to a higher plane...'.[71] The 'strategy' of annihilation was seen as a higher form of class struggle, leading directly to all out guerrilla war.

There was hesitation expressed at the Congress, but not on the principle of annihilation. Satya Narayan Singh, the Central Committee member from Bihar, expressed reservations at the annihilation of rich peasants on the grounds that they were not class enemies. As it turned out later, when Satya Narayan Singh raised the issue again both during Mazumdar's lifetime and after it, the matter was not settled to his satisfaction. There were rumours—later, when the disastrous effects of this turn had become obvious—that Vempatapu Satyanarayanan, the Srikakulam leader, had come with an alternate set of proposals, but there is no record of these. Satya Narayan Singh's objections, together with Mazumdar's reply—who emphasized that the enthusiasm of revolutionaries must not be checked and that they should be left free to decide exactly who was a class enemy and who was not—were circulated later in the Party, along with Sushital Ray Chowdhury's reservations and Mazumdar's reply to them. Despite his hesitations on this score,

---

[70] 'Political-Organizational Report adopted at the Party Congress', *Lalkar Weekly*, pp. 14–15.
[71] Ibid., pp. 16–17.

however, Satya Narayan Singh went along with the majority in proclaiming Charu Mazumdar the 'revolutionary authority'.

The attempt was to see in Mazumdar a leader of the stature of Marx or Lenin, or, more immediately, Mao, and to invest his pronouncements with the same aura or infallibility that was accorded those leaders. This raised some doubts, especially in the minds of intellectuals involved in the movement earlier with its cult of Mao. They were answered by pointing out that much as a baby on a giant's shoulders could see further than a grown man, similarly Mazumdar on Mao's shoulders could be expected to see further than the ordinary revolutionary. And Mazumdar had, to his credit, first the organization of Naxalbari, and now the 'annihilation line'. Certainly Mazumdar himself viewed the 'annihilation line' as his distinctive achievement to the course of the Indian Revolution. His authority though rested on the bases of his thought that made the evolution of such a line possible—namely his ability to read class character—the psychology of classes, and thus arrive at the style of struggle most suited to the Indian masses.

Speaking himself on the Political-Organizational Report while introducing it at the Congress, Mazumdar said:

Only by waging class struggle—the battle of annihilation—the new man will be created; the new man who will defy death and will be free from all thought of self-interest. And with this death-defying spirit he will go close to the enemy, snatch his rifle, avenge the martyrs and the people's army will emerge. To go close to the enemy it is necessary to conquer all thought of self. And this can be achieved only by the blood of martyrs. That inspires and creates new men out of the fighters, fills them with class hatred and makes them go close to the enemy and snatch his rifle with bare hands....

....The annihilation of the class enemy—this weapon in our hands—is the greatest danger to the 'reactionaries and revisionists all the world over.... We refuse to unite with these groups [i.e. other Maoists] because they are opposed to the annihilation of the class enemy, to class struggle and so are enemies of the people....

...Why am I against taking up fire-arms now? .... the use of fire-arms at this stage, instead of releasing the initiative of the peasant masses to annihilate the class enemy stifles it. If guerrilla fighters start the battle of annihilation with their conventional weapons, the common landless and poor peasants will come forward with bare hands and join the battle of annihilation.[72]

[72] Charu Mazumdar, 'On the Political-Organisational Report', *Workers Weekly*, pp. 22–3.

Thus, though the question of terror had not explicitly been raised, the turn to terror was explicitly endorsed, without calling it so. The 'annihilation line' was, it is true, still deeply imbedded in the rhetoric of agrarian revolution, but as became evident when the question of urban annihilation did come up later, there was no fundamental necessity that bound the 'annihilation line' to its practice in the countryside. And if the framework of agrarian revolution was ignored, or, as is more likely the case, presumed to be an unchangeable of the horizon of discourse, as indeed it was by the urban activists, Mazumdar's pronouncements quite easily fit into the validation of terror, of that specific kind—i.e. with mainly conventional weapons—practised by the CPI(M-L).

The injunction to urban dwellers to 'integrate' themselves with landless and poor peasants seems to militate against such a possibility. But the ambiguity of this word and the specific way in which it was appropriated by urban activists transformed this obstacle into the very validation of urban terror. Whereas these urban activists in their exodus to the villages had by and large interpreted integration as the adoption of the life-style of the villagers, they now identified it with becoming a part of the revolutionary struggle—and nothing could be construed as fitting the bill more than participation in urban terror. When, a few months later, Sushital Ray Chowdhury, writing under the pseudonym Purna, did bring up both the question of urban annihilations— that it had not been discussed prior to its implementation—and the question of statue-smashing (that those whose statues were smashed were in some cases people to be admired), Mazumdar replied unequivocally in favour of both and praised the enthusiasm of students and young people. Sushital Ray Chowdhury, an early partisan of Mazumdar's theories, fell from grace, and Saroj Dutta took over the task of editing *Deshabrati*, to which he had already been contributing. Dutta elaborated the theory of the urban 'actions' constituting some kind of a Cultural Revolution—at a time when they had become the main focus of Party activities. At the time of the Congress itself commenting on the inevitability of the victory of the Revolution, Mazumdar had cited the possibility of convening the Congress at all (in Calcutta) in conditions of repression as one of the main indicators.

Three factors guarantee the victory of the revolution. First, the revolution that has been delayed by more than twenty years brooks no further delay. Second, the revolution is taking place in the era of the total collapse of imperialism and the world-wide victory of socialism, the era of Mao-Tsetung thought. Third, we have been able to hold this Congress despite severe repression.[73]

Obviously, the urban terror formed a fundamental component of the revolutionary leaders' experience of the progress of Revolution, and provided grounds for their enthusiasm. But it never became the object of their theories, other than to bracket it out as a Cultural Revolution. That it was the logical culmination of their ethos and the coping stone that provoked the backlash that destroyed them was altogether out of the leaders' vision. The young who participated in it, however, did so with a consciousness of participating in the high tide of Revolution. The awareness of Srikakulam as a Liberated Area was an element of this consciousness, though not in any way fundamental, as was demonstrated when the struggle there was, shortly after, contained and then liquidated.

The high tide of Revolution that the young urban activists of the CPI(M-L) thought they were riding was a world-wide one. Much in the manner of Mazumdar himself, they were quick to look elsewhere, construe events symbolically and find a 'lesson'—a validation—of their own course of action. This is best illustrated by their construal of a world event that occurred almost at the time of the Party Congress itself. In May US forces invaded Cambodia. In a matter of days, large parts of the countryside which had been opposed to, or lukewarm to the communists, turned 'red'. Peking Review published before-and-after maps. Mazumdar interpreted the invasion as the beginning of the Third World War, a view rebutted by Mao Tsetung in his declaration of 20 May. But considerably after the event, interpretations current in the rank and file of the party held that the Cambodian events showed that the era had changed. Whereas in Mao Tsetung's own revolutionary fight the struggle had been to establish 'red' areas in hostile 'white' surroundings and by dint of effort try to expand them (the celebrated theory of red bases), with the Cambodian invasion it was the 'white' regions that were beleaguered and the red areas that completely encircled them. This view was ascribed to Mazumdar himself, and was cited as one of the arguments in favour of urban 'actions'.

In the months that followed the annihilation campaign gained momentum, and nowhere more so than in Calcutta. This does not

[73] Ibid., p. 24.

imply that annihilations, or indeed pro-Naxalite propaganda and organization, did not occur elsewhere. But compared to the scale of events in Calcutta, these were mere pinpricks blown up to star-bursts on the maps of India that began to appear on the walls of Calcutta and in the pages of *Deshabrati* and even *Liberation*. The occurrence of an annihilation became enough evidence to presume a region was well on its way to liberation.

All that seemed to remain was the inauguration of the People's Army. And with such a will to see it could it be a long way off? In October a peasant squad snatched rifles from armed sentries in Magurjan, on the Bengal-Bihar border. Two months on, in December, in line with his earlier predictions at the Congress, Mazumdar transformed this incident into the foundation of the People's Army. With the announcement, the squads in Calcutta, too, began to snatch the arms of the policemen they killed, though this activity in Calcutta perhaps predates the event in Magurjan, or at least the proclamation of its significance. With all this behind them, liberation perhaps seemed to be just around the corner, and to give an indication of the scale of this liberation, perhaps, assassins at the end of the year murdered the Vice-Chancellor of Jadavpur University. A teacher of the university I interviewed in 1983 found the event rather surprising for she had always found the students of Naxalite sympathies polite and usually well-behaved!

Suppression, Disintegration and Decline

The riotousness within the schools and colleges exhausted its fury in about a year. Exams in the middle of June 1971 were almost all held without anything untoward happening.[74] This is not to say that the so-called 'cultural revolution' died out completely, but certainly its main force was spent. Occasional cases of the defacing of portraits and statues continued to occur, but nowhere near the scale of these events in mid 1970. Annihilations continued to escalate. But whereas in the earlier period—for about a year since they first began in the city—they encountered little or no organized opposition, except from the CPI(M), this situation changed completely in the course of 1971. The first organized attempt was, of course, the invoking of anti-terrorist laws to cope with the Naxalites in September and November 1970 itself. But with the

---

[74] Ranajit Gupta, p. 1379.

unsettled conditions in the politics of the state, the implementation of these laws was rather restricted. For the general election in March 1971 to the Central Legislature, as well as the state legislature, the army was mobilized to ensure sufficient peace for the elections to be conducted in proper order, and being there it was deployed against the Naxalites then as well as later.[75] But the most important impetus to curb and destroy the Naxalites came after the fall of Ajoy Mukherjee's non-Marxist Democratic Front Ministry on 28 June 1971, when Siddhartha Shankar Ray was appointed Special Adviser to the Governor in the period of President's Rule. Both in his capacity as Adviser, by aiding and clearing the way for the police to handle Naxalite matters, and in his capacity as Congress leader by organizing the Congress volunteer squads, Ray evolved the two weapons that brought the Naxalites to heel.

In their heyday of almost a year and a half, the Naxalites in Calcutta had indulged in acts of the utmost brutality, even going to the extent of interpreting Mazumdar's 'He who has not dipped his hands in the blood of class enemies can hardly be called a communist' literally, to dip their hands in the blood of their murdered victims. The reprisals, when they were organized, were even more ferocious and undiscriminating in their violence. The police, if one is to believe one of their leading spokesmen, believed that the initiative for annihilations had passed out of the hands of mere students into those of the criminal underworld.[76] There is no denying that through the spread of the Naxalite politics, and its success, the bustees and their underworld population had been gathered into the ambit of the practice of political murder. Whether it was this that the authorities feared, or whether it was merely a convenient ploy for divesting their consciences of consideration for people they might have considered idealists, the authorities and critics of the CPI(M-L) were quick to point out the underworld connection. Whatever the significance of this connection, there were a large number of students and ex-students connected with the CPI(M-L) annihilation squads right until the end. And with the forging of a will and organizations to fight them, the counter-thrust was even more brutal than the thrust had been.

The Kashipur-Baranagar massacres of August 1971 were the first overt signs of this. But in a concealed way the police had always been

[75] Sankar Ghosh, *The Naxalite Movement: A Maoist Experiment*, Calcutta, Firma K. L. Mukhopadhyay, 1974, pp. xxii–xxiii.
[76] Ranajit Gupta, p. 1381.

party to such brutality with the extended powers placed at their disposal—arresting, torturing and executing without recourse to the law. The CPI(M-L) leadership for its part advised its cadre not to sue for bail, if arrested. Most of course were not granted bail. A few *did* take bail. The CPI(M-L) expected its cadre to school themselves in jail and then, with help from outside or without, to break out of jail. And there were quite a few such attempts at jail-break.

With the anti-Naxalite movement still gathering force, the Bangladesh war of liberation intervened, and cut the moral ground from under the Naxalites' feet. Robbed of the purity of their inspiring light, Chairman's China, they lived to see themselves robbed of their rhetoric of liberation by Congress activists who held out Indira Gandhi as 'Asia's sun of liberation'. It is quite likely that in this shift of morality and rhetoric, a shift in loyalty, especially among the underworld connections of the CPI(M-L), also took place. The disintegrating organizations of the CPI(M-L), loose at the best of times, lost all semblance of being organizations by the time the elections to the State Assembly came round in March 1972.

Forced finally to acknowledge something had gone wrong, Mazumdar was considering airing the criticisms that the Chinese leadership had put forward in 1970 (after the Congress when Souren Bose visited China), and conducting a 'self-criticism'.[77] He was also engaged in trying to build up a new organization, starting with a courier system. It was his first letter to his family sent via this courier system that was intercepted and led to his arrest. His death, the death of the CPI(M-L)'s 'revolutionary authority' left a movement in ruins with no one willing or able to undertake the task of building a revolutionary movement again. The CPI(M-L) survived in name and has grown again. But its legacy of terror still hangs as an enigma.

[77] Sumanta Banerjee, *In the Wake of Naxalbari*, Calcutta, Subarnarekha, 1980, pp. 264–8.

Chapter Six

'Semi-Feudal, Semi-Colonial'

The central concept of the Naxalite metaphysic was the characterization of the Indian economy as 'semi-feudal, semi-colonial'. There are reasons for calling this a *metaphysic*. First, the characterization is not so much the description of a state of affairs—an undertaking for which the Naxalites in any case lacked the diligent study and patience—as an injunction to action of a particular kind, i.e. the meaning of the characterization only emerges with respect to the strategy it entails. This characteristic the Naxalite discourse shares with most if not all Indian Marxist analysis. Second, the characterization does not so much refer to facts of the economy, in a 'materialist' sense, but to perceived experiences of personality which are reified into an economic terminology. Both these considerations point to the fact that to the Naxalite the formula (and it is a formula) of 'semi-feudal, semi-colonial' conveys a different meaning to what it does to the person who encounters the word in a text without recourse to the events in which it is located.

The characterization has been lifted from Mao Tsetung's characterization of the Chinese economy prior to the success of the Chinese revolution. Indeed, part of the reason for employing identical terminology was to give weight to the contention that 'China's Chairman is our chairman, China's path is our path'. But in the argument for a strategic identity a shift in the nature of the denotation of the formula has taken place. Whereas in the Chinese case the formula 'semi-feudal, semi-colonial' is directly aimed at expressing a manifest state of affairs with landlords and imperial powers in collaboration and contest, in the Naxalite case the formula has become metaphorical or, perhaps, ideational, claiming to penetrate a reality to its underlying truth when the manifest seems to contradict it. The nature of Chinese 'feudalism' set aside for the moment, there can be little doubt that the China Mao Tsetung writes of is ruled by landlords, warlords and imperial powers in collaboration with or in opposition to the Kuomintang at different times. In the Indian case, both the imperial power and the 'feudal' (if it is right to call it that) are concealed—if at all they exist—in a 'bourgeois democratic' independent

India. The prefixes semi-, therefore, which serve in the Chinese case to separate distinct regions of influence (in places the feudal power is dominant, in others the colonial, and the two collaborate) are intended in the Indian case to distinguish the nature of this feudalism and colonialism, i.e. it is not feudalism proper but semi-feudalism, and not colonialism proper but semi-colonialism. This difference of course is concealed under the identity of the phraseology which contends that in both cases feudal and colonial powers share the spoils.

The use of the 'semi-s' in the Naxalite characterization thus deserves further comment. Semi-feudalism accrues from a schema which sees the Indian economy (as all other 'underdeveloped' countries) as progressing from a state of feudalism to a state of capitalism, in which semi-feudalism is an intermediate state. In this sense of a transition from feudalism to capitalism the Naxalite events have provoked scholarly debate,[1] in connection with which the novel conception of the 'colonial mode of production' has been advanced.[2] 'Semi-colonial', more easily understandable in this schema of the 'colonial mode' as an agrarian economy open to the vicissitudes of the world market and thus of imperial interests, was, however, formulated before the concept of this 'colonial mode'. In this prior sense it implied an economy at the mercy of imperial powers not through political coercion, but through the exigencies of capital accumulation in an otherwise independent country. In this sense it was not far removed from the Leninist understanding of imperialism as the export of capital. For the mainstream of the Naxalites who joined the CPI(M-L), of course, it was feudalism that was the principal contradiction, though for Nagi Reddy it was imperialism.

Before examining in greater detail the meaning of the formula 'semi-feudal, semi-colonial' to the Naxalites, it is therefore necessary to say something about agrarian conditions in India and the question of the mode of production.

The Agrarian Question

With independence government concern with the countryside shifted decisively from questions of revenue and its realization to the production

[1] For a review of the debate scattered through various journals over a long period of time, see, for instance, Alice Thorner, 'Semifeudalism or Capitalism?', *Economic and Political Weekly*, 4 December 1982, pp. 1961–8; 11 December 1982, pp. 1993–9; and 18 December 1982, pp. 2061–6.
[2] Alice Thorner, p. 1997.

of food-grains and that of feeding the burgeoning cities. True, the shift in concern was not inaugurated with independence, for already under the British government, after the devastating Bengal famine of 1943, growing more food became a priority. Nor indeed was this concern so much a matter of explicit policy as that of the unstated but universally recognized assumptions of this policy. The explicit concern of agrarian policy at the time of Indian independence was with the legislation concerning *intermediaries*, and the dual interest with which it was linked—that of agrarian prosperity and that of land revenue. This dual interest had indeed always characterized the attempts at agrarian change and underlay the settlements of the British period which the post-independence legislation sought to undo. And centrally involved in the considerations that at one time or another led to the choice of a particular policy were the demands of social justice as the participants saw them.

The decisive shift in concern did not find explicit enunciation until almost a decade later, with the Ford Foundation Report on the urgency of the need to step up food-grains production and the measures required—in 1959. By this time the rhetoric of land-reform legislation had indeed shrunk to 'mere' rhetoric as the Report, paying lip-service to its objectives, mentioned cursorily the need to rush through land-reform measures and get on with the more pressing task of increasing production. Nevertheless, though the formulation of the shift in the concern of the government became explicit only a decade later, it already lay implicitly in the relative unimportance to which land revenue was consigned at the time of independence. In abolishing *intermediaries*, and devoting but little thought to the subject of agrarian revenue collection, already permanently fixed by the British, the government gave unequivocal expression to its lack of concern with the countryside as a source of finance. Land revenue being a state subject (and not a central one) the shift in orientation codified in the land-reform legislation served to mark a decisive shift in the relative powers of the centre and the states in favour of the centre.

Feudalism and Capitalism

In the Marxian sense of ideology, two ideological components enter into the constitution of European feudalism—the Roman laws concerning landed property, and the Christian religion. Politically feudal states are monarchies, and economically they are agricultural, with a proliferation of handicrafts. The relations of production are based on customary ties productive of community, which go hand in hand with an elaboration of relationships based on blood (construed today as kinship), related to a code of legitimate force in the defence of custom or blood.[3] It is this whole set of interrelated aspects of existence that is invoked by the word feudalism.

Capitalism on the other hand is seen to be characterized by an economic system based on machine industry and wage labour, the proliferation of economic organization itself, a legal system fundamentally concerned with private property, an ideology of individualistic consumerism (in which it is seen to differ from the Protestant otherworldly asceticism of its origin), and a political system of representative democracy.[4] The relations of production are of two distinct types, both premised on an alienated, abstract, or fetishized awareness of man implied by the description of this society as society proper in contradistinction to the community that describes feudal society.[5] The relations of production are established either in offices (or boardrooms, or restaurants or nightclubs) or on the factory floor. Germane to the analysis of the former is the legal construct of the person that forms the basis of contract, and the concern for profit.[6] Of more fundamental relevance to the latter is the process of mechanization that renders the workman an adjunct of the machine. Mediating between these two is the bureaucratic middle class that liaises with the owners to supervise the use of the machines.

In this presentation of capitalism I have not mentioned the important distinctions (from the point of view of Communist politics) between imperialism and capitalism (and from the point of view of liberal scholarship), between post-capitalist, or post-industrial, and capitalist or industrial.[7] Whereas the latter hinges on the evolution of

[3] In which rubric is subsumed the vassalage pointed out by Weber or Bloch. Max Weber, *Economy and Society*, vol. 3, eds. Guenther Roth and Claus Wittlich, Berkeley etc., University of California Press, chapter IV, and Marc Bloch, *Feudal Society*, trans. L. A. Manyon, London, Routledge and Kegan Paul, 1961.

[4] Perhaps, even more specifically, Calvinist. See Weber, *The Protestant Ethic and the Spirit of Capitalism*, trans. Talcott Parsons, 2nd ed., London, Allen and Unwin, 1930.

[5] Ferdinand Tönnies, *Community and Society*, trans. C. P. Loomis, Michigan State University Press, 1964.

[6] It is this element which the eighteenth century Scots sought to capture with the notion of 'civil society' subsequently taken over as bürgerliche Gesellschaft by Hegel and thus Marx.

[7] See, for instance, John Kenneth Galbraith, *The Affluent Society*, 3rd ed., London, Hamish Hamilton, 1977.

the bureaucratic middle class and what this implies for the nature of production and consumption, the former of earlier vintage emphasizes the evolution of financial organizations, the export of capital and the decay of the revolutionary potential of the European working class.[8] Both are concerned with defining a change they consider of fundamental significance in the character of capitalism, from the conditions that obtained at the time when that word first gained currency. Neither of these, however, is concerned with the question of property, which for Marx and the early socialists was the issue of greatest relevance. Marx himself, faced with the beginnings of this transformation in the evolution of joint-stock companies (the property question) rationalizes it as the transcendence of capitalism within the ambit of private property.[9]

As far as concerns the question of property, the most significant development in the world since the question was last discussed in its generality is the evolution of collective and co-operative forms of property, though these as the two distinct types—national property and corporate property *per se*—confront each other ideologically as socialism and capitalism. Common to both is the redefinition of individual ownership, either as custom or as law, to adapt to conditions in which the collectivity stands forth as a legal person.

But it is not these post-Marxian considerations that are of relevance in understanding the term semi-feudalism, which postulates an intermediate state of development between what is considered some essence of feudalism and some essence of capitalism. In this view feudalism is customarily construed as a predominantly agricultural society characterized by customary ties and the assertion of force to maintain law by landlords against their dependent tenants, and capitalism as a predominantly industrial society characterized by alienated individualism and relations dominated by contract. By a peculiar twist, not insignificant, the development of the one into the other is seen as being indicated by the monetization of the economy, though other indicators, such as wage labour and the reinvestment of surplus to expand production, are also seen as relevant. It is the monetization in the face of customary relations enforced by violence regardless of law that is seen to constitute the specificity of the mode of production called semi-feudal.

[8] See, Lenin, *Imperialism, the Highest Stage of Capitalism, Collected Works*, vol. 22, Moscow, Progress Publishers, 1964, pp. 185–360.
[9] Karl Marx, *Capital*, vol. III, Moscow, Foreign Languages Publishing House, 1961.

Money does of course have a central relevance to the existence, let alone the understanding, of any civilization, not to speak of mode of production. But it seems obvious to me that the notion of its relevance at work in the concept of semi-feudalism is simplistic and distorted, if not fundamentally wrong. Before going on to discuss this error itself it is more helpful to understand the grounds of the error. The error is constituted of smuggling in the Christian ideology to understand facts of an altogether different, Hindu ideology. For whereas the Christian ideology distinguishes clearly between the service of God and the service of Mammon, the response of the Hindu ideology is neither so categorical nor uniform over the *varna*s, or perhaps *even jati*s, on the question of money. Thus, the attempt to equate monetization with capitalism falls far short of its intent as usury is not the cardinal sin in India it was in medieval Europe, and coexists happily with non-monetary customary rights, and in fact is itself permeated by them. The zamindar, whose continued existence seems to be the proof of semi-feudalism, is simultaneously usurer.

As a characterization semi-feudalism by its inadequacy raises a host of problems, the answer to which is necessary for understanding the meaning conferred on this word by those who use it.

The Relations of Production and Property

The strategic implication of calling India a semi-feudal and semi-colonial country was, for Charu Mazumdar and the Naxalites led by him, the identification of feudalism as the principal contradiction, and the *jotedar*s as the main enemy of the people. This to the Naxalites is its denotation. It is through this deflection of what is usually denoted by a mode of production that the central tenet of Marxism is, for the communists, that of the existence of class struggle. The Marxist standpoint in scholarship in India, and in acute form today, consists of the argument of class struggle as the motive of History, and of the attempt to construe these classes. There is some doubt as to what fundamentally constitute classes, particularly in the present, but the concept of class itself is seen to constitute an advance on the understanding of non-Marxist scholarship which emphasizes the caste and religious aspects of Indian society as constitutive of its nature. In the case of the active revolutionary, the centrality of this question derives from the connection it establishes between his cosmology (the characterization of the state) and his commitment (to the Revolution) by providing a target for his aggression. And though Charu Mazumdar might have not found it necessary to comment on the general configurations in Indian society, he *was* certain that jotedars were the main enemy of the Revolution.

The jotedar represents the survival of the erstwhile 'intermediary' of the Intermediaries Abolition Acts of the states that in British times had made land-revenue settlements with them. At the time that intermediaries were the only sources of revenue-collection they were known as zamindars in Bengal and elsewhere, and taluqdars in Oudh. Jotedars then were a variety of sub-infeudatory, or a mass of such, that gradually grew up between the zamindar or taluqdar and the actual cultivators, from the time when these settlements were first made until the arrangement was abrogated. Such sub-infeudation was not only characteristic of the regions of so-called zamindari settlements, but of *raiyyatwari* regions as well, where in theory the government had come to an agreement with the actual cultivator as to the amount of his 'tax' or 'rent'. The situation that prevailed at the time of independence was that of a series of individuals arranged in a hierarchy based on legal agreements appropriating parts of the surplus of the cultivator, before that portion due to the government was delivered up to it. In broad theoretical terms this development can be seen as the divergence of conditions *de facto* from conditions as they were formulated *de jure,* such that intermediaries develop between the presumably exhaustive definitions of the legal code. But this is itself a legal formulation that obscures the process of law. It is more accurate to say that the legal definition of the lowest status, by conferring rights on it, transforms it into a privileged position, leaving the lowest still lower and still undefined. This is part of the character of law and the legal system in India. But to return to the jotedar, the person implied is the person paying land-revenue to the government but not cultivating the land he 'owns'.

The legislation abolishing intermediaries was supposed to have abolished just this class of persons, and the accompanying legislations on land ceilings to have rendered it impossible. Yet no one in India today doubts their continued existence and influence, though the exact dimensions of their influence and its nature is a matter of dispute among Communists. Communists are however unified in seeing them as undesirable, though there is a variation in the actual emphasis of this undesirability. To some, they are a brake on economic progress, to others an inhuman and unjust imposition on the abysmal poverty of the Indian peasantry. To most they are both, though few would claim, as perhaps a Marxist should, that they are considered unjust because they check the production of wealth.

Whether they actually do this, i.e. check the production of wealth, must remain doubtful. On the one hand, with their continued existence rural wealth has nevertheless increased, and certainly the production of food-grains has; on the other, though the abolition of intermediaries has not been total, it would be foolish to argue that in fact no change had taken place. But the argument that relates the change in the productivity of Indian agri-culture to the implementation of the land-reforms legislation (the CPI avowedly, and the CPI(M) covertly, in that it sees its principal agitational platform in the implementation of land reforms) is at variance with the CPI(M-L) view of the nature of the parliamentary process and the nature of the law. But then this view is different from the non-revolutionary variants of Communism in a significant way. For the revolutionary Communist, the question whether the existence of jotedars increases production is of relative, or perhaps even supreme, unimportance, and the only consider-ation on the question of wealth is that of the justice of its relative distribution. An. attempt (of a very peculiar sort) has indeed been made theoretically to show the irrelevance of this class of jotedars in the increase of agricultural productivity. It has been argued by Amit Bhaduri that in so far as the jotedar invests his surplus it is in usury, but this criticism overlooks the fact that *any* investment if it yields a return is caught up in the production, indeed expan-sion, of wealth, for without such a return on the investment is impossible. But, if one consults the available sources on the nature of agriculture, one finds the jotedar class involved in a variety of occupations besides its con-sumption of rent, though not actually cultivating its land, either in the sense of using wage labour, or that of working personally.[10]

More significant for the CPI(M-L) is that the continued existence of the jotedars, despite legislation against them, indicates the fraudulent nature of law. Parliament is seen as a talking-shop to fool the people, and the system of law enforcement through corruption. that maintains the jotedars in power as the reality and thus true intent behind the legislations. Certainly the Naxalites have here arrived at a crucial insight into the nature of social organization and law, in a word of property. They point, unerringly, to the most glaring fact of the situation as regards these, namely the divergence between law and fact. They do not push on to the theoretical conclusion to

[10] A. Ghosh and K. Dutt, *Development of Capitalist Relations in Agriculture, a Case Study of West Bengal* 1793–1971, New Delhi, Peoples Publishing House, 1977, p. 66.

be drawn from this, i.e. the divergence between legal property and social relations of production. Not explicitly. But it lies implicit in their notion of force constituting the legitimacy of property. Obviously this cannot ever wholly be the case, for, in addition to force against transgression, a consensus adequate to muster the force to punish transgression is necessary in society. This consensus, when it achieves national scope, can be codified as law, but only after the consensus has been established on an explicit doctrine that 'underpins' this law, in the Indian case the Constitution. And yet, as subcultures of nation-wide scope, it is possible to have consensus groups *without* a codified body of doctrine on which law is based, relying for legitimacy rather on the unspoken assumptions of the culture in which they exist. They form systems of law in a sense (as criminals do too) which stand outside the law, and on some grounds by this very *outside-ness* against it. This, indeed, is the insight that the peculiarities of the contemporary Indian situation point to—that there exists a difference between existential relations mediated by conceptions of ownership and these as they are codified in legislation concerning property. Indeed the Marxist postulation of the development of property relations presumes a divergence between relations of production and property relations[11] when in fact we have Marx's explicit statement in direct contradiction equating the two.[12]

The reason for this contradiction in the Marxist problematic is not difficult to see. It lies primarily in an identification of the person in law with the person in life, in presuming that the legal person lives on the street at the same time that the legal system is considered part of the superstructure. Certainly it is the attempt of Law to speak of living persons as they are, but this attempt is codified in the attempt to determine who has broken the law. The grounds of contemporary justice hold individuals individually responsible for their acts, and only as such responsible individuals are persons a concern of the law. And mediating between the ideals of peace and order to which the law aspires and its administration lies the social organization encoded as 'due process of law'. Equality in the eyes of the law is a blindness to the conditions in which the law exists.

[11] Especially in the conception of a revolution which replaces one set of property relations by another which has developed as relations of production without legal sanction inside the former. K. Marx, Capital, vol. III, ed. F. Engels, London, Lawrence and Wishart, 1960, p. 861; also K. Marx and F. Engels, *The Communist Manifesto*, Harmondsworth, Penguin, p. 85.

[12] Karl Marx, *Capital*, vol. I.

But if law is part of the superstructure, it nevertheless exists in a particular relation to the relations of production that forms its base. Without claiming universality for conclusions it would be fruitful to examine the relations in contemporary Indian society.

The *Peskar*

The distinctive peculiarity of the Indian legal system is the institution or status-role of the *peskar*. This is the peon concerned with forwarding the relevant file to the lawyer concerned with a case. The distance between 'legal person' and the person without social attributes, i.e. the property-less, is quantified in the sum necessary for a passport, but also bypassed by the power of influence, which incorporates kinship but is not exhausted by it. And bribes, as everywhere, establish the uneasy coexistence of police and criminal. In addition to these factors of interest in the sociology of law, the Indian example in further complicated by the esotericism of the law, codified in a foreign language, in a country where illiteracy is the rule, modelled on that of a country that was the foremost imperial power of the last century and the 'mother of parliaments'. The lawyer and the peasant inhabit different worlds spanned by a universe of discourse and enforcement, mediated by relations whose ambit of possibilities is essentially determined by those in the relations of production in which the peasant himself is enmeshed. The world of the lawyer is a sub-culture of the English-using urban culture, and that of the peasant a sub-culture of the illiterate rural culture. They might share a religion, but if this is the Hindu there might still be worlds that separate them. As individual human beings, as persons subject to the law, there is nothing that divides them, but to think that because of this unity they would share similar conceptions about themselves or about property would be an illegitimate conclusion. The legal and identity definitions of the two are premised on radically different kinds of experience, and entail different experiences of property. Ideally speaking the lawyer would merely translate the awareness of the peasant into a legal form, and yet the law allows for no existence of the intermediary, who, at least in the understanding of the Naxalites, rules the countryside.

The modes by which intermediaries have retained their hold on the land has been by transferring their rights to kin or fictitious persons or simply not declaring their ownership.[13] These, however, pertain to their relations with the government. In their relation to the peasant, things either have not changed or have changed in a way that does not threaten their existence as intermediaries, at the very least, if indeed in actual fact they do not actually buttress it. Besides which there is intermediar*ism*, the letting out of land by those with title to it, which is by no means restricted to the class of hereditary intermediaries. It is these, the inter-mediaries and those engaged with intermediaries, who span the two worlds of the Law and the peasant.

Property in Land

Without going into the prejudices and claims of various authors on the subject, all of them without exception have been aware that the ideas current about property in land in India prior to the arrival of the British were considerably different from those that the British espoused. The difficulty of determining as to what exactly these ideas were in India in the absence of some one authoritative text were compounded by the insistence on regarding the idealized notion of Roman *Dominium— usus, usufructus, abusus et vindicatio*—as determinant of the actual status of property holders (of land) in the occident. Before considering what this interaction of two 'codes' of property resulted in, it is necessary to say something about the 'codes' themselves.

The state of affairs in India, as the British found it, though the product of a great civilization, was itself the outcome of a prior interaction between a Hindu order, relatively unbroken, stretching back to the beginnings of Indian civilization, and a Muslim conquest. The amalgam that resulted had elements of both the Hindu view of affairs and the Islamic view of affairs. In this, though the Islamic view and civilization extended far beyond the borders of India, the Indian evolution of Islamic practices in India was peculiar to the subcontinent. The logical starting

---

[13] See S. K. Basu and S. K. Bhattacharya, *Land Reforms in West Bengal*, Planning Commission, Govt. of India, Oxford Book Co., 1963, pp. 64–77, regarding *mala fide* transfers, and Ratan Ghosh, 'Effect of Agricultural Legislations on Land Distribution in West Bengal', *Indian Journal of Agricultural Economics*, vol. XXXI, no. 3, July–September 1976, p. 45, for the continued concentration of agricultural holdings.

point for considering the state of affairs and the conceptions relating to them seems therefore to be Hindu India and Hindu conceptions.

Students of Hindu law have remarked that rooted as it is in *dharmik* conceptions, it does not, as Roman law does, permit of custom as a source of law.[14] As to whether this is a biased simplification of the same kind as that which relies on the abstract conception of Roman property to argue for its distinctive particularity in the matter of land, and one moreover based on an insufficient acquaintance with the dharmik literature, is not a matter that can be definitively settled here. It is important to note merely that the Hindu code of laws is concerned wholly with dharma, and thus with a normative orientation that is, for lack of a better word, 'religious' in character, thus perhaps not rooted in custom in the way that word is construed in Roman (and Germanic) jurisprudence. But equally central to the understanding of the question is the distinction made by anthropologists between a Great and Little Tradition as the characteristic dualism of the Hindu religion. This dualism though not coterminous with the distinction between doctrine and custom, overlaps it to a great extent, and coincides in its broad features with the distinction made in the dharmik literature between *sastrik* and *laukik* aspects (or elements) of Hindu practice and belief.

The terms sastrik and laukik are of wide diffusion in the dharmik literature and convey different senses about a central defining axis of meaning depending on the context. Literally they denote not so much a logical opposition as a differentiation that achieves clarity with respect to the peculiarities of Hinduism. Sastrik means of, or derived from, the *sastras* (the authoritative texts or merely doctrine) where laukik means of, or rooted in, the populace. Though this is their specific denotation, this is not precisely the sense in which they are always used, though central to usage is their invariant counterposition as mutually exclusive categories.

An adequate discussion of the distinction would call for a detailed knowledge of Hindu beliefs and practices, and a thorough discussion of sociological modes of analysis. For our purposes here, I would draw attention to a sociological implication of a doctrine in which such a distinction is crucial. The distinction itself would distinguish between

[14] Robert Lingat, *The Classical Law of India*, translated from the French with additions by J. Duncan M. Derrett, Berkeley etc., University of California Press, 1973, p. 176.

the beliefs and practices of those with adequate knowledge of the sastras, and thus perhaps an intellectual stratum, and those for whom such knowledge was either not necessary or not the rule. Such a distinction not only divides the community of practitioners, but distinguishes between the bases of their practice, and more fundamentally characterizes orthodoxy itself in a dualist fashion. Such a culture is not merely distinguished into a culture of the élites and one of the masses (as indeed Gramsci contends all religions apart from the Catholic establish), but sets up divergent sources of authority within the culture, though 'in the ultimate analysis' it is the sastrik that is true.[15] For the sastras themselves, the laukik element, though recognized, remains *terra incognita.*

Over this fundamentally dualist culture, in which the laukik component remained essentially unexplored, was imposed Muslim rule and the codes of Islamic law. Islamic law itself is also, as the dharmik law of the Hindus, 'religious' in character, but differs from the Hindu as being binding only on believers, with the concept of belief, as in the Judaeo-Christian tradition, central to the doctrine. As regards the relations with non-believers, they are regulated by Islamic law into one of three kinds—conversion, extermination or enslavement.[16] The evolution of Islamic law, and particularly in Hindustan, developed the significant fourth relation added to the original three in the attempt of imperial Islam to cope with subject peoples, that of amicable relations with non-believers who payed tribute.[17] By the imposition of Muslim rule, the royal apex of the dharmik hierarchy was nullified, and the whole of the corpus of Hindu thought consigned to the laukik oblivion in which many creative elements of even earlier Hindu thought had taken shape. True, this did not mean the end of Hindu thought, but its evolution in a form to which the concept of dominion was not central. It is for this reason, perhaps, that when the British arrived they found that the terms indicating ownership, particularly of land, were all Islamic in origin.

[15] Antonio Gramsci, *Selections from the Prison Notebooks,* ed. and trans. Quintin Hoare and Geoffrey Nowell Smith, London, Lawrence and Wishart, 1971, p. 328.
[16] Joseph schacht, *An Introduction to Islamic Law*, London, Oxford University Press, 1971, p. 130.
[17] Asaf A. A. Fyzee, *Outlines of Muhammadan Law,* London, Oxford University Press, 1955, says 'the Mughal rulers of India... applied the Hindu and Islamic laws to their subjects conformably with their own views ...' (p. 42).

Early Hindu ideas on the subject of property, if not adequately explored even today, were even less well known or widely known when the British first undertook their investigation. Even at that early date it was recognized that the ancient Hindus distinguished between ownership and possession.[18] The very awareness of this distinction would, in principle, if extended to land, permit the evolution of a concept of landed property (in the Roman sense) and a validation for rent. But one cannot take such a simplistic view of affairs for the evolution of the idea of property in land is in some ways radically different from the idea of property as it concerns movables and consumables. Scholarship has nevertheless less established the fact of private ownership, communal ownership and royal ownership of land as independent categories in ancient India.[19] Early British debate, centred on the question of royal or private ownership being universal, is in this context meaningless, for it imposes terms borrowed from the reality of European feudalism on to conditions where such considerations are irrelevant. The debate did however aid in the formulation of the policy of land settlement that the British later adopted, and however misplaced the attempt to determine the universal state of property may be, it does seem germane to inquire into the relations that existed between various types of property and the relative place of each.

Muslim conquest, whatever else it did, effectively ended the form of Brahmanical communal ownership that Hindu kings had patronized. Indeed with the arrival of the Muslim conquerors the whole of the property question, until then one presumes a matter of some consensus, is thrown open to confusion and doubt. With claims of absolute sovereignty on the one hand by despotic monarchs, and those of independent chieftains on the other, grounds were created both for the speculation into the character of property as such, and for the later 'feudal' construal of this state of affairs. Indeed it is to approximately this time that the divergence of opinion of Hindu sastris on the question of property date. The difference of opinion concerning the character of property as such has arrayed on one side the Bengali school of Jimutavahana, Raghunandana, etc., and on the other the *Mitaksara*, the *Smrticandrika*

[18] Julius Jolly, *Hindu Law and Custom*, trans. Batakrishna Ghosh, Calcutta, Greater India Society, 1928, p. 196.
[19] U. N. Ghoshal, *The Agrarian System in Ancient India*, Calcutta, University of Calcutta, 1930.

and other works of the south and west; the former maintain that ownership is sastrik, and the latter that it is laukik. Jolly construes the terms as here denoting religio-scientific in the former case, and temporal in the latter.[20]

The inflation of royal prerogative, so stressed by some of the later British administrator-scholars, actually pre-dates the Muslim conquest.[21] But it is only with this conquest that this prerogative gains institutional form. It is a moot point as to whether Islamic law is in any way instrumental in this transformation, the existing state of scholarship arguing rather for the absolutist aspirations of the Muslim monarchs to which their relationship with the interpreters of Islamic law are wholly incidental, and particularly so in the matter of land relations.[22] It is in this period that we see the formation and consolidation of a bureaucratic stratum of land administrators (*ijaradar*s, later *mansabdar*s), dissociated on the one hand from the ownership of land and on the other from the purely technical exercises of assessment and reportage to the crown (the province of officials such as the *muqqadam*s, etc.), tied for their very existence to loyalty to the throne.[23] Significantly, in these circumstances, the juridical literature is devoid of speculation into the origins and nature of property, much more so landed property.

Property in land becomes the object of speculation and investigation after the British acquire their *diwani* in Bengal. To the considerations that are brought to bear on the question of this property, significant is the observation that they are coloured by the European experience of the replacement of bourgeois relations by feudal relations. The question, to begin with, concerns the absolute ownership of land, the justification, even later, being that this formulation was aimed at determining the just rights of the state and the intermediary (the landlord).[24] The

[20] Julius Jolly, pp. 198–9.

[21] R. S. Sharma, *Indian Feudalism: c. 200–1200*, University of Calcutta, 1965, p. 196.

[22] W. H. Moreland, *The Agrarian System of Muslim India*, Cambridge, W. H. Heffer and Sons, 1929, p. 19.

[23] Irfan Habib, *The Agrarian System of Mughal India* (London, published for the Dept. of History, Aligarh Muslim University by Asia Publishing House, 1963) quotes a saying: 'an official (hakim) of a day could in a moment remove a *zamindar* of five hundred years and put in his stead a man who had been without a place for a whole lifetime' (p. 180).

[24] The difference between the terms 'rent' and 'tax', mentioned earlier is connected with this discourse. Absolute ownership justified the use of the term

question was nevertheless opened and authority was sought in the customary usage of times past, in so far as this was recorded. This speculation and investigation, whatever its scholarly results, culminated in the Permanent Settlement of 1793, which recognized the 'proprietary interest' of intermediaries on the condition of their prompt settlement of the revenue demand of the government.

Intermediaries and Intermediarism

The term intermediary itself sets up a problematic in which there are only two legitimate claimants to the usufruct of the land—the cultivator and the state between whom the intermediary mediates. This is indeed the bias that underlies the use of the term in the legislation that abolishes the right of the intermediaries to a portion of the usufruct. This bias has a much earlier provenance, and originates in the British desire to bypass such intermediaries, particularly in the case of the taluqdars of Oudh. Between 1793, when the Permanent Settlement was made with the intermediaries of Bengal (when the desire of the government had been to create a prosperous countryside under the stewardship of zamindars), and 1856, when the settlements in Oudh were first made attempting to bypass the taluqdars in the collection of revenue, the British attitude towards landed proprietors in the subcontinent had undergone a *volte face*. The revolt of 1857 did much to restore the legitimacy of the taluqdars, but the bias against intermediaries, implicit in the very use of the term, was already settled, and nowhere more so than in Bengal. The revolt which served to establish the proprietary interest of the taluqdars inaugurated in Bengal the legislation (1859) directed towards protecting the rights of the tenants and curbing the interest of the zamindars.

Recent scholarship has directed attention to the evolution of the class of zamindars in Mughal times, and even earlier, as a class relatively free of the despotic overlordship of the Muslim rulers though sometimes subject to them.[25] This literature, though very satisfactory in some respects—particularly in highlighting the elements of continuity in pre-Muslim and Muslim India, and in Mughal and post-Mughal India—falls short in others, particularly in explaining the development of agrarian

---

'rent' for the state's appropriation whereas 'tax' or 'revenue' viewed the proprietorship of the beneficiary in a more relative light.

[25] See Irfan Habib.

property, indicated not least by the fact of its inability to account for the varied uses of the term zamindar. To the British this regional variation— indicating a landlord of the European type in Bengal and a 'mere' farmer in the northwestern region—was confusing enough to lend support to the use of the term intermediary.

With this literature that emphasizes the continuity in the evolution of land relations, it becomes problematic whether the British legislation that 'instituted' and recognized them did in fact make any difference to the relations actually existing in the countryside. It seems fairly obvious from the scholarly work of recent decades that the revenue farming, to call it by its proper name, that the British instituted as the legitimation of the proprietary interest of the zamindars in Bengal had been a cus- tomary practice of post-Mughal Bengal, at least.[26] Nevertheless it has been argued that the recognition in law of proprietorship effectively changed the actual notions and practice of proprietorship, whereas, con- versely, it has also been argued that the successive legislations regarding proprietorship did not in fact change anything.[27] The latter is of course belied by the large volume of litigation concerning land proprietorship, particularly in Bengal, though the former is obviously too naive to be true.[28] The most prevalent prejudice considers the land settlements of the British a crucial turning point in Indian history, a view which today for lack of overt characteristics by which to indicate this fixes upon the inauguration of the alienability of land. As to whether the British actu- ally inaugurated such must for the present remain a matter in doubt; what is indubitable is merely their yoking of proprietary interest to the collection of revenue. And as far as alienability is concerned, though in principle this may well have been the effective content of the proprietary interest, the Hindu laws of inheritance were in practice an effective bar to the exercise of this alienability as late as the seventies in Punjab. But the crucial change wrought by the Britishis undeniable, for it extends not just to legal concepts and this or that particular change in land

---

[26] M. N. Gupta, *Land System of Bengal*, University of Calcutta, 1940, p. 11. See also Irfan Habib, pp. 181–2; S. Nurul Hassan, 'Zamindars under the Mughals' in *Land Control and Social Structure in Indian History*, ed. Robert Erik Frykenberg, New Delhi, Manohar, 1979, p. 18.

[27] Narendra Krishna Sinha, ed., *The History of Bengal (1757–1905)*, University of Calcutta, 1967, p. 53. See also, especially, A. Ghosh and K. Dutt, p. 1.

[28] Narendra Krishna Sinha, ed., p. 129.

relations, but the institution of a new legal code and a new legal system, governing among other things land relations as well. In the institution of the British rule lie the foundations of the law and order that the government of India defended against the Naxalites. The principle, if indeed principle is to be sought, distinguishing land relations in British and post-British times from what came before, is to be found in the rule of law that is instituted for proprietary interest.

Whatever may have been the difference that this made to the intermediaries, and there is no doubt that this was considerable, little attention has been directed to the fate of the legislation concerning tenants. In Bengal in 1859, and later elsewhere in India, tenancy protection rights were proclaimed that upheld the right of the tenant to cultivate the land that he had done so by custom. Distinction was made between 'occupancy' and 'non-occupancy' (or tenants-at will) tenants, conferring on the former heritable, alienable rights in the cultivation of the soil. The distinction between the two rested in a proof of twelve years of occupancy. As will be obvious, such legislation created for those with access to it rights in the land every bit as valuable as that of the zamindar, provided they were aware of it and capable of proving their right. Sub-infeudation, cited as the bane of the Indian, and particularly Bengali, agriculture, prior to the abolition of intermediaries, accrued just as much from the legislation concerning occupancy tenants as that of the power of the zamindars to further delegate their task (or privilege) of revenue collection.[29] And to the understanding of this development, caste, the ubiquitous institution of Indian society, is central, as to the development of sub-infeudation in areas under raiyyatwari settlements.

Indeed it is this very sub-infeudation that illuminates not only the proprietary interest of the intermediaries, but the whole character of the impact of the British legal code on Indian land relations. Sub-infeudation, the effectual outcome of the transplanting of British legal dicta onto Indian soil, illustrates the actual amalgam of property that resulted, the laukik working out of British sastrik principles. By the fact of the peaceful defence of proprietary interests—whether of the intermediary or that of the tenant—heritable, alienable rights to the usufruct were created that could be delegated. This element of sophistication had indeed formed a central element of ancient Indian conceptions of property, in

[29] Sir Francis Floud, *Report of the Land Revenue Commission Bengal,* Alipore, Bengal Government Press, 1940, pp. 33–4.

which *jajmani* relations were transferable. The legislation that abolished intermediaries abolished only the superstructural British legitimation of property in land, without throwing into question either its premises or those of the Indian society in which it had taken root.

Daniel Thorner, arguing from accomplished facts without considerations of legitimation, characterizes the Indian countryside as consisting of three classes—*malik*s, *kisan*s and *mazdur*s.[30] It is my contention that a consideration of the legal status of each of these and the legitimacy of their practices, together with the. rationale for them, is more revealing of the character of the Indian countryside and indeed of the Indian polity as a whole than any summary categorization of the type that Thorner offers.

Before closing this section a word needs to be said about the bias of the legislation abolishing intermediaries. Motivated both by concerns of social justice and the imperatives of increasing production, the logic in the use of such a term as intermediary is one that is fundamentally directed against the realization of rent. Indeed, the attempt to curb rent—both rural and urban—has formed the substance of the agreement between the socialistic aspirations of those in power and those opposed to it. As such it enters into the mentality of the Naxalites too, but more importantly as the rhetoric of the government which to the Naxalites is contradicted by its acts. While not forming the whole content of their semi-feudalist contention, the question of rent forms its economic core, as that of the rationale abolishing the rights of intermediaries.

The Formula and Parliament

While neither feudal not capitalist, nor in a state of development from the former into the latter, the government legislation abolishing intermediaries does aim at a transfer of rights from superior landholders to actual cultivators, eliminating rent. It is to this rationale and its noncompletion that the term semi-feudalism refers—though in the Naxalite discourse the question of rent or that of the legal situation is never overtly taken into account. It does, nevertheless, underlie their criticism of the parliamentary process that in their rhetoric and strategy

[30] Daniel Thorner, *The Agrarian Prospect in India*, Delhi, University Press, 1956, p. 4.

constitutes the expression of bourgeois democracy—the achievement of Indian independence.

It is thus that the question of feudalism is inextricably connected in their doctrine to the question of colonialism. For if the institution of parliament is a fraud, both its own legislations concerning relations in land and its very essence itself as the expression of India's independence of colonial powers are thereby nullified. And it is impossible to doubt that their opposition to parliamentarianism, as the fundamental doctrinal issue, is what distinguishes them from and opposes them to the CPI and the CPI(M).

But whereas the question of feudalism receives repeated emphasis, the question of colonialism only becomes important in the Naxalite discourse with the advent of the urban movement. It is when students are attacking their educational institutions that a rationale for this is offered by suggesting that in so doing the students are attacking the decadent colonial education system. This system is neither identified with curricula, nor the use of the English language, but with the nature of the ideals—the nonviolence of Gandhi as opposed to the martial prowess of the Rani of Jhansi—and the function of these ideals in perpetuating the exploitative system (of feudalism). The question of colonialism is thus, in a sense, something thrust upon the CPI(M-L) ideologues by the urban movement, after they had excluded Nagi Reddy from their fold for espousing its centrality. By this and the way in which the problem is tackled in their literature, two conclusions seem inescapable. The first is that whereas the contradiction concerning feudalism pertains to the base, that concerning colonialism pertains to the superstructure, and second by this very fact and in contradiction to it, the colonial mentality is far more pervasive than the feudal one. To so draw the implicit contradictory conclusions of the CPI(M-L) metaphysics may seem far fetched, but it derives its legitimacy from the attempt to explore the unstated interconnections of their rhetoric, always put forward as a unity and, more importantly, felt to be so.

While completely wrong in their sociological orientation, choice of words and understanding of the Indian economy, the Naxalites intended by their use of the term 'semi-feudal semi-colonial' to draw attention to the twin concerns of rural poverty and exploitation and the relative weakness of Indian voices on the international stage. These indeed form the predominant concerns of a great deal of Indian political thought and action. Where the Naxalites diverged completely from customary thinking was by the use of this formula emphasizing that, despite the evolution of parliament (the pride of many), conditions were essentially the same as in pre-revolutionary China, where no such institutions existed. The attack on the jotedar proclaimed simultaneously the disillusion with parliamentary democracy and the desire to see India a great power.[31]

[31] Sunil Sen, *Agrarian Relations in India* (1793–1947), New Delhi, Peoples Publishing House, 1979, has an interesting discussion of the emergence of jotedars on pp. 8–9.

Chapter Seven

The Existential Ideology of the Naxalites

A great lie in history; as if the corruption of the Church were the cause of the Reformation! This was only the pretext and self-deception of the agitators—very strong needs were making themselves felt, the brutality of which sorely required a spiritual dressing.

—Nietzsche

There are still people around proud to call themselves Naxalites, though what the epithet conveys now is considerably different from the days when it first gained currency, or in the explosive years 1970 to 1972 when Naxalites dominated the political scene of Calcutta.

The change is, to the superficial, a matter of degree—of the extent to which Naxalites are willing to go to achieve their aims. And indeed this has been the dominant attitude towards the Naxalites throughout the time they have been of significance in India. The press and public opinion has characterized them as 'extremists', rather than 'terrorists', though they themselves have always identified themselves as 'revolutionaries' and continue to do so. But, as the term 'extremism' indicates, the claim to fomenting revolution is one that incorporates questions of method that are as important as these claims themselves. In any case, it is the methods professed, if not universally practised, that served to distinguish the early Naxalites from other Communist groups, and equally that can distinguish the early-Naxalites from those of today. Charu Mazumdar's distinctive contribution to the theory of revolution consisted of considerations on the *method* of making it.

And yet, if we are to treat of the Naxalites with the seriousness they deserve, we cannot leave the question of their commitment as one of mere methods. Methods are fraught enterprises, and a discussion of methods is never far from a shift in fundamental ontology. It is as such a querulousness about fundamental ontology that the Indian dispute on methods of ending poverty or achieving socialism presents itself to the discerning observer. What makes this fundamental ontology difficult to determine is the pragmatic cast of the questions asked. The unanimity of the pragmatism in the face of an extant conflict points unequivocally to a disjunction in the universe of shared meaning. Questions of method gather up orientations to the fundamental reality that forms the ground of their questioning. That those orientations that underly the questioning can in fact be disjointed, despite a shared rhetoric of the goals of this questioning, is attested to by the fact of opposed, and perhaps equally tenable, answers to the questions of method. Most importantly, the discussion of methods iluminates what is entailed in the understanding of this 'method' itself. It is this that opens the path to a comprehension of the fundamental ontology that informs this striving.

Mazumdar's methods are geared towards precipitating a Revolution. It is not the alleviation of poverty or even the achievement of power that concerns him immediately, but the bringing about of this cataclysmic alteration of the relations of power.

The distinctively modern feature of modern India is the emergence of political philosophy and the growth of the political into the dominant discourse. This has been accompanied by a shift in the evolution of the meaning of being Indian. At the same time that a face has been formed to front the world, the world has indicted the Indian for the thing he is. And a soul has been forged, a *volk* defined. It straddles races, languages, peoples, religions, traditions, jobs and wealth,. It defines itself as a nation.

This nationalism has had a twofold aspect—enunciating ideals, programmes, the deed's of discourse and the discourse of deeds. In its early Hindu formulations it presents itself as *karma-yoga*, the transformation of existenz into Being, a reversal of the classical Brahmin problematic of *seeking* Being-in-existenz. Karma-yoga, as it is enunciated at the origins of nationalism, is a doctrine of detached but complete engagement with the world. From the perspectives of the believer it has meant a shift from the contemplative life to the active life, the pursuit of tangible achievement in preference to spiritual excellence, even if desire is in the process doomed to extinction. As a Gandhi one hounds this desire into the deepest night and there destroys it as a personal task. A will to power has emerged. It has had three names in Hindi—*swarajya, Ramrajya,* and to the mobs who kill in the name of *ahimsa, Gandhi-rajya.* Swarajya was what the earliest Indians called it, and Ramrajya was Gandhi's choice—a

Ramrajya that, for the current schools of political history, was crucially inaugurated by the Quit India movement and the transfer of power. Independence constitutes the political achievement of nationalism.

In the realm of ideals it has propagated the notion of the Motherland and argued in Sanskrit—*Jananijanmabhumishcha swargadapi chira gariyasi* (the mother and the mother-land will always be preferable to the abode of the gods). One's land of birth is transformed into the land of one's choice. Efforts to make it what one would like it to be become a duty. Whereas those who see in the internationalism ('China's Chairman is our Chairman, China's path is our path') of the Maoist Naxalites an insult to their sense of national pride and demand an Indian pedigree of greatness, those who admire the Naxalites, construing just this sense of duty as nationalism, see the Naxalites themselves as the proof of this pedigree. And, indeed, the motherland is often invoked in Charu Mazumdar's writings, but as an infernal place exploited crucially by the jotedar—*Jotedar-Rajya*. The term is never used. But this is seen to have been the outcome of the independence that is celebrated as the national event, along with Republic Day—an outcome that left the basic structure of society unaltered. Ramrajya has meant parliamentary democracy, a deliberate deception for the rising tide of the masses that fuelled this nationalism, the illiterate rabble who could kill for Gandhi-Rajya. Killing the jotedar becomes the realization of the ideal of—Revolution!

This Revolution has, as historical myth, its provenance in the Bolshevik, and, more importantly for the Maoists, in the Chinese revolutions, and as a fact of history in India its enunciation in the circles of terrorists who peopled the political stage in the first quarter of the twentieth century. Whereas the Marxist terminology of the former determines the categories of the discourse, the existential elucidation of Revolution is only accessible as the latter. In other words, whereas the concepts in which Revolution is spoken about derive from the Marxist-Leninist-Maoist literature, the terms in which it is perceived and presents itself as historical and personal choice are rather defined by the submerged and proscribed terrorist literature. Documents of Russian terrorism, which must have moulded the sensibility of Revolution of the Bolsheviks, are inaccessible to me. In the case of the Indian terrorists it is the recourse to violence and firearms in the cause of the nation that comes to distinguish this group of political agitators from the Congress. The Congress was construed by the English to be a legitimate successor because its organizations and leaders survived—not just the repression of a hostile government but the apathy that is as inevitable as enthusiasm. In opposition to the Bolshevik case, the development of the possibility of legitimate political movement in India crucially altered the situation and the aspirations of revolutionary groups, to begin with at the immediate origins of nationalism, and later again during World War II and subsequently for the communists. To the terrorists' descriptions of the revolutionary character of an act, the communists brought an additional perspective of mass agitation. It is to this developing idea of Revolution, formulated by terrorists, embellished by communists, both as theory and practice, that Charu Mazumdar has made a definitive contribution.

The theoretical tradition to which Mazumdar himself links his speculations is the Marxist-Leninist-Maoist. In the materialist metaphysic of these schools, the Revolution that Charu Mazumdar says he wants to bring about is the New Democratic revolution. This is to establish the rule of the vast majority of the nation, composed specifically of the peasantry, the proletariat, the petty bourgeoisie and the national bourgeoisie, upsetting the rule of the landlords, the comprador bourgeoisie, the US imperialists and the Soviet social-imperialists, who constitute a tiny minority.[1] This is a formulation that Mazumdar shares with all other Maoists, and does not form his own distinctive contribution. The terminology in which what became for Mazumdar Jotedar-rajya was codified, defined India as a semi-feudal, semi-colonial country. Mazumdar's distinctive contribution to the idea of Revolution lay in another dimension—in the attempt to grasp its existential unfolding as praxis. He ventured to describe the qualities of a revolutionary and the process of making revolution as directives in the fulfilment of a historic necessity. Mazumdar's own theoretical contribution to the Marxist-Leninist-Maoist tradition is thus one which cannot comfortably be addressed within that tradition, other than as the generic 'petty-bourgeois revolutionism' or 'individual terrorism', though it brings to that discourse a powerful critique, theoretical and practical, of 'Revisionism'.

To understand this 'revisionism', on the other hand, it is necessary to have recourse to the initial formulations of revolution in terrorist tracts. Mazumdar's view of the revolution is unarmed peasants turning ferociously on their armed oppressors, killing them and snatching their weapons to found an army that will liberate the whole country. It removes the recourse to firearms that in the earlier image had been an

---

[1] See Programme of the CPI(M-L), quoted in the last chapter.

integral part of revolutionism, and in fact even denounces it. What stands revealed is the unadorned unleashing of violence—'annihilation', murder. And certainly the phenomenon of Naxalite terrorism itself is utterly unlike anything in the history of the world.

Revisionism and Its Critique

The beginning of the process lies in the problematic of Indian communism and its radical sections. The communist movement in India is by and large concerned with industrialization, and in a broader perspective with development. The crucial question occupying centre-stage in communist theory—political theory that is (in so far as there is a coherent body of thought in India that one can call communist)—is 'Why is it that India is not yet an industrial nation?' This question, obviously, subsumes the problem of poverty that forms the central locus of liberal democratic thought, though it might be true to say that a fair section of the theorists are drawn to the communist movement because it promises some kind of programme for the practical elimination of poverty. It is not uncommon to find tendencies in the thought of the communists, not always overtly expressed, that extol the virtues of the poor in comparison with the rich. I mention this here because this trend is of greater importance when we come to consider the revolutionary sects.

As far as the chief question of communist practical political theory is concerned, i.e. 'Why is it that India is not yet an industrial nation?', the revolutionaries and all those radicals who consider themselves 'left of the CPI(M)' fundamentally change the formulation of the question and the thrust of their politics by asking, 'Why is it that India cannot industrialize?' The implications of this reformulation are perfectly clear. From the chief question of communist theory it is possible to draw conclusions of piecemeal reform, parliamentary struggle, and a belief that some sections of the national elites are oriented in the same way as the communists are, whereas the formulation of the 'ultra-left' and the revolutionaries makes a clean break with the process of political decision-making characteristic of post-independence India. Such was the starting point of the break of the revolutionaries within the CPI(M) from the CPI(M), and their attempt to gather around themselves activists and intellectuals.

The All-India Co-ordination Committee of Communist Revolutionaries (AICCCR) adopted as the first article of its creed that the ruling elites of India were incapable of destroying those elements of the social structure that were an obstacle to progress, an obstacle to the industrial and agrarian prosperity of the nation. The problem of agrarian prosperity is particularly important, for though the CPI(M) had also cited as one of the failures of the CPI (from which it broke) its incorrectness in arriving at a true evaluation of the role of the countryside, the AICCCR, in its turn, differed from the CPI(M) regarding the status and importance of the countryside in the revolutionary process. In both cases it was a question of degree rather than a clear-cut decision for or against. In theory and as a matter of principle, all varieties of communists agreed that the countryside was an important location of the revolutionary process, but the relative importance that they attached to it was a matter of difference, and the degree of practical attention that the different sections were willing to devote to the countryside marks them off from each other. For the AICCCR the countryside was crucial and the area where all energies needed to be concentrated to begin the revolutionary process. This theoretical consideration served to orient the AICCCR in its own political agitation, but the principle over which it disagreed overtly with the CPI (M) was the question of the possibilities of parliamentarism. The AICCCR came to consider the participation in the parliamentary process as itself suspect and contrasted this mode of 'mobilizing' the masses with the method of direct revolutionary agitation bypassing the mechanisms of conciliation set up by the state. It viewed the participation of the CPI (M) in the parliamentary process as one of the chief indications that it had turned 'revisionist'. It was with revolutionary activity in mind that the AICCCR characterized India as a 'semi-feudal, semi-colonial' country.

It might seem odd to phrase it in this way, i.e. to try to show that *from* the choice of a particular strategy, a particular theoretical characterization *should follow*. But to do so would merely fit the facts of the case. This is sufficiently indicated by the fact that no scholarly effort was expended in trying to determine the politico-economic determinants of the Indian social system. This is, of course, not to say that no evaluation of any kind was involved in the characterization of the Indian economy as 'semi-feudal, semi-colonial'. But this evaluation was largely the impressionistic generalization of activists about their own activity and its results. Of course, also, there is a general sense in which a characterization follows, or to put it in Marxist phraseology, 'expresses' a choice of strategy in even such a work as Lenin's *Development of Capitalism in Agriculture*. But, nevertheless, the fact that in the case of the AICCCR, in marked contrast to Lenin, the attempt at scholarly disputation was dispensed with is significant from three points of view: the first is that it expresses an impatience with scholarly undertakings, an impatience the implications of which come to be elaborated more explicitly in the evolution of the CPI(M-L), and particularly under the leadership of Charu Mazumdar; the second, that it reverts to the experience of activists for the 'real' 'test of truth', again an aspect the implications of which are elaborated in the practice of the CPI(M-L); and the third, that it pulls down theory to the level of those who are called upon to use it, again an aspect that comes to full flower under the leadership of Mazumdar.

The break with revisionism is accomplished simply by the denunciation of hypocrisy—the most significant social criticism from a moral standpoint, or should one say a religious one. What is denounced is not the doctrine, which to the revolutionary seems just as true as to the revisionist he denounces. The revolutionary reacts against the interpretation of doctrine by the revisionist which leaves him (the revisionist) free to controvert its spirit, both in the context of its social realization and, more importantly for the revolutionary and even more so for the terrorist, in the context of his own personal life.

In the case of communist terrorists this shift in the nature of theory is particularly marked, acutely obvious to the participants (the terrorists themselves, the law-enforcing authorities, and all those who follow these goings-on with some interest), though not perhaps consciously articulated. Nevertheless, this shift is characteristic of terroristic theory, whether of the right or of the left. Also, whether of the right or of the left, the metaphysic in which this personalized (perhaps one should say psychologized) doctrine is articulated is almost invariably a historical one. History is, however, interpreted ethically, in so far as it makes sense to the terrorist and the agents of history are held personally responsible for the state of affairs or outcome. To some extent, a historical metaphysic goes along with most contemporary doctrines of political action as the basis of understanding and political commitment. What is peculiar to the terroristic ethos is the psychologized, personalized interpretation of this metaphysic. To illustrate, one could say that in the case of non-terroristic social doctrines the metaphysic accounts for the nature of the state of affairs without overtly judging people as individuals, whereas in the case of the terrorist the personal judgement itself simultaneously accounts for the order of things and dictates the choices of the terrorist. Whereas almost all active participants in overt political activity seem to have a sense of impersonal and objective social tendencies in terms of which they are aligned, and indeed personally committed, the terrorist understands these tendencies (still impersonal and objective despite this inversion of the customary view) only in so far as they can be interpreted in terms of personal commitment.

A significant strand of the recent Marxist revolutionism, intimately associated with terrorism (though the founders repudiate this association) has in fact elaborated this manipulative interpretation of a fatalistic history. The thinking of what is commonly grouped together as the Frankfurt School is an important case in point. The encounter that spawned this thinking, that with Nazism, deemed by Adorno to be beneath theoretical contempt, is of course one that throws the whole question of the relevance and efficacy of social theory into question, at least in the sense in which the Frankfurt School itself understood it. And the despair with theory, the possibility of the construction of a history meaningful to men, or at any rate to the theorists, forms a deep undercurrent in the ethos of at least Marxist terrorism and revolutionism of the recent past. This despair has, no doubt, a double-edge. On the one hand it springs from the deep-rooted anti-intellectualism of the dominant pragmatism of our times, in the face of which the revolutionist feels himself powerless, from the standpoint of which he is condemned to futility; on the other, it is directed as a ferocious criticism against all those who merely theorize and do not act. The personal stake, paradoxically the stake of all implicated in society, thus becomes the criterion by which the revolutionist judges others and, certainly, himself—and (obviously, as the whole world proclaims), a stake in mere ideas is no stake at all.

For the conservative ideologists, whether of the right or left, the question of capitalism is fundamentally the question of private property, and the division into classes that such a categorization presumes, as sketched out in 'The Communist Manifesto' of Marx and Engels. For the New Left the inadequacy of this characterization stems from the impossibility of equating private property with persons, as involved in the growth of supra-individual property-owners and in corporate ownership; the development of privilege without any designation of this privilege as property; stemming from these the difficulties of delineating classes and their exploitative or progressive character; and most of all the disjunction between property in law and property in fact, and as a corollary of this, the disjunction between 'private' property in production

and 'personal' property in consumption. The New Left thus finds difficulty in subscribing unequivocally to an equation of the transcendence
of capitalism with the abolition of private property in its nineteenth-
century sense.

In the common ethos that informs the rank and file of the New Left,
capitalism is then identified with an amalgam of two concepts, one
drawn from the ethos of turn-of-the-century German Social Democracy
and Bolshevism, i.e. the power of money as embodied, theoretically, in
Finance Capital, the other drawn from a vulgar sociology of the present
day, i.e. the profit motive. These two economic determinants of the
inner reality serve to characterize the notion of capitalism and the doctrine of socialism aimed at its transcendence as an economic doctrine.
The configuration in society of this economic reality is fleshed out as the
concentration of power (certainly in post-War economic sociology,
though in some measure even in pre-War writings) and the *capitalist*
aspiration towards the containment and disruption of monopolies. The
New Left, though calling attention to the concentration of economic
resources, is centrally concerned with the coagulation *of political* power,
arguing for a connection between the two, but not making a direct
equation between them.

For the radical and revolutionary sects of the New Left, capitalism
itself cannot be encapsulated by depictions of its social configurations.
Marxist analysis has to inform, and be informed by the examination of
the individual, whether through the philosophy of existentialism or the
psychology of the personality. Thus capitalism itself comes to be defined
as 'inner reality'.

The most developed exponents of this theory of capitalism as an
inner reality are the French philosopher Sartre, and the German-
American philosopher Marcuse. The work of both of these takes the
form of a criticism of bourgeois humanism, the first from the pessimis-
tic standpoint of violence as the necessary bond at its basis and indeed
at that of any community, the latter from the standpoint of the pessimis-
tic disavowal of a dispensation from history that will transcend the
one-dimensional man that stands at the apex of bourgeois humanism.[2]
The earlier Gramsci, with his more optimistic, if only theoretical, thrust
towards a consideration of the problems of 'superstructure', locates the

---

[2] Jean-Paul Sartre, Critique of Dialectical Reason, New Left Books, 1976. I take
this to be implied in the discussion of Being-in-the group, pp. 581–93.

impasse of Marxism in a *concept* of ideological hegemony, one drawn on unconsciously, as spirit of the times, by both Sartre and Marcuse. In common sociological discourse this illumination of the inner realm as an asceticism with heroic overtones goes back to Weber himself.

The critique of revisionism is, in line with this, one directed at the inner world, but an inner world that finds expression only in an outwardly directed materialist metaphysic. For Charu Mazumdar and the terrorists, the critique culminates in the 'annihilation line'. The line itself becomes the critique of revisionism, unveiling the betrayal of the Revolution by the revisionists. It is what Mazumdar sees as his distinctive achievement and forms the distinctiveness of the Naxalite terror. To the revisionism of words it counterposes, as argument, the revolutionary act—and thus transposes the ground of metaphysics. It is, indeed, as the exploration of this ground that their existential ideology is elucidated. The appeal to truth becomes a matter of experience, rather than of fact—and there again, the privileged experience of the revolutionary cadre.[3] As such an unveiling, the 'annihilation line' brings to the surface the implicit metaphysical premises of Mazumdar's standpoint, a standpoint that informs his epistemology just as much as his ethics. In fact, ethics is epistemology here, for knowledge is partisan.

The Madhyabitta

The process, if such it is, of the evolution of the urban terrorism within the CPI(M-L) is one of the failure of the 'peasant line' to yield any lasting success, of the 'retreat' to the cities, and forced by the necessity of maintaining their distance from the revisionists (or indeed, of giving adequate expression to the sensibility that denounced the whole existing communist movement as revisionist) rushing headlong into the practice of terror.

When one speaks of the terrorists one is talking of intellectuals largely, for the most part students or ex-students, though of course others, among them industrial workers as well, though not as a significant proportion. The organizers of the CPI(M-L) too were, throughout, largely students or ex-students, and mainly from metropolitan centres.

[3] After these events, but elucidating in a more general way this partisan epistemology, see R. P. Saraf, *Scientific Dialectics*, which contends the 'dialectics' is only appreciable by one who adopts the proletarian standpoint.

Their interaction with the local cadre, led by the leaders' fulminations against revisionist organization to view even these leaders' authority as an unwarranted and revisionist imposition, certainly contributed to the disintegration of the party. Equally, the need for maintaining the established hierarchy in the interests of coherence and continuity in the face of these very leaders' avowals of accommodating the cadre in the leadership might well have contributed to the precipitation of the terroristic line, though not the terroristic ethos. The ethos clearly 'belongs' to the stratum of the intelligentsia who broke with revisionism. I put the 'belongs' in quotes not to show that there is a logical connection between the social circumstances of these revolutionaries and their thought, or even that there is a necessary progression in the evolution of communist culture of which these people, as embodiments, are the natural outcome, or even that by its nature terrorism is an ethos restricted to intellectuals, but because in the circumstances in which this occurred the ethos developed as the specific form of action (of the understanding of action) of this intellectual stratum. Others participated in terroristic acts, but not necessarily with this ethos. Indeed, the ethos made it possible for a large number of criminals to be turned overnight into heroes, who did not by that transformation undertake to share in the ethos itself.

To say that the revolutionaries (as they saw themselves) came from the bhadralok is today a commonplace. Though it is not possible from the existing evidence to prove any statement as to which section of the bhadralok the university students came from, it seems likely that most of them were madhyabitta, and certainly in Presidency College the large part of the students from *sahebi* backgrounds, or from families with overt sahebi aspirations seem to have kept away from the movement, though some of them did join. In the case of the schoolboys, however, one can be more specific and locate the support for the so-called 'cultural revolution' exclusively among children of the madhyabitta, considering that the English-medium schools were not harmed.

The revolutionaries themselves, however, even if they talked of themselves as madhyabitta occasionally in conversations, saw themselves essentially as belonging to the petty-bourgeois class of the Orthodox Marxist schema—neither bourgeois nor proletarian but somewhere in-between, though not necessarily owners of petty property. (It is, of course, intriguing theoretically as to whether the privileges enjoyed by this class are compatible with traditional notions of property, or entail the necessity for a deep revision of the notion of property, but I shall not go into that here.) As petty bourgeois, the large majority of college students at least saw themselves as belonging to a fundamentally despicable stratum of society, largely redundant in the revolutionary process, until they made a conscious effort to change themselves. Guilt was not altogether absent from their enthusiasm for the agrarian poor who were exploited, since certainly few if any of them suffered from a sense of personal injustice as cause for joining the movement.

Though informed by this guilt, their appropriation of the class-identity imposed on them by the metaphysic was essentially a nihilist one, akin to Heine's support of proletarian revolutionaries convinced that with their power his *Book of Songs* would be used 'by the grocer to make paper-bags to hold coffee or snuff for the old women of the future'. This appears most clearly in their rejection of theory of a conventional kind, and their search for a new kind of theory, as in the old communists' search for a new kind of party. In the case of the schoolboys, the guilt perhaps did not run as deep, as clearly they could see more privileged sections of their own stratum going to English-medium schools, though certainly they did not because of that see themselves as vanguards of the revolution (a positive self-definition) or even as essential parts of the revolution, as the official theory had it, else they would have attacked English-medium schools as well. The sense of personal devaluation, so strong among the college students, must have existed among them as well if one is to account in a satisfactory way for their attacks being limited by and large to the institutions they were in. True, it is not possible in the examination of their motives to exclude gratuitous insult to authority or at any rate a revolt against it, but this too in a muted form dictated by the fundamentally nihilistic perception of the world and primarily (*as* nihilism) of self.

With the development of student violence in Calcutta, the revolutionary leadership, principally Charu Mazumdar and Saroj Dutta, bent over to accommodate it in their theory and laid emphasis on the *revolutionary* character of this petty-bourgeois class. It was on these grounds that Mazumdar rebutted the criticisms raised against the terrorism in Calcutta. That he was bending, however, despite the revolutionary role attached to this class in the overall schema of the People's Democratic Revolution, is attested to by his many admonitions to the college students to 'integrate' with the peasantry. The subtle shift from 'fundamental' to 'operative' ideology, so subtle as to have been glossed over by contemporary apologists for Mazumdar, was organizationally and politically of the utmost importance, and spiritually in the case of Mazumdar and his devouter followers fuelled the subsequent pronouncement about the New Man.[4] Certainly the Calcutta terror enhanced the enthusiasm of Mazumdar (if not all his followers) to the extent that he could see the seventies as the decade of liberation. Mazumdar saw in these youth, petty-bourgeois or not, a developing cadre (or so he thought) free from the sin of original revisionism that lay at the heart of the existing communist movement and its cadre. And what argued for this freedom was their spontaneous and (or so Mazumdar thought) unselfconscious violence, their active will to destroy, their *unspoken* nihilism.

Elements of Naxalism which are common to the whole of the Indian intelligentsia, such as the devaluation and forceful overturning of the Gandhian dictum, need to be distinguished from the elements of the ideology specific to Bengal and at the root of the widespread and brutal terror in Calcutta. As one of these, perhaps one of the most important, the slogan 'He who has not dipped his hand in the blood of class enemies can hardly be called a communist' plays such a crucial role in the transformation of the agrarian line into one of urban terror and determines the form it takes. Blood, of course, is a resonating term in any culture, and most revolutionary rhetoric toys with it. It would be significant to recall the 'Blood' written on the wall with the spilt wine in Dickens' *A Tale of Two Cities* with the ominous warning from the author that there would be a time when that vintage too would flow abundantly.

As I have shown in Chapter 3, the associations of blood are, quite clearly, not the same in Bengal, apart, of course, from the equation of *roktopat* (bloodshed) with violence. To convey the Bengali significance of blood, I shall again quote a passage, cited earlier in Chapter 3, for ease of argument here.

---

[4] The distinction is made by *Martin Seliger, The Marxist Conception of Ideology*, Cambridge University Press, 1977:

'Party ideologies, and also the more abstract political philosophies (when they refer to matters of immediate political significance), must relate to circumstances which demand compromise over, and even contradiction of, some of their basic tenets. Since in the course of such deviations fundamental principles are not necessarily renounced or altered, all political argumentation normally bifurcates into two interacting and intersecting dimensions: the dimensions of fundamental and of operative ideology, as I call them.' p. 4.

Rokto [blood] is a Bengali construct which refers to blood as a substance, enduring and persistent, a permanent attribute which is recognized in the male line,
transmitted by men through the reception and acceptance (grohon kora) of the
male seed (sukra, bij) by women after marriage. Blood is shared by all persons in
the male line, and the direction of the line itself is recognized through lines from
male to male. Blood then is a symbol for a relationship among persons and
groups of persons. It differentiates classes of relationships and categories of related
persons. It expresses one of the most important concepts in what, by now, we
may call Bengali kinship: the idea for a certain kind of relatedness in conjunction
with the idea of the person, the idea of relative, the idea of marriage, the ideas of
issuance and linearity—all of which together define 'kinship' in Bengal.[5]

and

Blood (*rokto*) creates semen, several drops of the former to one of the latter.[6]

Both of these serve to show how the act of killing 'class enemies' is
equated with depriving them of their virility; how the whole class of
'class-enemies' are rendered of the same stock, though only by implication, in that the blood of one class enemy is much the same as that of
another; and how the 'annihilation line' is to be equated with uproot-
ing the whole class. True Charu Mazumdar in the 'murder manual'
hopes that this is what the peasants will say, but it enters very definitely into his own conception of the revolutionary communist, in so
far as this revolutionary communist is one who is 'integrated' with the
peasantry. In the case of the followers who practised the terror, the
slogan was of course interpreted as what perhaps it was meant to be—a
dividing line between communists and revisionists. But the most interesting of all are the fewer cases in which the injunction was interpreted
literally and hands were dipped in blood. Here the substance becomes
the embodiment of the symbol premised on it—a total inversion of
'reality'.

A second connotation of blood is the association with blood-
sacrifice, such an accepted part of the Calcutta way of life with its Kali
temple, for the intent, obviously, is not to kill all class enemies one by
one but to 'release the initiative of the masses' and, functionally, to rob

[5] Lina Fruzzetti and Akos Östör, 'Seed and Earth: A Cultural Analysis of Kinship
in a Bengali Town', *Contributions to Indian Sociology* (NS), Vol. 10, No. 1
(1976), pp. 111–12.
[6] Ibid., p. 121.

the administration of its eyes and ears.[7] The orgiastic-shamanistic goes hand in hand with the manipulative strategic so characteristic of the symbolic degradation of Reality or Being.

Nihilism

It is only to be expected that in a culture so dominated by politics as the Indian, the crisis of culture should only appear in an event of the highest political significance.[8] That the quarter from which this criticism of culture emanated should itself hold politics to be of fundamental significance, should see the world itself determined essentially in its political perspectives, and should seek to subordinate all its activities to a 'political' goal, is not accidental. As the radicals of the CPI(M-L) put it and as many leftists of all hues still proclaim—'Politics in command!' That within the CPI(M-L) this politics came increasingly to be inter- preted in an abstract and then a symbolic manner, and finally identified itself with a peculiar form of psychological theory, cannot detract from the fact that for these radicals the reality of the world was in the last instance 'political'. But in this politicization of everyday life one should not lose sight of the fact that here there is a peculiar understanding of the word 'political', and there is a peculiar mode of conceptualization through which even economic terms come to be understood *psychologically*, and the whole drama of politics takes on a subjective-cultural cast.

What has happened here is of the utmost importance—one area of rational, conscious culture—the 'political' in the revolutionaries' termi- nology—has been superimposed on the whole of culture, and it is only within these confines that the reality of the world is interpreted. The 'method', if indeed one can reduce this procedure, its dynamic and its motivations, purely to a question of method, is not without historic

[7] This is not as far-fetched as it seems. Consider in this context the meaning and resonances of a humorous story current in Naxalite circles at the time of the terror:

A young Naxalite is spotted by someone at a Durga Puja *pandal* during the festivities then and challenged with his atheism. Without hesitation the Naxalite replies '*Ma-o to naksal*' (The Mother too is a Naxalite), punning on 'Mao'.

[8] Culture is not here used in the narrow meaning of Saroj Dutta's epithet of a 'cultural revolution' for the Naxalite urban violence, but in the encompassing sense in which economics is part of culture.

precedent; most notably in the work of Marx himself where the attempt is to impose the functioning of 'economic' categories onto the totality of the social world as it is perceived. But, as in the case of Marx's 'economics', the revolutionaries' 'political' comes to have a wider significance and a more specialized use than the term has in everyday life. And, as in the case of all attempts at a justificatory metaphysic of action, the wellsprings and essential character of their own conceptual system, and indeed their very action itself, escapes the formulations designed to orient and explain them. Not a small part of this failure is attributable to the generalized use that the term 'political' comes to occupy in the revolutionaries' rhetoric. But the more significant causes of this failure lie in what the mode of understanding conceals, the area of experience that it does not care to formulate, in those elements of history and psychology that *underlie* the whole conceptual system of this ideology. Needless to say, the revolutionaries lacked the intellectual sophistication and the conceptual system to undertake such a 'self-examination', if indeed they ever had the motive for it. Nevertheless, the revolutionaries were convinced of the momentousness of both their action and their way of looking at the world. In this they were not mistaken, whatever may be the case with regard to the truth of the statements that they regarded to be self-evident. The period of terror in Calcutta and elsewhere in the world today is a question that aesthetics and social theory must come to terms with, if it is to make any claim to seriousness.

The supremacy accorded to politics in the media, and the overweening dominance demanded by political life in the revolutionaries' point of view, draw from different sources. The dominance accorded to politics in the media draws from the poverty of Indian society, and, one is tempted to say, intellectual life. Any attempt at a development of culture not organically linked to the traditional mould immediately becomes suspect and provokes the whole argument of the scarcity of resources and the strategic deployment of effort to meet the absolute necessities for sustaining social life. Despite this burden of poverty, culture has grown and *that* is the surprising fact, and not the derivative character of the work and, indeed, of the mentality of the avant-garde.

The revolutionaries, by contrast, saw in the predominance of politics an ethical imperative. It was not merely the case that in a country as poor as India it was irrelevant, even perhaps criminal, to demand more of culture than that it be used for the furtherance of political ends. The fact of the matter (to them) was that no matter how divorced from political or economic life culture or art may seem to be, it pursues (actively in most cases) political ends. In the last analysis there are only two kinds of culture—that *for* the people, and that *against* the people. Called upon to act, one must choose wisely and take care to see that one is actively for the people, if one is not to become historically entirely irrelevant. And as culture is in essence political, political life is the supreme expression of culture (even perhaps the indicator of 'being cultured'). Participation in the revolution is the highest activity to which people can aspire, and this participation demands that one bring political analysis to bear on all aspects of human life, and pursue in each case, and militantly, the interests of the people. We have thus two orientations to the supremacy of politics: the media pander to prevalent tastes and the revolutionaries attempt to change these tastes. There is however in the revolutionary attempt to change the prevalent tastes the assumption that the taste which accords supremacy to politics is a revelatory one. To the revolutionaries it reveals the fundamental character of the world they inhabit and provides the yardstick for measuring the worth of things. The difference in orientation only serves to underline the essential similarity of both—in that both attach the greatest importance to politics and to political events.

And yet the outbreak of the Calcutta terror, in spite of the fact that it was primarily a political event, owes its importance to its general cultural significance, rather than its purely political repercussions, even though these are hardly to be overlooked. The Calcutta terror was not a mass event like the Jacobin terror, yet it incorporated elements of that precedent while remaining fundamentally different. This fundamental difference concerns the internal orientation of the persons concerned and the role played by the terror in the two cases. In the one case it is linked with the realization of humanitarian goals, while in the other it is part of a process, and a mechanism of the expression of an ethos. In the one case it is organized, systematic and partakes of the nature of a spectacle, in the other it is the acting out of a symbolic rite that purifies, elevates and is by this fact part of the dialectic of emancipation. In the one case it is an affirmation of 'the general will', in the other it is an anticipation of this will. Both are negative and in that sense both are involved in a historic act of rejection, but the sentiments and personal reality underlying the two are fundamentally different. While the Jacobins merely realize the implicit, the Calcutta revolutionists are concerned with the explicit, despite the fact that they too can be considered in a sense the heirs of Jacobinism. The essential break with history, never achieved by the French Revolution, lies in the case of the Charuists in the acting out of the drama of nihilism—and in this lies their importance.

It is difficult to offer a precise definition of nihilism, or to transcend the surface transparency of Nietzsche's discussions. Historically (though that is not the first time the word was used), the term first came into general use in Russia to define, significantly, a type of revolutionist—a revolutionist devoid of any particular goal towards which he wished to move.[9] 'Here is the ultimatum of our camp; what can be smashed should be smashed; what will stand the blow is good; what will fly into smithereens is rubbish; at any rate, hit out right and left—there will and can be no harm from it', says Pisarev in formulating the nihilist position as it evolved in the late 1850s and 1860s in Russia. The attitudes and goals of this Russian nihilism were acutely presented and popularized, however, by Turgenev and Dostoyevsky.

It is, perhaps, from Dostoyevsky's discussions, or rather presentation, of nihilists that Nietzsche takes his cue. But by the time the idea reaches Nietzsche, it has lost the necessary connection with revolutionism, and is reduced to the fundamentally atheistic position, i.e. the lack of any universal interpretation of the meaning and significance of human action. The question is obviously connected with ethical considerations and Nietzsche is acutely aware of, and attempts to combat, Ivan Karamazov's contention that if there is no God everything is permissible.[10] The outbreak of Russian nihilism found its belated counterpart in Europe in the explosion of Dada.[11] It was only Nietzsche, psychologist and seer, who saw in the outbreak of Russian nihilism the symptom of *Europe's* decay and the presentiment of the European future. In Nietzsche's interpretation of nihilism there has been accomplished a fundamental shift in its meaning, from that of political or social action to the denial—active or passive—of values, drawing from the premise

[9] The first use of the term 'nihilism' occurs as early as 1799 in the letter of the philosopher Friedrich Heinrich Jacobi to his colleague Johann Gottlieb Fichte quoted in Hans Kung, *Does God Exist,* translated by Edward Quinn, Collins, 1980. p. 388.

[10] Fyodor Dostoyevsky, *The Brothers Karamazov.*

[11] Hans Richter, *Dada, Art and Anti-Art,* London Thames and Hudson, 1965.

that no grounds for values can be seen to exist.[12] Thus, 'nihilism' itself denotes two separated (though interrelated, as I shall show) types of orientation to the world—the first active and revolutionist, the other passive and apathetic. The two types of nihilism—revolutionist and apathetic—seem to be distinguished from each other, at first glance, on the question of political activity. Whereas the revolutionist proclaims the necessity of political action, the apathetic nihilist would seem to withdraw into a private universe—just as meaningless as the public domain he abandons as futile. But this surface distinction is illusory—there is a fundamental bond between both these types of nihilism and it is quite easy and frequent for one to pass into the other. Active nihilism is distinguished from passive nihilism by being an assault on values whereas the latter is merely a living in devaluation. Active nihilism might well be a response to passive nihilism. Both the revolutionist and the apathetic nihilist measure the world by some criterion, find it wanting, *then* turn to discover that the criterion is groundless. The revolutionist then persists in his activity as sufficient justification for itself, whereas the apathetic one withdraws from any kind of engagement, since it makes little sense to stake anything where nothing fundamentally is at stake.

Two points need to be emphasized: that the chronology of disillusion and action need not necessarily coincide with the facts of biography of particular individuals and that what essentially joins both is a demand for a meaning in human events that both feel cannot be fulfilled by an appeal to 'the facts of the case'.

To draw out of nihilism its psychological implication—the valuelessness of the world and, more profoundly, the valuelessness of endeavour, is in a deep sense the feeling of the valuelessness of the self. This is indeed the saint's premise, as Nietzsche sees it—and Nietzsche's own! Obviously such a nihilism does not preclude simultaneously a sense of great personal worth, but even where this exists, the worth consists precisely in the insight into the intrinsic worthlessness of the world and the self.

In this psychological form the nihilism of the English-educated university Naxalites is the despair with an education that makes greatness or even relevance impossible, of the Bengali-educated schoolboys with an education doomed to mediocrity and the second rate. It is only the university students who challenge the Enlightenment and its heritage—but by turn-

[12] The metaphysic of the 'Will to Power', a work he did not himself present for publication, arguably puts forward such a ground explicitly. The question of 'Thus Spake Zarathustra' is too complex to treat of in such a brief space.

ing away from it! The schoolboys, on the other hand, who attack their institutions directly, challenge rather the vernacular education that is the inferior heir of the Renaissance, *because* it is inferior, and boring to boot.

The devaluation of life of which Nietzsche accuses the saints, the religious and the philosophers is an accusation, for he sees in this the cause of why they have been devalued and are no longer believed. It is thus in the affirmation of 'life' (as Will to Power) as the opposite of what the saints, the religious and the philosophers have believed that he wishes to establish his claim to credibility. A similar dynamic pertains to the Naxalites' turning away from the academic (the pursuit of truth) in favour of the political (the pursuit of power).

Nietzsche's own philosophizing on the question of nihilism, for all its subtlety and complexity never assumes explicit shape. Obviously it is not the Russian Nihilists that Nietzsche means, but something of which they themselves are a symptom. The closest he gets to explicitness is the unpublished 'Will to Power' (would he have published it?)—

What does nihilism mean? *That the highest values devalue themselves.* The aim is lacking; 'why?' finds no answer.[13]

Again, significantly here, it is a question of what it means rather than what it is, and the rhetorical 'why' has no predicate. And this is not accidental, for if we are to attach a meaningful predicate to this rhetorical why it can be no other than the 'life' that underpins the Nietzschean metaphysic. An explicit awareness of nihilism would perhaps entail the rhetorical question, deemed unanswerable on the ground of any idea—'Why live?', in the face of a life that reduces such a question to absurdity. It is thus that Nietzsche sees in Buddhism—which woos extinction—the archetypal form of passive nihilism. To interpret nihilism in terms of values or goals as he does is to be unaware of the vital ground of the question, and to distance it to the decency of ideals. And why he should do so is as manifest as his attacks on any justification of life—he seeks in the act of destroying to create his own for-what. This is the active nihilism he extols. It is of course the 'higher men' (of the Nietzschean rallying cries) who ask for an answer to 'why live?', an answer that will encompass their lives as a whole. But life itself is prior and *forms the necessary ground of the question.* Nietzsche's achievement as philosopher becomes the investigation of the vital form of the question, his achievement as nihilist the destruction of the Christian answer. For the 'herd', life by itself is sufficient.

[13] Friedrich Nietzsche, No. 2, p. 9.

It is difficult to find a philosophy more affirmative of life, not as principle but as assertion of its reality, than the philosophy of Gandhi. Life above all, and a human life is what it seems to proclaim and demand—even at the expense of desire of which it is fully aware. And this need finds its concentrated expression in the doctrine of non-violence, a doctrine which in the assertion of its own life asserts equally the life of others, as well as the others' awareness of this its own life—and this as premise rather than conclusion! Without awareness of this its internal character, the philosophy functions, nevertheless, as the official philosophy of the Indian polity. It is as this official philosophy that the Naxalites attacked Gandhism, and symbolically portraits of Gandhi. The official creed of non-violence is challenged on the grounds of its hypocritical character, and assaulted on the grounds of its untruth. Violence is asserted as the dominating and dominant reality of the social world. In this overturning of values, the inner experience is the withdrawal of all verity, that can only be reclaimed, and that too only momentarily, in the violent act. The act itself has acquired the contemplative character, the character of argument that it sees as the untruth in the highest ideals it negates, and wishes to refute, to destroy. The inner contradictory character of this nihilism, as indeed of all nihilism (which devalues the highest values as the form of their realization), expresses itself in the dilemma that as life is affirmed in opposition to abstraction, life itself is fundamentally defined and experienced as abstract.

The abstract nature of their experience of life is most easily pointed out as far as its connection to their behaviour is concerned in the Naxalites' choice of 'class-enemies' to annihilate. To begin with, of course, these are the jotedars, so that the abstraction of their theory is fleshed in an embodiment that coincides with the practice of their life. With the inauguration of the Calcutta terror, these come to be ordinary policemen, CPI(M) activists, petty oppressors, political opponents. The class-enemies become those who symbolically embody the opposition to the course of the Revolution. And this should come as no surprise. It is merely the working out of the abstract and symbolical experience of what this Revolution is to consist of, premised on an abstract and symbolical perception of one's own life.

Comments on the Terrorist's Inner Life

For the terrorist reality is subjectively constituted and put to the test in practice. The notion of test, of the separation of the wheat from the

chaff, is not elaborated into a principle of organization. The overweening concern with organization comes to flower in the sects from which
the terrorist movement arose. It is the denial of any principle other than
that of doctrine in the unification of the autonomous bands of terrorists
that lies behind the technicist elaboration of the doctrine. It marks, in a
certain sense, the reappearance of the condottiere, in the sense that it
postulates the essentially warlike constitution of society. What the symbolism consists in is the transformation of a metaphor for describing
reality into a standard for personal life. This should draw attention to
the point that it is this concern with the self and its salvation that constitutes the meaning of the cosmology.

Nihilism, which proclaims the extinction of self, may seem to be at
odds with the vehement assertion of individuality in terrorism. But the
seeming opposition is illusory, for the type of individuality that is
asserted is that which is brought about by the analytical reduction of the
self to the 'ego' and the subsequent reconstitution of the 'with-world'.
The principle that human life cannot have a meaning at a different plane
of existence from its practitioners devalues the world as the spirit to
'psyche', at the same time that this psyche assumes symbolical form.
This is the double transformation that characterizes the with-world of
the terrorists.

True, the terrorist is overtly concerned in theory with the with-world.
The form that this theoretical interest in the with-world achieves in
practice is the community of shrunken concerns that the terrorist constructs in his organization. Good cheer and bonhomie replace the
reaching out of person to person, and the rationale of the meaningfulness of the relations remains as nothing else than the participants'
closeness to death. The imminence of and struggle in the face of death
reaches out to bestow its meaningful touch—the supreme validation;
the situation to which it all boils down; the final arrival of the ultimate
analysis—upon the constitution of the terrorist group as a reality different from the exploitative reality that confronts it. This is an illusion, for
what is accomplished in reality is the internalization of the abstract form
of rational relations which are the rule in society. The with-world that
the terrorist postulates in theory, however, is the radical counter-position
to the one he encounters in experience. The with-world becomes
Utopia—for it is denied in life, both that of the social life to which the
terrorist counterposes himself, and that which he experiences in his own
organization.

Despite his simplicity in matters of dress or life-style or debate, the terrorist's soul has been seized by a total and unreasoning desire for greatness. The form in which this greatness is defined is however one of negation, of opposition. The positive on which this is based is never formulated in the terms of the life of the terrorist but in a rationalist historical metaphysic. The act of the terrorist, at the same time, by itself rules out any formulation of a *tradition* to which it is bound—a scheme of thought within which its specificity can be located and in terms of which its competence in arriving at adequate solutions or relevant formulations judged. This is not to say that different periods of history do not exhibit terrorism, nor to deny the uniqueness of the modern type of terrorism (terrorism in conditions of democratic political organization), or to rule out the possibility of collecting and indexing a literature of 'terrorist thought'. But to unravel the meaning of this thought one will necessarily have to refer to areas other than that of terrorist thought itself. One will have to define that Other in resistance to which the terrorist sees his self validated. The form of this Other is, however, split into varied aspects, which, to the terrorist, are related in a pragmatic hierarchy with a fundamental definition. The validation of his own activity as significant and crucial lies at the basis of this fundamental definition.

The heroism of the terrorist is not logically derived from the metaphysic of history which he puts forward as his theory of the universe, but from the cultural clichés of the dominant ethos (the film culture, perhaps). The paradigm of heroic activity is assimilated by the acceptance of that which defines the human situation essentially in the aesthetics of low-brow culture. In this general form it is perhaps true of all revolutionary heroism and does not pertain to just the terrorist. What distinguishes the terrorist from the 'run-of-the-mill' revolutionary is that in the terrorist's case the ethic of heroism has become the significant locus of meanings rather than the end to which meaning is directed. The end to which the heroism is directed has become symbolical, a 'demonstrative' act, in two ways—by being staged in full view of, and for the benefit of, the powers which it thus symbolically attacks, and by the character of the act as a ritual of validation, translating the metaphysic to reality, welding it to the personal sources of meaning.

The terrorist is at once defender of his faith and the proof of its truth. He, like the saint, has chosen to live out his life as an example. He has seized his life and plays it out in the full glare of the stage. But, as his life becomes totally public, his ethos becomes totally private. The ethos of the circles which the terrorist inhabits cannot be discussed except in the form of homilies and fables at a second remove. The closing of the circle of authenticity—in that he defends his faith by his acts both in an ends-means nexus and in a symbolical way (in that he is the proof of its truth)—and the taboo against discussion of the personal are caught up in the experience of the self as abstract. The experience of his personality as abstract confers on his intentions a tendency to re-establish this abstraction on a worldly footing. Personal—in a double sense, directed against persons, and implicating his own person—violence thus becomes a significant mode of re-establishing the continuity between self and world.

The terrorist mania, that special form of insanity into which the unadjusted ex-terrorist lapses—the fear of being watched, the necessity for secrecy, the need to attack as the best form of defence and a host of other symptoms—seems superficially merely a case of the internalization of the strategic conception of society long after it has become irrelevant. But as to why *this* is internalized rather than the populist behaviours can only be explained by the persistence of the need for heroic existence. This indicates that, at least in its pathological form, the heroic definition rather than the historic metaphysic is central to the terroristic sensibility. For if the latter were central the mania would be open to modification. This does not altogether clear up the issue and it leaves the question of the sane terrorist unresolved. The argument for the centrality of the heroic definition of the self can be easily stated—the historic metaphysic has the status of dogma with which the terrorist has no intimate or even informed acquaintance. Vietnam is in his heart. He must plot the course of action only after the initial commitment has been made. Truth is not defined in a scholarly way but in an existential way. True, to say that his truth is defined in an existential way only opens up the investigation of the specificity of this truth for the terrorist sect with which we may be concerned. The difficulty is that it is not formulated philosophically, but, as with the movement towards heroism, forms the essential underpinning of the mode of being.

What is the positive vision of the revolutionary? Marxism has left—and drawn attention to—the motivation to revolt on a humanist ground. When the positive vision shrinks to the bare necessities, what becomes of the orientation that sustains the revolutionary's life? It is such a question that reveals what is meant by the essential nihilism of Charuist communism. The ethic of the revolutionary expands to engulf the whole of society. The revolutionary standpoint is seen as one that reveals the essential structure of society. The complex of revolutionary motivations, not necessarily those of the revolutionary himself, is seen as the revealing analysis of the social dynamic. The glorification of the negative sentiments throws into sharp relief the hollow pretentiousness of the culture of affirmation. The definition of the self as essentially in revolt draws attention to the depths of the spiritual dilemma in which the self finds itself unable to answer the call of the Self and of the Other simultaneously in a way in which murderous violence is not also posed. The meaning of man at once shrinks to those relations known, and demonstrable, and expands to become itself a metaphor for the whole cosmos (as in some such work as Mao's 'On Contradiction'). The whole of civilization is thrown into question.

Complexity of doctrine, discursive dialectics, destroys, perhaps, the monumental solidarity of the terrorist organization. This is not to say that the terrorist sensibility is incapable of accommodating subtlety (as it demonstrably possesses in the ambivalence of its attitude to the ruling ethos), or indeed that the doctrine is inflexible (denied by the shifting alliances in the evolution of the terrorist group), but that as an *organizational* principle the terrorist demands a clear, unambiguous and simple definition of goals. This may be imperative for all mass political organizations. But the revolutionary—and terrorist—organization is not a mass organization. The simplicity of the organizational principles characteristic of mass organizations is adopted as a ruling principle by this terrorist elite, that sees itself as an elite, perhaps because any step beyond the superficial simplicities will open up the chasm of contradictory, ambivalent and self-defeating (in the psychic sense) motivations that lie at the root of the terrorist's commitment. This commitment, on the other hand, needs to be continually restated and reaffirmed, if by nothing else than the terroristic act itself. The perpetually threatened status of the spirit lies at the basis of this, as of the strategic conception of society. Both are projections of the state of the terrorist's soul.

In a very fundamental sense, the 'class hatred' that Charu Mazumdar ensconced at the heart of the revolutionary process was the central experience of self-hatred of the Naxalite terrorist. As Mao had taught 'Fight self. Repudiate revisionism.'

Chapter Eight

The Heritage

And yet we know well:
Even hatred of vileness
Distorts a man's features.
Even anger at injustice
Makes hoarse his voice. Ah, we
Who desired to prepare the soil for kindness
Could not ourselves be kind.
                    —B. Brecht, translated by Michael Hamburger

As human beings and historical events, the Naxalites have a good side and a bad, and as human their bad sides are inextricably entangled with the good in an ambiguity that makes unequivocalness difficult. It is not difficult to decide that the Naxalites could not have hoped to present a viable alternative, for it is events that have demonstrated that they could not in fact do so. But they did so hope. And it is in the ambiguity of their relation to this hope and ours that we enter the domain of ideology. 'Ideology' does not denote that precise schematization of the world of fact that constitutes science but delimits a world in which not only the facts themselves but the facticity of facts are in dispute, where we deal with the question of the value of things and not just their price.

Value as a fact of human existence is the irreducible datum of social science. Whether it is possible to have a non-evaluative conception of value has been in dispute ever since Weber broached the plea for a value-free sociology. Whereas in the terms of everyday language it is perfectly possible to be passionately idealistic and respect facts at the same time, it is not clear how in a profounder sense passionate ideals can leave one's sense of reality untouched, this apart from all purely cognitive consider-ations as to whether our theories fit our facts or mould our facts. It is as the dubiousness of the enterprise of social science that the concept of ideology stands vindicated by its appropriation into popular discourse. Considering the phenomena of social life, it is impossible to avoid the question of the value of value, and the profounder social scientists have not indeed avoided it. But if the ground of their concern with the subject was a vindication of their discipline, their discipline now well-established, our engagement centres about what has become its crucial concept, that of ideology.

The meaning the doctrine of the Naxalites appears to have for non-believers is different from what it had for the believers. This is patently indicated by the programme of agrarian revolution linked to a policy of urban terror. Observers, sympathetic to the Naxalites have upbraided them for their policy of 'individual terror' and pointed out its incompatibility with the 'mass line' entailed in the Marxist-Leninist theory of revolution to which the Naxalites vowed allegiance. What has escaped these observers, however, is the mystery of the emergence of this policy of 'individual terror' from the very principles of 'mass line' that they invoke. To construe it in terms of the dichotomy of the policy of 'individual terror' and the 'mass line' indeed obscures the possibility of understanding the phenomenon. Far rather, question the meaning of the texts in which sentiments such as the 'mass line' are expresed to elucidate their meaning for the terrorists. And certainly in this business of counter-posing 'mass line' to 'individual terror', the more fundamental shift of location from the countryside to the cities is obliterated.

When we deal with the texts of Naxalite views we are quite clearly concerned with an ideology—with a system of ideas designed to confer meaning on human activity. The further question as to whether we are here dealing with a false-consciousness is, however, premature, for before this question can be posed the meaning of the text itself needs to be settled—because of the divergence we have already noted. Before one can decide whether ideology is a false-consciousness, one must become aware that ideology may, prior to that, be a false appearance of consciousness, one that may even in fact contradict the very premises of this consciousness. This is certainly the case with regard to the Naxalites. Before admitting its plausibility as a general rule, certain observations on meaning are called for.

The very possibility of more than one meaning being construed from a text indicates the experiential character of meaning. Meaning might indeed be objective, as Weber holds, but its objectivity cannot be rooted in anything other than the subjective.[1] The realms of intersubjectivity that render meaning in a particular sense intelligible are equally objective, but no privileged objective can be set over against a spurious subjective (as Weber does in his crititism of Simmel) in deciding the validity of a particular interpretation.[2] Certainly there is the overt linguistic sense as an objectivity and the meaning appropriated by a particular group may contradict this and so stand revealed as merely subjective, but in the case of the Naxalites it is precisely this subjectivity objectifying itself in acts that we are concerned with. The linguistic litany conceals the framework that invests it with meaning. And the reason for this concealment is quite clearly the legitimation that has been recognized as the function of *all* ideology. This legitimation, however, is not to be understood so much as a *post-hoc* rationalization (of which there are certainly glaring instances in the history of the Naxalites, and most prominently in the view of urban events as a cultural revolution in Saroj Dutta's writings) as the very categories of the positing of the cosmos having an evaluative and thus legitimating character.[3] To think of the Naxalite consciousness in the terms in which it expressed itself is a contradiction in terms, a contradiction that informs the urgency and totality of this consciousness. To think of the deceptive expressions of this consciousness in the terms of this consciousness is, however, not a contradiction, and forms the intent of this interpretation.

The standpoint that illuminates the Maoist rhetoric of the Naxalites and informs it is a nihilist one. The experience of self from which the metaphysic of emancipation is elaborated is a profound awareness of the devaluation of values, at base the valuelessness of this very self. The vindication of the self turns about the attempt, futile, to transform it, the revaluation of the world about the attempt to destroy it. Violence, which mediates the relation of the self to itself and to the world, is elevated to the status of a universal principle that illuminates society at the same time that it devalues its supreme values. The deliberateness of this violence transforms both the inner world of the terrorist and the outward targets

---

[1] Max Weber, *The Theory of Social and Economic Organization,* trans. A. M. Henderson and Talcott Parsons, New York, The Free Press, London, Collier-Macmillan Ltd., 1964, p. 88.

[2] Ibid.

[3] As in *Poob Akash Lal,* CPI(M-L) publication, cited in Sumanta Banerjee, *In the Wake of Naxalbari,* p. 238.

against whom it is directed into symbols that invest meaning on an otherwise devalued and meaningless universe. The Maoist rhetoric, for its part, codifies this meaningfulness in a discourse of *social* liberation.

The shift in fundamental ontology unfolds itself as a praxis. And it is as a praxis, in its degraded form as technique, that it is elaborated in the thought of Charu Mazumdar. Mazumdar appropriates the Maoist categories, investing them with a psychological and symbolical content to enunciate the strategy of terror. The terror when it develops, elevates Mazumdar himself to the status of a symbolic authority, at the same time that it relegates his Maoist metaphysic to a litany.

The categorical import of violence is, nevertheless, embedded in a situation that is distinctively Bengali. Both in how they perceive themselves and how others perceive them the peculiarities of Bengali society are significant. Thus, psychologically speaking, the experience of devaluation manifests itself as an assault on the intellectuality which underpins the Bengali pride in being Bengali, transforming the act by which it is challenged (the terror) into an intellectual act. The response to them, conversely, whether in support of them as self-sacrificing idealists or in opposition to them as terrorists, grasps them, if at all, as an intellectual challenge. Socially, the basis of the terror lies in the intellectual strata. But for the understanding of the terror itself, the most important consideration is the specifically Bengali colouration of the way in which the Naxalite discourse was appropriated both by the Naxalites and those who stood apart from them.

The distance between a literate and an existential ideology is thus quite clearly demonstrable in the case of the Naxalites. Its more general incidence is indicated by the work of the same philosopher who undertook to elaborate the lineaments and significance of European nihilism—Nietzsche. In the Nietzschean criticism of Christianity as a formulation *of ressentiment,* the distance which separates an articulated literate ideology from an implicit but informing existential ideology is vividly presented, though in conformity with the Nietzschean metaphysics existential ideology has here a purely psychological cast. True, the divergence of theory from intent is explored, if only cursorily, in the work of Marx, and is embedded in the contemporary understanding of the word ideology itself. But in the Marxian schema there is a consonance between existence and theory that, at least, Nietzschean thought challenges.

It is, indeed, no accident that the philosopher of nihilism should have struck upon the distance between theory (literate ideology) and existence (existential ideology, if construed here only as psychology). It is only with the experience of the nothingness of values that the distance between their formulation as values and the reality that they encode assumes the dimension of a problem. The fit between Word and experience, uneasy at the best of times, develops here into a veritable contradiction.

The humanitarian appeal of the Naxalites is not only at odds with their inhuman methods but with their experience of their own humanity. Both in their awareness of not being part of the destiny-laden crushed humanity in whose name they exercise the terror, and in their experience of this hatred of themselves as the ground of verity, they contradict the letter and spirit of the humanitarian aspirations to which they claim allegiance. Their defense of communist dogma only develops as an attack on communist history and communist organizations. Their positive vision, that of Chairman's China, is only fleshed out as the negativity of Revolution and the abyss of terror.

It is the power and actuality of this No-saying, for which they were crushed, rather than the chimera of their Utopian yes, for which they were admired, that they owe their significance in history.

Indian Communism and the Idea of Revolution

In historical memory, communism is as old as the Buddhist sanghas. The ideal of a communally shared life is, however, in no way considered a solution to all the ills that plague humanity. This is the case in all the practising communist ascetic sects in history and in our own times. Communism as a solution to social antagonisms has, however, almost always been associated with violent and revolutionary aspirations. Violence against the materially privileged has been considered by all revolutionaries, and among them also the communists, a sine qua non of the establishment of their millennium. Their millenarian aspirations have, however, produced little but further violence, and on the few occasions on which they have managed to secure seats of power, they have started by employing violence on their own companions and in the end, have themselves become victims of this violence. As to whether widespread and near universal bloodshed can be prevented remains a moot issue, but for as long as a relative peace prevails, revolutionary communists are among those who preach the virtues of violence and revolutionary disorder. Of course, they themselves claim that their vehement and total commitment to violence and disorder is in the service of an ideal of a resolution of all social antagonisms, violence, and indeed, all human suffering. In Europe, where these peculiar creeds originated, communist aspirations were linked to Christian perspectives, and even today the morality proclaimed by revolutionary communists is kin to Christian ideals of harmony, their activities, however, often being anything but harmonious. Whether religious or anti-religious, whether revolutionary or peaceful, communism is a moral doctrine, however dubious the moral behaviour of some of its practitioners.

The obsession with the idea of revolution and indeed radicalism, the compelling desire to *be* a radical and a revolutionary, and to be appreciated as such, perhaps begins in Germany with the student of Hegel—a thinker who considered European civilization superior to all

212 / *The Naxalites and their Ideology*

others—who came to be called the Left Hegelians. Whereas these students considered Hegel to be thoroughly conservative, they attempted to draw support for their radical and revolutionary 'pretensions from his attempt to synthesize the revolutionary aspirations of the French dethronement of their king, Christian theology and morality, and the fledgling authoritarian German ambition for a place in the European constellation. Hegel deployed a superimposition of the mathematical distinction between 'a' and 'not a', the linguistic 'yes' and 'no' on human existence and the course of history and intellectual life, with which he was only vaguely familiar. Through this process, he proclaimed an evolution through mutual antagonism and tension, culminating, of course, in the mind or spirit of Hegel himself who thought he had finally penetrated the logic of human achievement and was its absolute embodiment. His own grandiose view of himself was, in his mind or spirit, merely the philosophical expression of the fledgling German State, the absolute realization of the Christian God in the world. Drawing on such transcendent immanentism and its relative partisanship with the negative, the Left Hegelians in their various ways, posed as the revolutionary liberators of German, ergo human thought. One of these, Feuerbach, found the worldly embodiment of the Christian ideal of love in socialist and communist ideals. Drawing on all of those, Karl Marx, a Jew-turned-Christian-turned-militant atheist, claimed to have proved that in his works the inevitability of communist revolution had finally arrived as the end and goal of human aspirations from its beginnings.

From its probable beginning in the pamphlet of Lala Har Dayal while he was a student at St. Stephen's College, Delhi, Indian revolutionary communism has been permeated with this radical posturing. However, this is a posturing informed by an urgent and insistent angst to achieve the unprecedented and a consuming rage against the hollowness and shallowness of customary life. The desire to *be* a revolutionary and to *make* revolution is, in the case of the Indian communist, considerably at a loss as to what to do. The European Marxist cast(e) of this doctrine, and its early voluntary abdication of independent thought to the leadership of Stalin at the helm of the Third Communist International, has kept it anaesthetized to the customary life of the Indian population, however much at odds the doctrine is with all its ideals and values. Of course, in this, it is hardly alone. That faction of the huge nationalist upsurge that convinced the monarch of England and the British Isles to withdraw from India and then occupied the seats of power in this country, felt that the enslavement of India was a product of its loss of a scientific temper and that this fabled beast was the secret and the heart of the British and European superiority. It found itself in the same predicament as the communists—out of sync with the population it governed and administered—and busily set about trying to create clones through an ambitious educational thrust to transplant European learning to India and hopefully, some day, to beat the Europeans at their own game.

From the beginning, communists in India were faced with the dilemma of making revolution or organizing the masses. The birth of the Communist Party, as of a whole spectrum of socialist sects, is caught up with attempts to create mass organizations to transplant a European millenarian idea into the soil of an Indic self-absorption. From the early period, imitating the Hindu terrorists of 'Anushilan' and 'Jugantar', Bhagat Singh is among the revered martyrs of both the nationalist and communist causes. At just about the time of independence, there were two revolutionary episodes in the Communist Party, one the separatist Telangana movement and the other the abortive urban insurrectionary adventure under the leadership of Ranadive. Somewhat later, the Tebhaga movement in Bengal raised revolutionary hopes. For the most part, communists collaborated with the government and participated in the electoral process and trade union movement, contesting the ruling party where they could, provoking confrontation when it was possible, and using violence, though rarely armed, as often as possible. They were elected to power in Kerala under the leadership of E.M.S. Namboodiripad, though the government was later dismissed by presidential decree. The socialist spectrum included, as it does now, *all* the political parties in India contending for power, with the exception of the short-lived Swatantra Party founded by C. Rajagopalachari. However, before the 1960s, communists tended to be looked at askance, even though the word 'revolution' was never unacceptable. The French Revolution, the Industrial Revolution, the Bolshevik Revolution, and the Chinese Revolution were almost universally held in high esteem by intellectuals. Stalinism was contested by some, though certainly not by the majority, and vehemendy was upheld by the communists (it is worth mentioning here as an aside, that at the beginning of the disintegration of the Soviet Union, when the BBC had already broadcast the detention of Gorbachev under the excuse that he had been taken ill, the Indian government insisted on affirming this excuse, despite being in full knowledge of its falsity). Before the 1960s, there was considerable anti-communist sentiment in the country, not, as now, against their perceived double standards of an affluent lifestyle with protestations of partisanship with the deprived, but against their anti-property doctrine, their so-called materialism, and their violent practices. A strong, though not the ruling faction of the Congress Party was opposed to communism and the communists, though parties and sects hostile to the communists and communism, like the Rashtriya Swayamsevak Sangh (RSS) and the Proutist Bloc, were persecuted. In general, independence and the transfer of power had purged the ranks of those permitted a voice and a place in the educational establishments and the corridors of power of all non-Europeanist and anti-Europeanist elements.

For the most part in India, the popularity of the idea of revolution among the intellectuals to whom it appeals is that of a revolution in ideas. It is as an experience of conversion, *mata parivartana,* to begin with on a personal and then on a social scale, that the idea of revolution holds its greatest fascination for intellectuals, whether Indian or European—the perspective of a transformation of human mentality, of the human mind and heart and soul. It is customarily argued that Europe, the history of which is taken to begin with the founding of the temple of Apollo at Delphi in ancient Greece, has evolved through three stages to the present, the ancient, medieval, and modern, marked by different human orientations, mentalities, social arrangements, and ways of life. The times, the spirit of the times, and what is crucial to them, the human spirit, are argued to have evolved through three stages from the sixth century BC to the present. The non-European parts of the globe, particularly those older than the ancient Greek do not fit into this schema, though Marxists and particularly the Indian Marxists attempt to superimpose this pattern in toto onto what we know of India's past. In any case speculation, reflection, and debate about modernity has become a global feature and a variety of views is being advanced about modernity, our understanding of our own times, where we stand with respect to the past, and crucially, our probable future.

Of course, Indic and Islamic conceptions of time and history, theories of the human spirit, its nature and evolution, are quite different, as, need I add, the Christian including the European Christian. The European Christian view of history, inscribed into the Julian calendar used worldwide, divides time and history, the destiny of human life and the human spirit, with respect to Jesus Christ. All that comes before his birth is of one kind, all that follows is another. Modernity, in European Christian reflection, is a time of decay and moral decline, a precursor if not harbinger of doom and extinction, the cataclysmic and final Day of Judgement. Islamic views, kin to this, see doom and extinction imminent, and divide the calendar with respect to the life and times of Muhammad, but despite considerable historiography, do not offer much in the way of cosmic historical speculation, though marked by a deep and wide-spread perception of crisis (it is worth mentioning here, that some Muslims see the present as potent with the possibility of the Islamization of the globe). The Indic conceptions are perhaps the most far-ranging, and divide cosmic time into a regular cycle of the repetition of four *yugas* or ages, *Sat* or *Krita Yuga, Treta Yuga, Dwapar Yuga,* and *Kali Yuga* of falling moral worth and arrangements, marked by a cataclysmic *pralaya* or annihilation of differing scope and intensity, depending on the time-cycle, at the end of Kali Yuga. In the Indic view, we are in Kali Yuga and approaching pralaya.

The Europeanization of the globe has globalized the usage of the term 'modernity', and universalized perhaps the idea of modernity. The current concern and reflection about modernity is, to my mind, a grappling with the issues of the plurality of culture, differing conceptions of life, time, humanity, and history, itself a symptom of the decline of European hegemony and its universalizations, though heir to its globalization of intellectual life and rhetoric. No matter what the views to which we personally subscribe, our times are fraught and critical. However, the progressivist view of modernizers, which is the mentality of most ruling governments, remains most optimistic and complacent. Communists and their sympathizers in India, simultaneously products and agents of such Europeanization, share the sense of crisis and its millenarian import, consumed by desires to be active for such change, if only and for the most part as ideologues, claiming with the philosopher Marx that 'Philosophers have only interpreted the world, the point, however, is to change it'. The point at which such perceptions of the point coalesce and become pointedly critical, both personally and collectively for the Indian communists, is the *idea* of revolution.

Indian communist theory revolves around the idea of revolution, the question of its nature, the characterization of its stage (that is, a conceptual sum of the current situation in terms of Marxist and Leninist, and not to forget, Maoist rhetoric), and the issues of strategy and technique for precipitating this their overriding aspiration. The whole discourse is carried out in the esoteric jargon of the Marxist sects of the times, with what relation to the activity of these ideologues and their followers, it is difficult to say. Nevertheless, in this commitment to the revolutionary ideal, the valorization of violence for the sake of violence, though restricted to those whom the communists claim as their agents, is the overriding tenor of their rhetoric. Violent aggressiveness, termed militancy, is to them indicative of the revolutionary fervour that they themselves believe distinguishes them and that they wish to inculcate and see enacted in and by the masses. Such theory has informed the communist and revolutionary socialist sects in their organizational wrangling of leadership status. None of the communists in India claim to believe that communism is on the agenda. Most of them do not even believe that socialism is on the agenda, which in the work of Marx was supposed to precede mil-blown communism. Yet they feel an overriding urge to perpetrate violence and topple the government, and rule themselves. For most of them, if not all, their ideas remain at a remove from their personal feelings and lives, the idea of revolution being the only coalescence of personal feeling and public rhetoric. Most of the parliamentary communists have arrived at a conclusion that 'the time is not ripe' for their revolution. They content themselves with organizing, indoctrinating, and seeking votes, of course with a 'militant' edge to their activities. However, the revolutionaries amongst them and alongside them and opposed to them, of whom there are a not inconsiderable number are busy devising and arguing about ways to precipitate a revolution that will catapult them into power. There are some among them who are willing to be anonymous servants and sacrifice themselves for this ideal of power for the underprivileged, but only a select few. These few tend to see themselves as the incarnations of the revolutionary desires of the underprivileged and feel themselves called upon to serve by leading and ruling. For the most part, the ideal of revolution goes hand in hand with the aspiration to power, enacted preliminarily in the power to precipitate and make revolution.

The ideal of revolution takes a whole variety of forms all over the world. The sharing of a rhetoric of revolution makes for a solidary mutual back-scratching. From professional chairs in Europe and America to fashionable raggedly dressed students in the premier educational institutions of India to disaffected youth in the provinces itching to brutality, the revolutionary inspiration forms a chain of complicity and cupidity that makes for the possibility of a brilliant career peddling or claiming to peddle revolution. At the same time, the general tenor of European and Europeanized letters and academics, so at odds with the attitudes and orientations of even the European and American public, and in India at loggerheads with the sentiments of the lay public, itself inclines not only to a sympathetic toleration of such rhetoric, but an active inculcation of extremist and radical hype. Needless to say, this has not always been the case. Over the years since the end of the World War and exponentially since the sixties of the last century, the slow tide is almost now a deluge. Hardcore conformity demands a rhetoric of radical non-conformity.

Indian revolutionary pretensions have come a long way, when self-confessed partisans of a communist revolution—like the parliamentary communists—are active in trying to suppress communist revolutionaries, like the Naxalites, who take the terminology of revolution at face value as an injunction to kill and destroy. The face-off, if face-off it is, and not as usual in Indian politics, inside conspiratorial complicity and politic stratagem of convenience, changeable at a moment's notice, in the interests of power, is at its sharpest in Bengal, the scene of most of the earlier events outlined in this book. This book left Bengal with the crushing of the Naxalbari outbreak and the disintegration of the impulse to organize revolution, with the destruction of the organizations of revolutionaries inspired by Naxalbari and the leadership of Charu Mazumdar—raised to the status of the veneration of a cult by these very events. In what follows, I will try to sketch the subsequent follow-up leading to the looming of the Naxalite menace as again a spectre haunting Indian hopes of peaceful development—though, paradoxically, despite their considerably enlarged scope, nowhere considered as much of a threat as in the earlier events when they were a miniscule faction of perhaps largely symbolic relevance, except for the events of the Calcutta terror. The growth of the Naxalite influence in recent times still takes its inspiration from the events of Naxalabari and the leadership of Charu Mazumdar. But though violent events are more widespread, there is nowhere near the sense of threat and imminent catastrophe that marked the scene in earlier times. Part of it, no doubt, is a habituation to the sense of crisis and a living with uncertainty that continues to spread and grow more intense in a whole variety of ways, and not because or not merely because, as revolutionary communists like to believe, a communist revolution is imminent. Further, the Naxalite depredations are in regions of peripheral relevance to the governance and revenues of the country. Also, though a steady trickle of the highly educated still takes to revolutionary ways, we are nowhere near the critical situation in premier establishments that characterized the earlier events. One may also attribute the relative ease about the Naxalites to the shift in the intellectual ambience. The idea of communist revolution, once so dangerous to pedagogy, especially in institutions of higher learning, is now almost a settled orthodoxy touted from these establishments themselves, or at least never overtly challenged or disputed in the halls of academics, the opposition taking the form customarily of careful avoidance or oblique and muted aspersions of doubt. In this exodus from a freak fringe fashion of self-aggrandizing intellectuals to an entrenched political correctness, the idea of communist revolution has radically altered its non-conformity though not its non-conformist pretensions. Like the idea of equality, preached in our times by lords and ladies, the idea of revolution has become almost a settled mainstay of the workaday lives of university teachers and students. Where it is all leading is plain to those not overly educated. For the educated, perhaps a return of disputatiousness might prove useful.

Fresh Takers for the Mouldering Idea

The coming of age of the post-World War II generation in the sixties and seventies of the last century saw an explosive revival of the idea of communist revolution. Its icons were Mao, Che Guevara, and the Vietnam War. The Naxalites of India were part of this general discontent and what is more, tended to see themselves as so, even though not overtly allied with political activities at the international level. Bred in a progressive atmosphere of peace, party to its security, and avid consumers of its progressivist idealistic rhetoric, the generation found themselves party to a disillusion with conformity and sought their variable liberation or nirvana in drugs, sex, music, and politics. The Naxalites were the most extreme of this outburst of dissent.

Though the Naxalites take their name from the incident at Naxalbari in 1967, the defining attributes of the Naxalite view of revolution emerged only later. What was evident even at the time of the Naxalbari episode was only the aspiration to precipitate a revolutionary outbreak and the claim that in this confrontation, what was at stake was not material gain, but political power. What this might entail or how it could be intensified and spread was not clear at the time, and the following events and the growth of the cult of Charu Mazumdar is an experiment in and elaboration of just such an attempt. From the beginning, it was not the labouring poor of the nation or Bengal that Charu Mazumdar addressed, but first, the disaffected revolutionary activists within the communist movement and later, 'student-youth' (*chhatra-jubok*). His concern, throughout, was to commit them to a struggle for political power, and through and by their leadership engage the whole of the nation in a violent and protracted civil war. That he claimed to see such a war as already having begun was part his mystical-symbolic interpretation of the course of international and national history and part his conspiratorial view of this history as controlled by scheming manipulators. The sources of his revolutionary optimism were disaffected middle-class revolutionaries and student—youth with the potential to unleash the class-hatred of the labouring poor.

The most significant essay of Charu Mazumdar as far as the Naxalite desire to unleash violence is concerned is of course, 'A Few Words about

Guerilla Action', justly well-known as the 'Murder Manual'. It instructs revolutionaries to whisper into the ear of a likely candidate of the rural poor the suggestion to kill the local landlord, against whom the poor man is supposedly burning in hatred. With the deal fixed, the revolutionary is to organize a murder band in secret, kill the offending person, and the band to disperse to previously prepared hide-outs. When things have cooled somewhat the band is to return, harvest the enthusiasm at the murder with more secret organizations, and so on. At one stroke, the strategy removes all the paraphernalia of proselytizing and preaching Marxism–Leninism, and Mao-Tse-Tung Thought, or what have you, or organizing the rural (or urban) poor, and precipitates the rule of violence. This, to Charu Mazumdar's mind, and the minds of those who followed and still follow his lead and inspiration, was the 'creative' deployment of Marxism–Leninism, and Mao-Tse-Tung Thought. It was singularly opposed to the general tendency of communist attempts at organization, which Mazumdar and his followers saw as a futile parroting of its phrases and an attempt to unite the poor to repeat and further propagate these phrases. The conspiratorial murder gang replaces the time-honoured classes or study circles that had been held by the communists and revolutionaries among the labourers and assorted sundry (including, of course, middle-class intellectuals) to organize them for revolution. It also obviates all theoretical and philosophical rumination, heart-burning, and speculation both as to the state of affairs and the strategy and tactics one needs to adopt to organize a revolution—the burden of communist and even Naxalite 'theory', or what passes for it, even today. In these so-called theoretical exercises and disputations, oriented—as we are well aware—to unleash violence, the relations between the discussants and disputants turn, not infrequently, violent and murderous themselves. So, the vista of the so-called communist movement both internationally and nationally is one of mutually warring groups, each trying to kill the other when not actually engaged in killing 'class enemies'—unsuspecting policemen on duty, paid employees of the government, farmers or businesses, or the Tsar—of whom the dissenting faction is taken to be the most dangerous and violent. It took Charu Mazumdar, a Brahmin landlord from the foothills of the Himalaya, to unveil the ideal of revolution, touted even more stridently and ubiquitously by the Western and the Westernized well after these events, as the naked doctrine of murder by a gang of those dedicated (or consecrated?) to murder.

What remain are pretensions to the conquest of a property-less Utopia, though it does not figure anywhere even near the agendas of revolutionaries and avowed communists, and to the forcible interference of governments in ownership and personal property. This is the ideological nexus of the so-called 'liberal' and 'leftist' staple of the Western and Westernized academies and educational establishments, that the Indian government seems to see as the guarantee of its staying in power in the country, its sure road to all-round prosperity, and the ground of its ability to compete with and hopefully, some day in the not-too-distant future, outstrip the West. As for doing away with the sense of personality and personal ownership by the regulation of labour, property, and goods, it suffices to say that the enjoyment of the world and its goods is a personal choice and not a shared one. Foregoing these can hardly be enforced and is necessarily voluntary. My aspirations to status, respect, admiration, and power and pelf are neither open to scrutiny nor can they be murdered out of existence. My relinquishing of these can only be a personal decision, not open to even the most efficient of secret police organized by rulers. As for the so-called redistribution of wealth by governments, the large bulk of it serves to siphon goods and money from the Third World to the West, the rest to trap the unwary into suicidal sacrifice, and the people's spending sends the currency into the inflationary climb through which the government cheats those foolish enough to repose their trust in its manipulatory machinations. All governments, deeply in debt, reward those in power with a life-style of the grandeur of the most opulent of monarchs of the past, in addition to such personal gains as these are able to garner for themselves. Soviet Union or no Soviet Union, People's Republic of China, People's Republic of Vietnam, Cuba, Great Britain, or sovereign, democratic, socialist republic of India, all bear witness to this tendency.

In any case, what fires communist revolutionaries was not and is not the hope of a Utopia of the end of hatred entailed in what they see as class conflict, their outcries against exploitation and social inequality notwithstanding. Nor are the relations between individual communists particularly friendly or loving, even though they address each other as 'comrade'. The Naxalite fervour, as I suspect any and all revolutionary fervour, is not the hope of a golden future, but despairing violent anger at the unacceptability of the condition of things, when it is not itself an outright lust for power that they proclaim as their avowed end. It is the deep and sharp intensity of these emotions of hatred, produced paradoxically by a simultaneous aspiration to the highest values and an experience of their emptiness (when it is not just out and out envy and resentment), that is the driving force of their violence. It is the deep intensity of feeling that fires the sacrifice of those among them who so feel inclined.

The early period of Naxalism which my book treated was a tragic disaster, but as has been observed, 'The only thing we learn from history is that we do not learn from history' The destruction of the short-lived CPI(M-L) in West Bengal did not put an end to the efforts of erstwhile and fresh revolutionaries. However, for a long period, from 1972 to about 1985, there were no untoward incidents. When incidents of revolutionary murder and mayhem began again, it was not in Bengal, but in Bihar. In Bengal, after the tumultuous period of Naxalite revolution and Congress—CPI(M) counter-revolution, the CPI(M) enjoyed undisputed power with its allies for about 30 years, at least partly, by its promise of, if not extirpating, the 'Congsal' Congress and Naxalite terror and counter-terror, at least keeping it firmly out of sight. Not that these years in Bengal were prosperous or peaceful. The low-salaried white-collar and the blue-collar unions continued to be resentfully aggressive, the rhetoric against the 'bourgeois' strident, and the countryside violence-ridden. Fomenting these and capitalizing on them, the organizations of the CPI(M) and its allies permeated into the lowest echelons and highest intellectual enclaves, becoming an integral element of Bengali social life. From having been a leader in commerce and industry, West Bengal was transformed into a relative backwater, and the institutions of higher learning, once the cynosure of Indian culture, receded into relative eclipse. Part of the decline of West Bengal from its premier position is, of course, the rise of other competing nuclei, but part is certainly to be ascribed to the direction in which its leaders tried to take it, let us not forget, with the overwhelming appreciation and support of its public. These are, of course, the leftists, who clamour elsewhere, where they do not receive public support, about 'the manufacture of consent'.

After the disintegration and collapse of the early CPI(M–L) and the death of Charu Mazumdar, for quite some time, there was confusion and vexed soul-searching among those who still held by the perspectives of revolution. Most of the erstwhile revolutionaries abandoned active involvement in revolutionary activity and hastily began to try to rebuild their interrupted careers. Many of them of course continued to abide by

Naxalite perspectives and carried their propaganda into the streams in which they could find a reasonable livelihood. Also the perspectives on socialism of the Naxalites, if we for a moment ignore their signal blood-thirstiness, began to gain ground in the circles of electoral politics and within the Parliament itself. In the educational establishments, already favourably inclined to populist activism through the days of the nationalist struggle and hotbeds of dissent, vandalism, and the customary anarchy of student life in the days before Naxalism, Naxalite sympathies and the rhetoric of partisanship with aggressive, violent dissent began to be more and more fashionable. The agitation against the Mandal Commission saw the end of violent student protest that had been characteristic of Indian higher education almost from the days of its establishment in India. However, by this time, academic orthodoxy had turned overwhelmingly leftist and if not out and out preaching communist revolution, thoroughly welcoming of such ideas and permeated by the views of those Western writers, who, from their comfortable niches in European and American universities, clamoured to destroy privilege, so long as it was not *their* privilege. Today, the allegiance to leftist ideas in Indian academic circles is widespread and by many, considered a ticket to a secure academic appointment in this country or abroad.

From the death of Charu Mazumdar to the fresh outbreak of Naxalite violence in Bihar in 1985, Naxalites were not in the news. Immediately after the destruction of the Mazumdar-led CPI(M–L) many people in the CPI—the aristocratic and liberal cultured faction of the communist movement—as also quite a few other socialists, and humanitarians generally, were active in the relief and rehabilitation of erstwhile Naxalites, subjected to considerable suffering at the hands of the government and in its prisons. The revolutionary urge, however, had hardly been destroyed. Fresh takers to the idea of revolution were in considerable confusion as to what to do. The early period saw the repudiation of the annihilation line (that is, the strategy of the 'Murder Manual') by most erstwhile Naxalites and most other socialists and communists, but hardly by all of them. In any case, even among those who rejected the annihilation line as incorrect, the search for a correct path of revolution was a consuming passion. In revolutionary groups and groupuscules, discussion, splitting, forming, and splitting again were the order of the day. Most of the erstwhile Naxalites worked in other kinds of organizations, and some organizations of significance which were formed are active today and are sympathetic to the Naxalite cause when not actively engaged in perpetuating its perspectives. Though born in the heat of revolutionary fervour, and sympathetic to its perspectives, these organizations are active in a whole range of humanitarian efforts in defence of those persecuted for their crimes and innocents caught in the cross-fire between law and order and its enemies.

The Naxalite movement in Srikakulam in Andhra Pradesh had an independent origin, although it threw in its fortunes with the CPI(M–L) under Charu Mazumdar and its destruction coincided with the smashing of the CPI(M–L). In a similar, if not identical way, revolutionaries all over the country threw in their lot under the leadership of Mazumdar while it lasted. However, the leadership of Mazumdar was the guiding inspiration of many fresh revolutionaries like Asim Chatterjee who joined the Naxalite cause, and certainly of the Calcutta terror. The issue of the leadership of Mazumdar and the question of his status in the revolutionary pantheon was a matter of considerable importance in the discussions of the revolutionary groups and groupuscules deliberating their course of action after the smashing of the CPI(M–L) under his leadership. *All* those who later took to murder and violence and continue to do so today rank Mazumdar among the revered path-breakers of the revolutionary communist cause, even though they differ from each other in points of principle related to the interpretation of his teaching.

During the heyday of Mazumdar, Naxalite depredations were most marked in Bengal and Srikakulam in Andhra Pradesh. They were, however, evident in other parts of the country as well. Kerala has its own roster of Naxalite heroes and Punjab also witnessed some Naxalite murders and considerable Naxalite influence. In Andhra, I have already mentioned, revolutionary activity predates Mazumdar and has surfaced again. In Punjab, it is likely this blood-thirst was later absorbed into the Khalistan insurgency and subsequendy crushed, though a significant undertow continues in various avatars even today. In this context, it is worth mentioning that the insurgency in the north-eastern parts of the country, with which there is considerable leftist academic sympathy today, has in its formative period seen considerable revolutionary communist influence.

The resurgence of Naxalite violence (and I call it Naxalite consideredly) is caught up with the cult of Naxalbari and the 'annihilation line' of Charu Mazumdar. It has found unprecedented response from poor and uneducated caste-Hindus and tribals in various parts of the country. In the various regions in which it has developed, there is a considerable difference between the ideology and motivation of the intellectuals who lead and organize it and the ideology of the poor and uneducated who form its rank and file. True enough, the intellectual leaders themselves are hardly knit into a single organization, doctrinal issues of symbolism, strategy, and tactics dividing them into contending factions. But the poor and uneducated they lead have inner lives radically different from those of their educated leaders. The dynamics and the logic of their struggle thus differs over the regions in which they live, here associated with caste issues, there with tribal, elsewhere with vendettas, and always with envy, lust, resentment, and greed. Stripped to its 'Charuist' formulation, making revolution is baldly a matter of inciting hate to murder. The German scribe with a penchant for the prophetic pose, Karl Marx, once wrote, 'Events and personalities occur, as it were, twice in history, the first time as tragedy, the second as farce.'

Ideological Conflict

In closing, a few words about ideology again.

The Naxalite organizations today are highly diversified. A large number of people with varying concerns and interests are necessary to the movement in its present form. The battling battalions who murder and are killed are only the crucial front where the problem manifests in its unmanageability and the leading edge of the drive through which the Naxalites hope to realize their hopes. What *are* their hopes? In a word—power; dominion over India and finally the globe. To what end? These ends are framed in ideological terms—the esoteric jargon of the communist revolutionary sects. I have argued that the proclaimed formulated doctrinal ends for which they fight—and are willing to die—conceal the inner reasons for their commitment to their cause.

The leaders, the organizers, the spine, and the continuity of the movement are the revolutionary intellectuals. Without them there would be no movement. The Naxalite movement is thus not principally a rural, agrarian problem as the doctrine of the Naxalites argues, but a problem of the leading edge of the urban intelligentsia. And for these, it is a matter of doctrine (concealing the inner dissatisfaction and suffering from which it springs) for which they fight.

The mainstream of Western academic culture encourages and abets such doctrines. It is at odds with the opinions of the people it wishes to educate. If education has come to such a pass where it wishes to destroy itself, where are we?

Select Bibliography

Primary Sources

All India Congress Committee (Opposition). Election 1971. *Life and Property in Danger: Save It Now or Never.* New Delhi: 1971.

Andhra Pradesh Communist Committee (Revolutionaries). *Draft Programme* 1972.

CPI(M). Adopted by the Central Committee at its Madurai session from 18 to 27 August 1967. *Divergent Views Between Our Party and the CPC on Certain Fundamental Issues of Programme and Policy.*

———. Adopted by the Central Committee in its Meeting from October 5–9, 1968 in Calcutta. *Why the Ultra–'Left' Deviation: An Examination of the Basic Causes of Left Defections In Special Reference to Andhra.* Calcutta.

———. West Bengal State Committee. *Who is Responsible For Politics of Terror and Individual Murders? Open Letter to Shri Siddhartha Sankar Ray. Writer's Buildings, Calcutta–1, 7th July 1971.*

CPI(M) and Others. *Statement of Leftist Parties of West Bengal on West Bengal Election, 1972.*

Dutta, Saroj (Sasanka). Articles in *Deshabrati.*

Estimates of State Income And Its Regional Differentials in West Bengal. Bureau of Applied Economics and Statistics, Govt. of West Bengal, 1969.

Government of West Bengal Education Directorate. *Septennial Review of the Progress of Education in West Bengal for the Period 1957–58 to 1963–64.* Alipore: Superintendent Government Printing, West Bengal Government Press, 1970.

Mazumdar, Charu. Articles in *Liberation.* Articles cited:

'A Few Words to the Revolutionary Students And Youth'. *Liberation,* March 1970.

'"Boycott Elections!" International Significance of the Slogan'. *Liberation,* December 1968.

'Develop Peasants' Class Struggle Through Class Analysis, Investigation and Study'. *Liberation*, November 1968.

'Develop Revolutionary War to Eliminate War of Aggression Against China'. *Liberation*, October 1969.

'Fight Against the Concrete Manifestations of Revisionism'. *Liberation*, September 1969.

'The Indian People's Democratic Revolution'. *Liberation*, June 1968.

'It is Time to Build a Revolutionary Party'. *Liberation*, November 1967.

'March Forward by Summing Up the Experience of the Revolutionary Peasant Struggle of India'. *Liberation*, December 1969.

'Make the 1970's the decade of Revolution'. *Liberation*, February 1970.

'On the Political-Organisational Report'. *Lalkar Weekly* (Leamington Spa).

'One Year of Naxalbari Struggle'. *Liberation*, June 1968.

'Party's Call to the Youth and Students'. *Liberation*, September 1969.

'To the Young and Student Community'. *Deshabrati*, May 2, 1968.

'To the Youth and Students'. *Liberation*, April 1969.

'Undertake the Work of Building a Revolutionary Party'. *Liberation*, October 1968'.

'United Front and the Revolutionary Party'. *Liberation*, July 1968.

'Why Must We Form a Party Now?'. *Liberation*, March 1969.

Mitra, Pratap and Mohit Sen. *Communist Party and Naxalites*. Communist Party Publications, November 1971.

Purna. *On Statue Smashing*. Circulated Document of the CPI(M-L).

Sen, Asit. *An Approach to Naxalbari*. Calcutta: Institute of Scientific Thoughts, October 1980.

'Urban Guerrilla'. Unsigned Article. *Economic and Political Weekly*, 10 July 1970.

Periodicals

Deshabrati

Frontier

Lalkar Weekly

Liberation

Statesman Overseas Weekly

Secondary Sources

Addy, Premen and Ibne Azad. 'Politics and Society in Bengal'. In *Explosion in the Subcontinent.* Ed. Robin Blackburn. Penguin Books in association with New Left Review, 1975.

Altbach, Philip G. 'The Transformation of the Indian Student Movement'. *Asian Survey,* vol. VI, no. 8 (August 1966).

———. ed. *Turmoil and Transition: Higher Education and Student Politics in India.* Bombay, etc.: Lalvani, 1968.

Althusser, Louis and Etienne Balibar. *Reading Capital.* Trans. Ben Brewster. London: New Left Books, 1970.

Anderson, Perry. *Considerations on Western Marxism.* London: New Left Books, 1976.

Baden-Powell, B. H. *Land Systems of British India.* Oxford: Clarendon Press, 1892.

Baig, M. R. A. 'The Partition of Bengal and its Aftermath. *Indian Journal of Political Science,* vol. XXX, No. 2 (April–June 1969).

Bandopadhyay, S. 'Report on an Adda at Dr Surajit Sinha's House on 20th February, 1970'. In *Cultural Profile of Calcutta.* Ed. Surajit Sinha. Calcutta: The Indian Anthropological Society, 1972.

Banerjee, Debabrata. 'A Decadal Survey of the Labour Scene in West Bengal'. In *Problems of the Economy and Planning in West Bengal: Proceedings on a Symposium 24–27 February, 1974.* Calcutta: Centre for Studies in Social Sciences, June 1975. Cyclostyled.

Banerjee, Sumanta. *In the Wake of Naxalbari.* Calcutta: Subarnarekha, 1980.

Barua, Dipak Kumar. 'New Poets with New Lines: An Overview'. In *Studies in Modern Bengali Poetry.* Ed. Nirmal Ghose. Calcutta: Novela, 1968.

Basu, S. K. and S. K. Bhattacharya. *Land Reforms in West Bengal.* Planning Commission, Govt. of India. Oxford Book Co., 1963. Delhi, etc.: 1976.

Baumer, R. V. M. *Aspects of Bengali History and Society.* New Delhi, 1976.

Bengal Chamber of Commerce and Industry (Sponsors). *Supplement to West Bengal: An Analytical Study.* Calcutta: Oxford and IBH Publishing Co., 1973.

Bettelheim, C. *India Independent.* Trans. W. A. Caswell. London: MacGibbon and Kee, 1968.

Bhaumick, P. K. *Occupational Mobility and Caste Structure in Bengal: Study of Silda Market.* Calcutta: Indian Publications, 1969.

Biswas, Arabinda, *et al.* 'The Ethnic Composition of Calcutta and the Residential Pattern of Minorities'. Reprint from *Geographical Review of India.* Published by the Geographical Society of India.

Blackburn, Robin, ed. *Explosion in the Subcontinent.* Penguin Books in association with New Left Review, 1975.

Bloch, Marc. *Feudal Society.* 2 vols. Trans. L. A. Manyon. London: Routledge and Kegan Paul, 1961–2.

Bose, Nirmal Kumar. 'Calcutta: A Premature Metropolis'. *Scientific American* 213/3 (September 1965).

Brower, Daniel. *Training the Nihilists: Education and Radicalism in Tsarist Russia.* Ithaca: Cornell University Press, 1975.

Calcutta: People and Empire (Gleanings from Old Journals). Calcutta: India Book Exchange, 1975.

Carstairs, G. Morris. *The Twice-Born: A Study of A Community of High Caste Hindus.* London: Hogarth Press, 1957.

Chakrabarty, S. 'Concept of Bhadralok and Chotolok in Bengal Hindu Society: Some Observations'. *Bulletin of Anthropological Survey of India,* xix/2 (April 1970).

Chakravorty, Jagannath, ed. *Studies in the Bengal Renaissance.* Revised and Enlarged Edition. Jadavpur: National Council of Education, Bengal, 1977.

Chandra, S. *Parties and Politics at the Mughal Court 1707–1740.* Third edition. New Delhi: People's Publishing House, 1979.

Chattopadhyay, Prof. K. P., *et al.* 'Undergraduate Students in Calcutta: How They Live and Work'. *The Calcutta Review,* vol. 132, no. 1 (July 1954).

Chattopadhyay, Tapan. *The Story of Lal Bazar.* Calcutta: Firma K. L. Mukhopadhyaya, 1982.

Chauduri, K. C. *The History and Economics of the Land System in Bengal.* Calcutta: The Book Company, 1927.

Chowdhury, B. K. 'Land Reform Legislation and Implementation in West Bengal'. *Indian Journal of Agricultural Economics,* vol. xvii, no. 1 (January–March 1962).

Copley, Anthony. 'Student Protest: A Sense of Life's Demands'. *South Asian Review,* vol. 7, no. 1 (October 1973).

Coulter, Jeff. 'Marxism and the Engels Paradox'. *The Socialist Register.* London: The Merlin Press, 1971.

de Souza, Alfred, ed. *The Indian City.* New Delhi: Manohar, 1978.

Debi, Mahasweta. 'Sattarer Dashak O Tarpore'. *Sattarer Dashak.* Calcutta.

Desai, A. R. and S. D. Pillai. *A Profile of An Indian Slum.* University of Bombay, 1972.

Dostoyevsky, Fyodor. *The Brothers Karamazov.* 2 vols. Trans. D. Magarshack. Harmondsworth: Penguin Classics, 1958.

Durkheim, Emile. *The Rules of Sociological Method.* Trans. Sarah A. Soloway and John H. Mueller. Eighth edition. New York: The Free Press; London: Collier-Macmillan, 1964.

Dutt, K. 'Changes in Land Relations in West Bengal'. *Economic and Political Weekly Review of Agriculture,* December 1977.

Engels, F. *Dialectics of Nature.* Trans. C. Dutt. Moscow: 1954.

Feuer, Lewis S. *Ideology and Ideologists.* Oxford: Basil Blackwell, 1975.

Floud, Sir Francis. *Report of the Land Revenue Commission Bengal.* Alipore: Bengal Government Press, 1940.

Ford Foundation Sponsored Agricultural Production Team. *Report On India's Food Crisis and Steps to Meet It.* Ministries of Food and Agriculture and Community Development and Co-operation. Government of India, 1959.

Franda, Marcus F. *Radical Politics in West Bengal.* Cambridge, Mass.: MIT Press, 1971.

Freud, Sigmund. *Civilisation and Its Discontents.* Trans. Joan Riviere. London: Hogarth Press, 1951.

Fruzzetti, Lina and Akos Östor. 'Is There a Structure to North Indian Kinship Terminology?' *Contributions to Indian Sociology* (NS), vol. 10, no. 1 (1976).

———. 'Seed and Earth: A Cultural Analysis of Kinship in a Bengali Town'. *Contributions to Indian Sociology* (NS), vol. 10, no. 1 (1976).

Fruzzetti, Lina, *et al.* 'The Cultural Construction of the Person in Bengal and Tamil Nadu'. *Contributions to Indian Sociology* (NS), vol. 10, no. 1 (1976).

Frykenberg, Robert Eric, ed. *Land Control and Social Structure in Indian History.* New Delhi: Manohar, 1979.

Fürer-Haimendorf, C. von. 'Caste and Politics in South Asia'. In *Politics and Society in India.* Ed. C. H. Philips. London: George Allen and Unwin, 1963.

Fyzee, Asaf A. A. *Outlines of Mohammadan Law.* London: Oxford University Press, 1955.

Galbraith, John Kenneth. *The Affluent Society.* 3rd Edition. London: Hamish Hamilton, 1977.

Ghosh, A. and K. Dutt. *Development of Capitalist Relations in Agriculture, A Case Study of West Bengal* 1793–1971. New Delhi: People's Publishing House, 1977.

Ghosh, J. C. *Bengali Literature.* London and Dublin: Curzon Press; Totowa, U.S.A.: Rowman and Littlefield, 1976.

Ghosh, Kalicharan. *Famines in Bengal 1770–1943.* Calcutta: Associated Publishing Company, 1944.

Ghosh, Rattan. 'Effect of Agricultural Legislations on Land Distribution in West Bengal'. *Indian Journal of Agricultural Economics,* vol. XXXI, no. 3 (July–September 1976).

Ghosh, Sankar. *The Naxalite Movement: A Maoist Experiment.* Calcutta: Firma K. L. Mukhopadhyay, 1974.

Ghoshal, U. N. *The Agrarian System in Ancient India.* Calcutta: University of Calcutta, 1930.

Gordon, Leonard A. *Bengal. The Nationalist Movement 1876–1940.* New York and London: Columbia University Press, 1974.

Goudsblom, Johan. *Nihilism and Culture.* Oxford: Blackwell, 1979.

Gramsci, Antonio. *Selections from the Prison Notebooks.* Ed. and trans. Quintin Hoare and Geoffrey Nowell Smith. London: Lawrence and Wishart, 1971.

Guha, Ranajit. *Elementary Aspects of Peasant Insurgency in Colonial India.* Delhi: Oxford University Press, 1983.

———. *A Rule of Property for Bengal.* 2nd ed. New Delhi: Orient Longman, 1982.

Gupta, B., *et al. CPM Terror in West Bengal.* New Delhi: CPI Publication, October 1970.

Gupta, Biplab Das. *The Naxalite Movement.* Bombay: Allied Publishers, 1974.

Gupta, M. N. *Land System of Bengal.* University of Calcutta, 1940.

Gupta, Sankar Sen. *A Study of Women of Bengal.* Calcutta: Indian Publications, 1970.

Habib, Irfan. *The Agrarian System of Mughal India.* London: Published for the Dept. of History, Aligarh Muslim University by Asia Publishing House, 1963.

———. 'Social Distribution of Landed Property in Pre-British. India'. *Enquiry,* Winter 1965.

Heidegger, Martin. *An Introduction to Metaphysics.* Trans. Ralph Manheim. New Haven: Yale University Press, 1959.

Hilferding, R. *Finance Capital.* Ed. Tom Bottomore. London: Routledge and Kegan Paul, 1981.

Horkheimer, M. and T. W. Adorno. *Dialectic of Enlightenment.* Trans. John Cumming. London: Allen Lane, 1973.

Hula, Richard C. 'Political Violence and Terrorism and Bengal'. In *The Politics of Terrorism.* Ed. Michael Stohl. New York and Basel: Marcel Dekker Inc., 1983.

Husserl, Edmund. *Cartesian Meditations, An Introduction to Phenomenology.* Trans. Dorion Cairns. The Hague: Martinus Nijhoff, 1973.

Inden, Ronald B. *Marriage and Rank in Bengali Culture. A History of Caste and Clan in Middle Period Bengal.* New Delhi etc.: Vikas, 1976.

Inden, Ronald B. and Ralph W. Nicholas. *Kinship in Bengali Culture.* Chicago and London: University of Chicago Press, 1977.

Irani, C. R. *Bengal and its Communist Challenge.* Bombay etc.: Lalvani, 1968.

Jain, S. C. *Agricultural Policy in India.* Bombay etc.: Allied Publishers, 1965.

———. *Problems and Policies of Indian Agriculture.* Allahabad: Kitab Mahal, 1963.

Jaspers, Karl. *Philosophy.* Vol. 3. Trans. E. B. Ashton. Chicago and London: University of Chicago Press, 1971.

Jawaid, Sohail. *The Naxalite Movement in India.* New Delhi: Associated Publishing House, 1979.

Johari, Dr J. C. *Naxalite Politics in India.* Institute of Constitutional and Parliamentary Studies, 1972.

Jolly, Julius. *Hindu Law and Custom.* Trans. Batakrishna Ghosh. Calcutta: Greater India Society, 1928.

Joon-Chien, Doh. *Eastern Intellectuals and Western Solutions.* Ghaziabad: Vikas, 1980.

Jung, Carl. *The Integration of the Personality.* Trans. Stanley Dell. London: Kegan Paul, Trench, Trubner and Co., 1940.

Kabir, Humayun. *The Bengali Novel.* Calcutta: Firma K. L. Mukhopadhyay, 1968.

Kakar, Sudhir. *The Inner World.* Delhi: Oxford University Press, 1981.

Kane, P. V. *History of Dharmasastra.* Vol. ii, part I. Poona: Bhandarkar Oriental Research Institute, 1941.

Küng, Hans. *Does God Exist?* Trans. Edmund Quinn. Collins (Fount Paperbacks), 1980.

Labour in West Bengal 1973. Dept. of Labour, Govt. of West Bengal.

Larrain, Jorge. *The Concept of Ideology.* London: Hutchinson, 1979.

Laushey, David M. *Bengal Terrorism and the Marxist Left.* Calcutta: Firma K. L. Mukhopadhyay, 1975.

Leach, Edmund and S. N. Mukherjee, ed. *Elites in South Asia.* Cambridge: Cambridge University Press, 1970.

Lenin, V. I. *The State and Revolution.* London: Martin Lawrence, 1933.

————. *Collected Works.* London: Lawrence and Wishart; Moscow: Foreign Languages Publishing House.

Lichtheim, George. *The Concept of Ideology and Other Essays.* New York: Vintage Books, 1967.

Lingat, Robert. *The Classical Law of India.* Translated from the French with additions by J. Duncan, M. Derrett. Berkeley etc.: University of California Press, 1973.

Lubell, Harold. 'Migration and Employment: The Case of Calcutta'. In *The Indian City.* Ed. Alfred de Souza. New Delhi: Manohar, 1978.

Lukács, Georg. *History and Class Consciousness.* Trans. Rodney Livingstone. London: Merlin Press, 1971.

Macintyre, A. C. *Marcuse* (Modern Masters). London: Fontana, 1970.

Maine, Henry Sumner. *Ancient Law.* New edn. London: John Murray, 1930.

Majumdar, R. C. *Glimpses of Bengal in the Nineteenth Century.* Calcutta: Firma K. L. Mukhopadhyay, 1960.

Malik, Yogendra K. *North Indian Intellectuals, An Attitudinal Profile.* Leiden, E.J. Brill, 1979.

Mannheim, Karl. *Ideology and Utopia.* Trans. Louis Wirth and Edward Shils. London: Routledge and Kegan Paul, 1936.

Mansubhain, G. S. ed. *Crises in Indian Universities.* New Delhi etc.: Oxford and IBH Publishing Co., 1972.

Mao Tse-Tung. *Complete Works.* Vols. 1–5. Peking: Foreign Languages Publishing House.

————. *Quotations from Chairman Mao Tse-Tung.* [The Red Book].

Marais, Eugène N. *The Soul of the White Ant.* Trans. Winifred de Kok. London: Penguin Books, 1973.

Marx, Karl. *Capital.* 3 vols. Trans. Samuel Moore and Edward Aveling. Moscow: Foreign Languages Publishing House, 1961.

————. *A Contribution to the Critique of Hegel's Philosophy of Right.* Trans. Annette Jolin and Joseph O' Malley. Cambridge: Cambridge University Press.

————.'Introduction to a Contribution to the Critique of Political Economy'. In David Horowitz, *Marx and Modern Economics.* London: MacGibbon and Kee, 1968.

Marx, Karl and F. Engels. *The German Ideology.* Ed. C.J. Arthur. London: Lawrence and Wishart, 1970.

————. *Collected Works.* London: Lawrence and Wishart, 1976.

Mason, Philip, ed. *India and Ceylon: Unity and Diversity.* London, etc.: Oxford University Press, 1967.

McLane, John R. 'The Decision to Partition Bengal in 1905'. *The Indian Economic and Social History Review,* vol. ii, no. 3 (July 1965).

Mepham, John and David-Hillel Ruben eds. *Issues in Marxist Philosophy.* Vol. 3. *Epistemology, Science, Ideology.* Sussex: The Harvester Press, 1979.

Misra, B. B. *The Indian Middle Classes.* Delhi: Oxford University Press, 1968.

Mitra, Sisirkumar. *A Marvel of Cultural Fellowship.* New ed. Bombay, 1967.

Mohanty, Manoranjan. *Revolutionary Violence, A Study of the Maoist Movement in India.* New Delhi, 1977.

Moreland, W. H. *The Agrarian System of Muslim India.* Cambridge: W. H. Heffer and Sons, 1929.

Morris, M. D. 'Economic Change and Agriculture in Nineteenth Century India'. *Indian Economic and Social History Review.* Vol. iii, no. 2 (June 1966).

Mukherjee, Dr Amitabha. 'The Transformation of Caste'. In *Modern Bengal: A Socio-Economic Survey.* Ed. S. P. Sen. Calcutta: Institute of Historical Studies, 1973.

Mukherjee, P. N., *et al. Left Extremism and Electoral Politics. Naxalite Participation in Elections.* Draft MS for restricted circulation. New Delhi: ICSSR, July 1979.

Mukherjee, Radhakamal. *Economic Problems of Modern India.* Vol. 1. London: Macmillan, 1939.

Mukherjee, S. N. ed. *Elites in South Asia.* Cambridge: Cambridge University Press, 1970.

Nagaraj, K. and Ratan Ghosh. 'Land Reforms in West Bengal', *Social Scientist*, vol. 6, no. 6/7 (January/February 1978).

Nair, Kusum. *Blossoms in the Dust: The Human Element in Indian Development.* London: Gerald Duckworth.

Nanterre Students. 'Why Sociologists?' In *Student Power.* Ed. A. Cockburn and R. Blackburn. Harmondsworth: Penguin, 1969.

Nicholas, Ralph M. 'Ritual Hierarchy and Social Relations in Rural Bengal'. *Contributions to Indian Sociology*, no. 1 (December 1967).

Nietzsche, Friedrich. *Complete Works of Friedrich Nietzsche.* Ed. Oscar Levy. London and Edinburgh: T. N. Foulis, 1911.

O' Malley, L. S. S. *Modern India and the West.* London, etc.: Oxford University Press, 1941.

Overstreet, Gene D. and Marshall Windmiller. *Communism in India.* Berkeley and Los Angeles: University of California Press, 1959.

Palit, Chittabrata. 'Calcutta—The Premature City: A Study in Urbanization'. In *Modern Bengal: A Socio-Economic Survey.* Ed. S. P. Sen. Calcutta: Institute of Historical Studies, 1973.

Pandubhai, S. L. 'The Voluntary Institutions of the Marvaris in Calcutta'. In *Aspects of Society and Culture in Calcutta.* Ed. M. A. K. Siddiqui. Calcutta: Anthropological Survey, 1982.

Pareto, V. M. *The Mind and Society, a treatise on General Sociology.* New York, Dover, 1963.

Payne, Ernest A. *The Śāktas.* London, etc.: Oxford University Press, 1933.

Philips, C. H., ed. *Politics and Society in India.* London: George Allen and Unwin, 1963.

Problems of the Economy and Planning in West Bengal: Proceedings of a Symposium 24–27 February 1974. Cyclostyled and bound for the Centre for Studies in Social Sciences. Calcutta, June 1975.

Raha, Kironmoy. *Bengali Theatre.* New Delhi: National Book Trust, 1978.

Rai, Haridwar and K. M. Prasad. 'Naxalism: A Challenge to the Proposition of Peaceful Transition to Socialism?' *Indian Journal of Political Science*, XXXIII, 4 (October–December 1972).

Ram, Mohan, *Maoism in India.* Delhi: Vikas, 1971.

Ramanathan, G. *Indian Babu (A Study in Social Psychology).* New Delhi: Sudha Publications, 1965.

Ray, Anil Baran. 'The Communal Attitudes to British Policies: The Case of the Partition of Bengal 1905'. *Social Scientist*, vol. VI, no. 5 (December 1977).

Ray, Satyajit. *Our Films, Their Films.* Bombay, etc.; Orient Longman, 1976.

Ray Chaudhuri, Tapan. 'Indian Nationalism as Animal Politics'. *The Historical Journal,* vol. 22, no. 3 (1979).

Richter, Hans. *Dada: Art and Anti-Art.* London: Thames and Hudson, 1965.

Risley. H. H. *The Tribes and Castes of Bengal.* 2 vols. Reprint. Calcutta: Firma K. L. Mukhopadhyay, 1981.

Rosen, Stanley. *Nihilism.* New Haven: Yale University Press, 1969.

Roy, Ashish Kumar. *The Spring Thunder and After.* Calcutta: Minerva Associates, 1975.

Roy, Manisha. *Bengali Women.* Chicago and London: University of Chicago Press, 1975.

Roy, Ranajit. *The Agony of West Bengal.* Third edn. New Age Publications, 1971.

Saha, P. *History of the Working-Class Movement in Bengal.* New Delhi: People's Publishing House, 1978.

Samanta, Amiya Kumar. 'The Terai Upsurge'. *The Calcutta Historical Journal,* vol. vi, no. 1 (1981).

Sankaracharya. *The Works of Sri Sankaracharya.* Srirangam: Sri Vani Vilas Press. Memorial Edn.

Saraf, R. P. *Scientific Dialectics.*

Sarma, J. *Caste Dynamics Among the Bengali Hindus.* Calcutta: Firma K. L. Mukhopadhyay, 1980.

Sartre, Jean-Paul. *Critique of Dialectical Reason.* London: New Left Books, 1976.

Sayer, Derek. *Marx's Method: Ideology, Science and Critique in Capital.* New Jersey: Humanities Press; Sussex: The Harvester Press, 1979.

Schacht, Joseph. *An Introduction to Islamic Law.* London: Oxford University Press, 1971.

Seliger, Martin. *The Marxist Conception of Ideology.* Cambridge: Cambridge University Press, 1977.

Seminar. 'Indian Intellectuals'. No. 222 (February 1976).

Sen, Asok. *Iswar Chandra Vidyasagar and His Elusive Milestones.* Calcutta: Riddhi-India, 1977.

Sen, Ranen. 'What is Happening in West Bengal?'. In *CPM Terror in West Bengal.* New Delhi: CPI Publication, October 1970.

Sen, S. P., ed. *Modern Bengal: A Socio-Economic Survey.* Calcutta: Institute of Historical Studies, 1973.

Sen, Sunil. *Agrarian Relations in India (1793–1947)*. New Delhi: People's Publishing House, 1979.

Sengupta, S. *Caste Status Group Aggregate and Class*. Calcutta: Firma K. L. Mukhopadhyay, 1979.

Shah, B. V. 'Students' Unrest—A Sociological Hypothesis'. *Sociological Bulletin*, vol. xvii, no. 1 (March 1968).

Sharma, R. S. *Indian Feudalism: c. 200–1200*. University of Calcutta, 1965.

Shils, Edward. 'Students, Politics and Universities in India'. In *Turmoil and Transition: Higher Education and Student Politics in India*. Ed. Philip G. Altbach. Bombay: Lalvani, 1968.

———. 'The Academic Profession in India'. In *Elites in South Asia*. Ed. Edmund Leach and S. N. Mukherjee. Cambridge: Cambridge University Press, 1970.

Siddiqui, M. K. A., ed. *Aspects of Society and Culture in Calcutta*. Calcutta: Anthropological Survey, 1982.

Singer, Milton. *When A Great Tradition Modernizes*. London: Pall Mall Press, 1972.

Sinha, Narendra Krishna, ed. *The History of Bengal (1757–1905)*. University of Calcutta, 1967.

Sinha, Pradip. *Nineteenth Century Bengal: Aspects of Social History*. Calcutta: Firma K. L. Mukhopadhyay, 1965.

Sinha, Surajit, ed. *Cultural Profile of Calcutta*. Calcutta: The Indian Anthropological Society, 1972.

Spratt, P. *Hindu Culture and Personality: A Psycho–Analytic Study*. Bombay: Manaktalas, 1966.

Statistical Abstracts India 1970. General Statistical Organisation, Dept. of Statistics, Cabinet Secretariat, Govt. of India. Delhi: Published by Manager of Publications, 1972.

Stohl, Michael, ed. *The Politics of Terrorism*. New York and Basel: Marcel Dekker Inc., 1983.

Sumner, Colin. *Reading Ideologies. An Investigation into the Marxist Theory of Ideology and Law*. London, etc.: Academic Press, 1979.

Sur, Dr A. K. *Folk Elements in Bengali Life*. Calcutta: Indian Publications, 1975.

Taylor, Ian and Laurie Taylor. *Politics and Deviance*. Penguin, 1973.

Thorner, Alice. 'Semifeudalism or Capitalism?' *Economic and Political Weekly*, 4 December 1982, pp. 1961–8; 11 December 1982, pp. 1993–9; and 18 December 1982, pp. 2061–6.

Thorner, Daniel. *The Agrarian Prospect in India.* Delhi: University Press, 1956.

Thorner, Daniel and Alice Thorner. *Land and Labour in India.* London: Asia Publishing House, 1962.

Timberg, Thomas A. *The Marwaris.* New Delhi: Vikas, 1978.

Tönnies, Ferdinand. *Community and Society.* Trans. C. P. Loomis. Michigan State University Press, 1964.

Tripathi, Amales. *Vidyasagar: The Traditional Moderniser.* Calcutta: Orient Longman, 1974.

Weber, Max. *The Protestant Ethic and the Spirit of Capitalism.* Trans. Talcott Parsons. Second edn. London: Allen and Unwin, 1930.

————. *The Theory of Social and Economic Organisation.* Trans. A. M. Henderson and T. Parsons. New York: The Free Press; London: Collier Macmillan, 1964.

————. *The Sociology of Religion.* Trans. Ephraim Fischoff. London: Social Science Paperbacks in association with Methuen and Co. Ltd., 1966.

————. *The Religion of India.* Trans. Hans H. Gerth and Don Martindale. New York: The Free Press; London: Collier Macmillan, 1967.

————. *Economy and Society,* 3 vols., eds. Guenther Roth and Claus Wittich, Berkeley etc., University of California Press.

Weiner, Myron. 'Notes on Political Developments in West Bengal'. In *Political Change in South Asia.* Calcutta: Firma K. L. Mukhopadhyay, 1963.

Wiebe, Paul D. *Social Life in An Indian Slum.* Delhi, etc.: Vikas, 1975.

Wittfogel, Karl A. *Oriental Despotism: A Comparative Study of Total Power.* New Haven: Yale University Press, 1957.

Woodhead, Sir John (Chairman). *Famine Inquiry Commission Report on West Bengal.* Delhi, 1945.

Index